ZERO AT THE BONE

Rewriting Life after a Snakebite

Erec Toso

The University of Arizona Press

Tucson

The University of Arizona Press
© 2007 Erec Toso
All rights reserved

Library of Congress Cataloging-in-Publication Data
Toso, Erec, 1956–
Zero at the bone : rewriting life after a snakebite / Erec Toso.
p. cm.
ISBN-13: 978-0-8165-2591-1 (pbk. : alk. paper)
ISBN-10: 0-8165-2591-9 (pbk. : alk. paper)
1. Toso, Erec, 1956– I. Title.
PS3620.O87Z46 2007
814'.6—dc22   2006032829

Publication of this book is made possible in part
by grants from the Department of English and the
Writing Program at the University of Arizona, and from
the Ada Pierce McCormick Foundation.

Manufactured in the United States of America on acid-free,
archival-quality paper containing a minimum of 50% post-
consumer waste and processed chlorine free.

12 11 10 09 08 07   6 5 4 3 2 1

Zero at the Bone

For Kyle, Sean, and Megan

For the storytellers, the teachers

A man walking along a desert path sees an unmistakable shape and nature tells him to freeze. He then backs up noiselessly and hides behind a rock. There, heart pounding, he waits for the path to clear. After a while, he peeks over the stone, eyes wide to see more clearly. There is no movement.

Finally, he approaches that spot on the path and stares down at the serpent. There is no creature. It is only a bit of sisal rope. Relieved, he picks up the rope and pulls it taut. It unbraids into cords and then strands and then fibers, and then he is left holding . . . nothing.

—Buddhist proverb on the ways of the mind

After his period of sitting under the Bodhi tree, or Tree of Enlightenment, Lord Buddha sat for seven days under a great banyan tree. Then he left that tree and went to a tree called the Tree of the Serpent King, Muchalinda. Muchalinda was a huge cobra who dwelt in a hole among the tree roots. As the Buddha meditated, unmindful of his surroundings, a large storm arose. Muchalinda crept out of his hole and wrapped himself seven times around the Buddha, keeping the Buddha's head dry with his great hood.

—Myth of snake as guardian and protector

Contents

Zero at the Bone

1 / Steps

No gravel crunches beneath my sandals as my feet rise and fall over desert soil recently soaked by a summer thunderstorm. No force of will can change my course. In this dream I am numb, deaf, caught in a nebulous, deterministic fog, at once cold and suffocatingly hot with fear. Ponderously slow, I play out the scene again and again. There can be no change in the outcome.

Air, heavy with residual heat and thick with monsoon sultriness, passes by and around me like water in the wake of a passing ship, swirling vapors, ghastly trails of gray mist. I want to run, to leap to one side, or back, to summon the survival imperative embedded in every cell, but am so heavy with inertia I cannot resist. I am locked in a slow and inevitable sequence.

As I take my next step, fang sheaths retract, a jaw unhinges, and fangs thrust forward. Thick muscles in the shape of an S contract, straightening the body, driving home a surprise sucker punch driven by defensive reflex. The twin spears pierce the skin of my foot. Venom sacs compress, injecting a large dose of poison deep into the side of my foot.

I cannot scream or move. I am suspended, held by bonds I cannot see, growing, growing, bloating to obese flapping sheets of flesh. I am sliced up the middle, divided, exposed, and vulnerable. That can't be me I see in a mirror, nor is it death standing there beside me. I want to laugh, to deflect the embarrassing absurdity, but can only stare and endure.

A large rattlesnake retreats into the night, leaving me flayed, swollen, suspended in a web woven of silence.

I climb out of sleep into greater strangeness. I pursue but cannot catch something in a receding dream as I recognize morning light coming through the blinds. I turn to a sound, almost a word. Luna, my dog, nuzzles the side of the bed, knocking the slats with her tail—a muffled, paintbrush-on-wood alarm clock. Tock. Swish. Tock. Swish. Tock.

The sepulchral comforts of the bed and my wife's warm nakedness cannot keep me under the covers. I have to rise. It is now October, and the mornings feel suddenly and, to me, unnaturally chilled. It is already time to shut down the evaporative coolers for the night. Soon, we will turn them off completely, sliding the metal damper into the duct before firing up the furnace. I don't know how this happened. In some ways, I am still living in August, the hot, monsoon time in Tucson. The past two and a half months have passed by without me, and the gap between then and now disturbs me, puzzles me, will not let me rest.

It is when I swing my legs over the bed and get ready to slide on a T-shirt and shorts—minimal, insulating comforts, a modicum of modesty—that I remember my foot. It is still bandaged, sore, and swollen a full two months after the rattlesnake bite.

Oh yeah. That. I hobble to the toilet as Luna limps arthritically along-side, ready for her morning walkabout in the dry riverbed that passes beyond our front yard, on the other side of the big mesquite. The vapors of sleep are still swirling around me. Known and imagined lovers, friends, messengers, brothers, and something menacing have accompanied me through the long and cool night.

Summer here in the desert has broken, just yesterday. I wait for this time: the days of clear, intense light and cool breezes. Daytime heat just a few days ago was still punishing, hovering right around 100 degrees. Today, though, will be cool.

My foot throbs, aches, and stings, something like what I imagine an amputee's phantom pains to be. I am delighted to have my pains arise from an existing limb, and it reminds me that I will have to change the dressing this morning. At one point, the surgeons discussed the possibility of having to take my foot, but here it is still, a tired refugee, wrapped in gauze and Ace bandage.

It complains as I hop on the good leg, first a sting, then an ache, then a burn as if it can't make up its mind what to send as a message to my sleepy brain. I wiggle my toes as I sit on the toilet—no standing for a while—and scratch Luna beneath her collar. Her white muzzle rests on my wrist, and she looks straight at me, her dark brown eyes framed by black lines, natural eyeliner. She used to be yellow, but has turned white around her noble lab nose. She is getting old, sleeping now next to my wheelchair when I write or work at my desk rather than wandering up the wash or chasing blacktail jackrabbits.

I feel shell-shocked. I don't know what to make of my dreams or of the speeding world around me. I have lost my bearings and a sense of my place in time. I should now be halfway through a semester of teaching. But am instead at home, crippled, watching the parade that is the working world from the base of a tree on a distant hill. The sounds of the marching waft up on the breeze, and occasionally I see a wave from someone in the passing throng, but mainly it is quiet. And I sit. Like Rip Van Winkle, I'm not sure what day or year it is, only that I am waking up after being long disconnected and far away from my daily routines.

I find the wheelchair in the living room, the only place unblocked by doors too narrow for it to pass through. I wheel over to the computer, delighted by the gliding ease of the chair. It wheels in tight circles and coasts straight ahead without effort. Even when I sit in a regular chair now, I catch myself reaching for the wheels.

Luna is not yet ready to go out after all. Neither am I. She lies next to the chair as the machine begins to boot up. This time has become a ritual. I must write my way into and through these last two months. I have to find a way to embrace the trauma and to release it. I know there are words that can loosen this tangled knot in my head.

I'm not even sure who I am or what I value anymore. I love quiet. I want peace. I know that I want to pay more attention to my place and to my life and to those who cross my path or who share their days with mine. I feel very simple and cringe at the prospect of complicating things, of speeding up, of scrambling up the scree slopes of making a living, of going back to work, of the noise of my previous day-to-day life.

The words will come. This open space with no story to guide it cannot last. I am full of opportunity and urgency, images and pulsing emotions. It is time to write these last few months, to find in them the thread that opens, that illuminates, that binds the loose pieces of discord to some kind of truth. The story will have to reveal itself, rising as it does out of the corner of sight, summoned forth by questions and desire. I have to learn the language of hunches and tugs of the gut, to squeeze from mute fragments the living blood of this world I now inhabit.

I begin to write the morning of that day, an unexceptional one other than being longer than most, a day of transition, a day inscribed by one chance encounter.

2 /Day Begins

It is morning. I run toward the eastern mountains, the Rincons, still in their shadow before the sun rises over the crest. Only drunks, mystics, sleepy laborers after a graveyard shift, and lunatics are up at this hour. Which am I? Granite crags in the Catalinas, to the north, are lit above me. Light is traveling down the range. This is my time, the nether world between light and darkness, the interstice of the crepuscular edge. A raven calls from a perch high in a cottonwood. The day has not yet begun; all things are possible.

Rattlers should be under cover or torpid at this time of day I remind myself, but watch the trail anyway. If I see one, I'll be ready to step aside. No big deal. Just part of being out in the desert. Some friends who run with me during cooler seasons don't agree. "Too risky," they say. They run on treadmills this time of year. When a mountain lion was spotted recently near here, they said "better to kill the thing."

It has been dry, scary dry, for years now. Even the monsoons, our quirk of wind currents and ocean moisture that collide over the desert Southwest, have been sparse for almost eleven years. Water, thirst: the linchpins and fear of desert life. Records for days without rain and consecutive days over 100 degrees seem to fall as the years go by. The monsoon this summer, too, has been spotty, but promises something today. Air tingles and prickles the skin with heat and density. Something has to give.

The prickly pear are shriveled and shriven, wrinkled and absolved, beyond caring, cleansed by light, heat, and fasting, like the biblical heart, and the saguaros have been stressed by the miserly conditions to sunken, hollow thinness. Gaunt as teenaged boys, they stand flat and black as spiny cardboard cutouts against the lightening sky. This time of year their silhouettes usually show a plumpish bulging around the middle because they have drawn so much water into their hydrophilic cores. They survive now because they submit to the purifying scarcity, emptiness, and economy that is the desert. It is not in the heart of a wild thing to complain.

Almost a hundred thousand acres burned in the mountains north of Tucson this summer. The fires came down the slopes dangerously close to million-dollar homes in the foothills. Where the slurry bombers dumped flame retardant on the slopes north of town, the charred ridges are streaked red. I remember the thick pine duff, ready to ignite, that snapped and crunched as we ran along a trail near the summit of Mount Lemmon in June. Still no rain.

But we hope; we wait for the monsoon, that wind pattern that pulls moisture up from the Sea of Cortez and swirls it over the Sonoran Desert. It threatens, but does not yet deliver. A few thunderstorms, single-cell microbursts, here and there across the valley, have torn the hell out of power lines and uprooted storage sheds, but no towering purple monsters that fill the horizon, charge into the city, and beat it up, turning streets into torrents of foaming chocolate sand waves. No, not a single gully-washer to show for the season.

The air is saturated today, so humid that the swamp cooler will blow only wet, hot air, like the stale breath of a sleeping giant, and droplets of sweat will rise from pores to join each other in a glistening film on those who work outside, away from relief of air-conditioning. That humidity is a good sign, and the dew point is up to sixty-eight degrees. Uncomfortable, yes, but it's a small price to pay for rain. A seed cloud is already building over the peak ahead of me.

The trail winds though the desert brush, the creosote, jojoba, cholla, and sotol. The stately saguaros stand sentry over the valley, extending high up the arid slopes. I have to watch for loose rocks that can roll, tear, and paralyze an ankle. In the washes, the dry drainages between the ridges, it is still cool, the air fresh from high in the mountains. At night, the cool air drops down the canyons like invisible waterfalls, pulled by the tug gravity has on its higher density. I cross these early morning streams, kicking sand up around my ankles with my stride. It collects at the cuff of my shoes and chafes against sunburned skin. The streams of air are at flood stage, cool air still swirling downstream. By midmorning the tide of temperature will change. This afternoon, sun-heated air will turn the flow back on itself and will race uphill, condensing as it rises, cooling and falling and turning into an unstable mass of wind, ice, and electricity, the mysterious fury of a thunderstorm; we hope.

For now, though, the cool air reigns. I focus beyond the far mountains, to a horizon that I cannot see, and pick up my pace. I attend to my breath, feeling it rushing in and out my mouth. I feel the tension rise and fall in my neck, the ache of strain come and go in my legs. I watch thoughts and try to stay out of their grasp, their demanding dramas. All I am doing right now is running. The ground moves steadily by beneath my stride.

I pride myself on the speed and strength of my pace. I have worked at them for years, watching my time for the mile drop, even as the numbers marking my age climb. Running is mine. I have no one to answer to, no one to serve. It is the one place I find order, the one place of extravagance. And I jealously protect it, hoard it, justify it. To myself and those who know me I am a runner. I revel in that, wash myself in it. Running is solace.

Days pose questions that running helps me answer. Chaff sifts out the cracks of my mind, leaving those things that need attention, examination. I write my syllabi, compose letters of recommendation, make sense of my marriage, and then check the locks on mental doors that I do not open. "Let's not go into that," I hear Edward Abbey say, that explorer of the world outside who declined invitations to examine the canyons inside. The words leading there don't come to me either; my heart goes hard when certain subjects come up. It bars entry, switches on the security system, lets threat trigger the lockdown of emotions under siege. Those questions are off-limits and are like the rain that never makes it to the ground, the virga, the walking rain. My heart waits for words that might come, someday, but that linger high in the air like raindrops that never fall.

Closing the door on burning questions does not silence them or send them into exile. No, to the contrary. Unanswered, they fester and gather strength and set out to get the attention they need, by poisoning if necessary. The poet Robert Bly says that men and women carry a long black bag behind them. That bag contains all that is blotted out, pushed aside, unrecognized, repressed, and denied. It is a bag filled with sorrow, fear, and ghosts. I dragged my bag through the desert that morning, kicking up rocks, raising a rooster tail of dust, knocking over dead teddy bear cholla, picking up fallen prickly pear pads, ocotillo spines, and rabbit turds. I can almost hear the scraping of it, and my heart tells me it is there, like an invisible cinder block harnessed to my shoulders, or an ironwood cross plowing a trail through the sand.

There are questions I am not strong enough to entertain, that are too big to digest: the desert that has gone from trail to subdivisions—gleaming blots on the desert skin, hung with "no trespassing" signs; the inadequacy I feel as a father of two young boys growing faster than I can understand; my mother wasting away from Alzheimer's in a nursing home two thousand miles away. No, unanswered questions don't go away, but linger and taint the day with dread. In the world beyond running I have little control. My days feel jumbled, chaotic, entropic, tangled, impossible to comprehend or sort through. My mind dances around the big questions, the direct lines to feeling out of control, all of which lead to a grief that I am sure will smother me.

I let them sit there, like boulders in the streams of my awareness, and go back to the simple push of foot against the trail. Run. Just run. Often, if I run long enough, I forget they are there. Then I feel euphoric, relaxed. It is a place I return to when I can.

I keep running. Yes, that is better. Just settle into the rhythms.

I surrender to the heat, to the ebbs and flows of tension. I allow the discomforts, the pains, to go and come, rise and fall.

I run until the pain begins to dissolve, break up, loosen its grasp. The heat turns my body to chills, a strange paradoxical sensation, and I watch the pain as the chills and shivers run up and down my arms. The periphery of sight goes dim and blurry, but the center stays focused and I continue to look through it. I speed up. As I accelerate, my hands begin to tingle and the tingling spreads up my arms and then legs toward my trunk, slowly, steadily. I push harder, approaching a sprint. Just as the tingling works its way over my whole frame, I reach the end of the run, tap the bar, stop the clock, bend over and breathe. Yes, here, with the hydraulic surges of blood in my ears, arms, and thighs, I am home, alive. And here I want to weep, but don't, unless the effort has been great, beyond anything I can handle. After hours of running, sometimes at the finish line, I let the tears come, from where I do not know. But now my back, neck, and arms feel loose and full and in tune. The desert and I absorb each other's heat.

I feel at home here in the rhythms of breath that are part of long-distance running—the only time I feel content, light, awake. Once someone asked me if I was ever really happy, and I had to answer that I was not, except after an effort long enough to throw me against "the wall," a place where the body begins to burn itself for energy to keep going. It was only after this kind of effort that I let my guard down, that some numbness fell away. I made the inferential leap that movement frames the story that comforts. And I want to move faster.

Light travels down the alluvial slope that extends to the foothills and valley. It has reached the floor, setting the day in motion. The starting gun fires, and the invisible rider who controls the clock digs his hot spurs into the flanks of dreaming workers. It is time to get going. The bag catches up to me and the muscles again go tight with the need to keep watch over the struggling figures inside.

I walk the last stretch to the house before showering the cold shower of necessity, hurry, and livelihood.

The rest of that morning I didn't see much. As a college writing teacher saying good-bye to the freedom of summer, I was reluctant to let go of that peace, time, and space. My thoughts were my own on break, but now the transition back to teaching meant I would give up the rambling, free, and utterly captivating freedom of unstructured time. I had learned somewhere that vacations were good and work was bad. In fact, I am sure there is a banner somewhere beneath the family coat of arms that states, "Life is not something to enjoy; it must be endured."

As I and the boys packed up for school, I noticed the easel and paints I had set up in the corner of the living room. I was halfway through an oil painting of Cochise Stronghold showing imposing granite spires catching the light of a rising sun, but finishing that would have to wait for the top layers of painted detail. The colors now were just a wash, and the precipices looked flat, dead, and amateurish. I resented the reminder of things left undone, and the prospect of not being able to focus on it tore at my gut.

"Come on, let's go," I told the boys, with a hint of menace in my voice. They were not used to getting up and were still busy munching down toast as they packed their rudely oversized backpacks. They both needed haircuts and were showing hints of gangling adolescence. When I was their age, I hated my father and his incessant barking to hurry up and hop to.

This business of being rushed got under my skin. The irritation poured over me like a chemical wash. Why, I wondered, had I caved in to this life? I was more like my boys, a teenager hiding in the skin of a man in middle age. I looked shaved, combed, showered, ready to lead and teach, but felt harnessed, domesticated, and hitched to a plow at the start of planting season. It had not been my vision to be a householding teacher, a worker bee. Many years ago, in my picture of the future, I was not going to be one of those who were bent to the will of the Man, the organization, the machine of the corporate state. I was going to be different.

"We're leaving in six minutes, and if you're not in the car, I'm leaving without you," I said as I turned and marched out the door. The boys started to blame each other. "If Sean would only hurry up," or "Kyle is so selfish, he never gets ready on time." But the three of us filed out to the Jeep. Always eager to be pressed into service, it started up when asked, began burning oxygen and exhaling greenhouse gases, ready for another day.

Vapors left after the brief overnight sprinkle rose in a sweltering vengeance from the pavement as we pulled out of the gravel drive and onto the four-lane highway that crosses the big wash on its way toward the city limits. We joined the river of commuters.

This day in particular had to be the worst, I told myself. To start with, it was the first day of school for my kids and the first day back at work for me. My two sons were in junior high at two different schools and I needed to get them up early and drive them in for their orientations and early classes. They both complained bitterly about the end of summer, about the beginning of homework, about new, starchy shorts, about the punishing heat of August in Arizona. School, the heat, new, starchy clothes—all great reasons to complain and feel justified doing so.

I did not disagree. We drove to the various schools in my old Jeep, its paint peeling off the hood, its spare tire rattling, listening somewhat unsympathetically to the news on the radio: war, fear, celebrity scandal, hunger for something better. We joined the other commuters, many of them busy doing anything other than driving: talking on the phone, sipping coffee, trimming beards, glossing lips, drying hair, catching up on last night's DVD, flossing teeth, teasing out kinks, plucking curlers, solving sudoku. This multitasking, rolling carnival had a soundtrack, a video track, and was going to look good, or die trying.

We plied the currents of traffic and distraction across town, jockeying for position, careful not to get caught behind a city bus and the delays it would cause. The boys then dutifully hauled their backpacks and band instruments into their separate schools. I spurred my mule of a car down the boulevards of Tucson toward the university. The picture of my boys—their impossibly skinny arms and legs, the load of backpacks, lunch bags, trumpet, and saxophone they carry—is etched onto my mind. I can see too the responsibilities of homework, practice, and submission to authority weighing them down. The image lingers. They are growing away from me, being handed over to a smokeless assembly line that will stamp and shape them into men, into workers. I don't let the thought go any further, nor do I weigh or measure the implications. I know my time with them is short, but I can't see past my own problems—having little to show for years of work and a life that is not the life I imagined when I was younger. I have my own burdens to carry.

I could not shake the tape loop reminding me it was my first day back, and I had to shake it, had to get ready. It was up to me to present at the training session for new graduate teaching assistants. Talking the whole while to myself, I wound my way through the maze of streets to an off-campus parking spot on a neighborhood street. A litany of complaint and faultfinding chattered on behind my eyelids: it's too hot; I don't want to go back to work; I'm losing this race; I have failed—failed to keep the roof from leaking, failed to raise my boys well, failed to gain any kind of respect or notoriety for my writing. The words, my love of words, the passion for finding the right ones, all seemed to have stayed on vacation. There it was again, in the pit of my stomach, that searing fear of something. Quick, on to something else.

Failed on all fronts—yeah, that's it. I see my failure all around me. In the eyes of my colleagues, in the arrogance of rival writers, in the piles of ungraded papers, in the paltry paycheck I receive for showing up and conducting classes with students who don't much care, who see me as a roadblock that takes up time on their way to fun and freedom. Blah. Blah. Blah. In short, although I did not like it, I saw failure everywhere because it was in me; it was the filter, the lens, through which I taste and perceive the world. The talk was poison, and it would not rest or change until something supplanted it—necessity, distraction, or crisis.

I came to a stop curbside and switched off the life-supporting AC, without which there would likely be no metropolis in the desert, no shopping malls, no golf courses, no sushi bars, no tanning booths, no custom homes climbing the ridges, insulting and scarring the mountains with roads bull-dozed to vain hideaways. Air-conditioning is the lifeline to population and prosperity, the comfort that makes the summer bearable. The momentum of noise did not slow, even after the radio was silent. The steamy morning flooded the interior, setting my skin aglow with the prickly monsoon sweat. So much for the shower.

I threw open the door and got a blast of sun to go with the moist air before I went through the routine: put the locking bar, the Club, on the steering wheel, disconnect the faceplate from the radio and put it under cover in the storage console between the seats, extract the ignition kill from beneath the dash, unfurl the windshield shade and slip it into place, lowering the visors to hold it there. Done.

They say that Jeeps are the number-one stolen vehicle in the number-one town in the country for auto theft. They say; they say . . . It's already been broken into a couple of times, so I have to take these precautions. All part of the urban desert experience. Trust in Allah, but tie your camel.

I stepped outside the truck, and the dog began to bark. The fibers of muscle in my neck and shoulders went tight with hot anger. I have been parking in the spot for several years when I can't park on campus. This dog, an overweight but otherwise handsome Queensland heeler, knew me. But he barked as if I'd slipped through a window and was abusing his mistress.

I reacted.

I began to taunt the dog under my breath, to call him names. He is the Dim Dog. The Dumb Dog. The dog wanting another brain cell so that he can rub the one he has against another. The dog that needs to shut the fuck up. He stood there, hopping with rage, behind his wrought-iron gate and howled, snarled, and yipped, calling in reinforcements, sending out the alarm that the perimeter had been breached.

I was so tense I could barely remove my bike from the roof rack. When I finally did, I pedaled away in a foul humor, a cloud of irritation leading the way and trailing behind me as I rolled toward campus.

Yes, the day was a normal one.

I slung my book bag over my shoulder, clipped on my bike helmet, and finished the last two miles of my commute to the university.

I noticed the tires were low and that the day would probably be a scorcher. Clouds were already gathering around the peaks of the mountain ranges. They would likely become full-blown thunderstorms by the afternoon, possibly drenching me on my return trip to the Jeep.

Sweat pasted my shirt to my back and leapt off my forehead by the time I locked the bike outside the office. I felt rivulets of sweat running down my chest as I unlocked the door with resignation and reluctance. I then calculated and traced the time I would spend at each of my duties, keeping my attention on that moment when I would finish, ride back to the car, go pick up kids, and go home to rest. I have to admit I just wanted to sleep away this workday.

That, I knew, would have to wait.

I loaded two diet sodas into my book bag. Like bullets into a bandolier, they stacked nicely next to each other. The caffeine would help get me through the morning, would help mask my indignation that summer was ending.

I trudged off to the orientation meeting, eyes marking the expansion joints in the sidewalk as they passed beneath my step. What was that saying? I mused . . . step on a crack and break your mother's back? Not that my mother, now into the advanced stages of Alzheimer's, would be much worse off. That thought precipitated greater gloom, greater turbulence in my mental air. I hunkered down into my task. It was as if I were carrying some massive weight in my book bag that pulled my attention downward. What I really saw was not the cracks, nor much of anything in the world around me, but the scenes of where else I felt my life should be.

The elsewheres ran the usual range of distraction and daydreaming. I thought I should set up my life to be more free, maybe move to Montana and get a big dog, a sheepskin coat, and write muscular action novels about climbing mountains or running rivers, or outrunning and foiling the greedy corporate evildoers. They would be novels that were simple, good, and true, that saw the big picture without turning away, that said what needed to be said. Or I reviewed lost loves from college days. I wondered what other lives I might be leading if I had taken a different path. Maybe I'd work in a studio out back behind somewhere rustic, a bit brooding, romantically scenic, like a beach in the Northwest, lonely with seagulls calling overhead, where my paints would not have to be put away every school year, where I would have time to write. I just did not think my life would be like this, not so much the duties and routines but the nagging heaviness of it, the leaden body.

In general I felt that life had dealt me someone else's hand, that I was sitting in for someone, that I was playing out a provisional existence waiting for my real life to begin, that . . . that . . . on and on. Exactly what real life was I didn't know, but it had to be something other than the one I had. I was waiting for the real and absent owner of this life to return and to resume his days so that I could get up and begin my own life, one much more glamorous than the one I was playing out.

So I walked, eyes on the curbs, cracks, and crosswalks, book bag obeying the traffic laws of gravity. My walk to the general meeting signified the end of free time and the initiation of another school year, the grip of responsibility, where my time would no longer be my own but at the beck and call of the Program. It is easy to find an enemy in authority. I would soon speak to a large group about teaching, about policies, about things necessary but only vaguely interesting. I would do my job, go through the motions, and, in the process, provoke questions that I didn't want to answer. I just wanted to be left alone. Yes, just left alone. But that would not happen, not today anyway.

I approached and then entered the auditorium where the meeting was about to take place, and I saw my colleagues, some friends, and the new graduate students whom I would advise. People organized themselves into clusters of conversation, and I was swept up in the talk, excited by some of it, bored by some of it, but occupied. I was surprised again by the youth of the grad students. They looked to me like freshman college students. How had it happened, I wondered, that they were so young and that I was so old? There were about thirty of them, and they were full of hope, life, and enthusiasm. I had to admit they were beautiful, healthy people at the opening doors of a career in academics.

What had happened here? When I was a freshman in college, I found words. My mother had given me books she loved, had set the kindling of reading at my feet and struck the flint, repeatedly, and I had read, had found something in Sinclair Lewis, Theodore Dreiser, and others, but had not yet begun a self-sustaining burn. Literature had been her church, her guiding light. I did not quite understand what she saw there. Literature took her away from the day to day, which she dealt with only reluctantly. For her, life was a burden to be borne so that one could find time to read. But after I left home for college, words began to pour out of somewhere, showing me thoughts I did not know I had, a world I had no idea existed, in a voice I knew dimly that I had to follow. I dreamed to be here, to be a teacher, to write whatever it was that was the truth hidden in telling detail and image. But here I was living my dream without the vision or passion. They had gone out of reach, under cover. In their place, duty ruled, and I obliged. Papers piled up.

I walked through the door to begin another semester as the weight of it settled on me. A future stretched before me, a chain of tasks all of which pulled me away from the brooding over something I did not understand. I had become a mule, a cargo carrier, a cop of sorts. Had teaching changed or had I? I met with the graduate students, and I got swept up in the momentum of the task. I presented, drawing from the well of years of experience to prepare them to teach their first classes, to uphold the university requirements and attendance policies. I tried to shelve my reluctance and to be helpful, to speak from my own humanity to theirs.

The hours passed in the lockstep progression of seconds, dragging a heavy past, burdened by a dreaded future. "Time is what keeps the light from reaching us," writes Meister Eckhart. His words echo somewhere, but get lost. They sound vaguely insane and dangerous. I was frozen in time, numbed by its oppressive grasp. I had learned too well that work was something to endure, never to enjoy, and dutiful son that I am, I played my role to keep my mother close. The grad students reminded me of myself in earlier days, faces eager, a little afraid. I gave them what I could, but could squeeze no more help from the spring of my being by the end of the day. I had performed the work I was asked to do—had shown them parts of the campus, had eaten lunch with them, and gone over ways to organize their syllabi. For three hours I had led a discussion with them, all in a circle, about teaching, about fear, about the substantial undertaking of running a college writing class. They looked to me for guidance, and I felt a spark of excitement that I quickly extinguished. The invitation was there, but I declined, watching the clock.

Then the workday was over. I left the gauntlet of leadership and reentered the steam of monsoon summer. The promised storm had gathered and lit the mountains with lightning. I knew I would get wet on my bike ride back to the Jeep and I did, but it did not bother me. It was such a relief to have gotten through the first day that the rain felt good, cleansing even. The rain fell hard and cold as lightning struck very near. I pedaled awkwardly across campus, keeping my loaded book bag on my back. It had a tendency to swing forward, pulling even heavier on my shoulders. I rode fast on poorly inflated tires through streets filled with silt-filled rivers of runoff. Cars slurped through the running streams, stoplights went out when power was cut, and I navigated as well as I could the back roads to the car, the Dim Dog barking, the schools where I picked up my boys efficiently and uneventfully.

None of this lived up to the standards I felt my life should fulfill. There was something I felt I should be doing, something that would give me energy rather than just wear me out. I listened again to the radio as the three of us worked our way across town to home, to dinner, to more of the news, and then finally, blissfully, narcotically, sleep.

3 / Darkness and Silence

O beautiful
Darkness and Silence
the two eyes that see God;
great staring
Eyes.
Robinson Jeffers

The air that night was thick and inescapable, its density blanketing my senses as I shuffled quietly across my front yard. It smelled of rain-soaked creosote, tasted like tar. Low clouds, hung with humidity, an afterglow of the storm, rested still in space, ghosts dancing in front of a lead curtain of overcast. Drops, stubbornly resisting their fall to earth, still hung on the paloverde branches.

I walked ahead of my two sons, Kyle and Sean. We had been swimming in the community pool and were returning home. Normally, I close up the pool, put the cover on the spa, shut off lights, store pool toys. But that night I had finished before they were done playing and walked ahead of them, leading them by about ten feet or so. I could hear them roughhousing behind me, relieved, like I was, that the first day of school was now history. They jostled each other like puppies, goggles hanging from their necks. I felt as heavy as they were light.

As I stepped forward through the dark, sound muffled by the thick blanket of air, scent stifled by rising vapors, vibrations dampened by soil saturated and loose, a rattlesnake tasted the air with its heat-sensing pits and its delicate tongue.

I walked in a cottony somnolence beneath the arbor of wild, untrimmed trees. The branches wept drops, bent low to the ground with their weight of water, and brushed my brow, an attempt to rouse my sleeping soul. But I did not heed them. I was swimming in a stream of noise and anxiety that was telling me how much I had to do the next morning, how worried I was about it going well, how much I resented having to put it all together and put my introverted self in front of so many people. I might as well have been sleepwalking.

I can only imagine the sequence of events that unfolded as I shuffled blindly forward in the dark. The snake, its venom sacs full of expectation, turned to flee as the gap between us closed. Unable to escape, the snake likely turned again and prepared to rattle a threat, to ward off the approach of a bone-crushing creature, but it was too late for flight, too late for threats, as my foot fell very near the snake's body.

No one can know how a snake perceives the world, what it sees from eyes that have never blinked, how it can wait coiled for days next to a mouse trail, alert as a samurai, still as stone, for a rodent that may or may not pass within striking range.

What the snake felt or thought is beyond the grasp of my imagination, but its actions were as clear and defined as blueprints. As I walked toward the light of the front porch of our house, a rattlesnake struck the side of my left foot; venom glands on the snake compressed, sending venom through the delicate ducts and into the hollow, syringelike fangs, which had extended beyond the protective fang sheaths. The snake had likely disarticulated its jaw in order to extend the curved fangs outward. The fangs, between one-half and three-quarters of an inch long, then penetrated my skin and sank deep into the soft tissue on the outside of my arch. Venom then passed almost instantaneously through the discharge orifice into the muscle of my foot.

If I had been wearing boots, carrying a simple light, or even just tapping the ground with a walking stick, I might have heard a faint "tick" as fangs struck something inanimate, leaving a harmless stain, or I might have seen him ahead and then stepped aside to admire the pattern of rhomboid scales, or I might have just startled my trespassing neighbor. If . . . then I would have sidestepped injury, would have continued the uninterrupted trajectory of my life. But he and I crossed paths in the shadows. Like colliding pinballs, each of us was knocked off course and sent spinning onto another, this one new, untraveled, unforeseen.

I froze, wondering what had just happened, and tried desperately to divert the boys from whatever it was beneath me. My thick foot, hungry heart, worried bones, and softening gut—all this ephemeral assembly of cells, chemistry, distortions of reality, and electrical impulse—all became subjects to sudden harm. As sophisticated as a syringe, the delivery system did its work. Then the snake rattled a dry leaves whir.

What happens in one's mind when life decelerates from supersonic distraction to a standstill of awareness? Do neurons short-circuit? Do endorphins or adrenaline or dopamine chemically alter the workings of it? Do the vibrations of the molecules suddenly freeze like the child's game of red light/green light? Does God tap you on the noggin with a wand that allows light to enter between the spaces left by stillness and illuminate, or perhaps disrupt, the inertia of habit? Is it all these things? Is it none of these things?

Are we forever in exile until just before we die and get to see what is really at work on this lovely, lonely, harried planet? Do we finally give up feeling distinct and reconnect to that which has sustained us all along?

Does the kundalini energy of Hindu stories, the internal snake that rests coiled at the base of the spine, suddenly travel up, circling vertebra by vertebra, to the sleeping mind, where it delivers a bolt of energy?

Hell if I know.

We may never know, but my world was temporarily suspended outside of time by the surprise waiting for me in the summer heat of my front yard. In that gap of no time, no hurry, no motion, fear took a vacation. No time to be afraid. And anxiety fell through the windows that opened as my ship of a life suddenly dropped anchor.

This was something I could not explain when others later asked how it was. When they heard about it, they assumed that I sped up even more, that fear and worry and anxiety somehow redoubled their efforts to keep things moving. It seemed the answer to crisis: to keep moving, to keep accelerating fueled by catastrophic stories and skin-tingling danger. Yes, the stories we tell about snakes came to life, awakened by what others saw as my front yard abomination. The stories reared their hoary heads, awakened by a deep-seated, mythological fear.

Some would see in the bite the realization of a nightmare. Others a random, freak coincidence of nature. A few saw it as an unprovoked attack by a demon. No one was neutral.

For me, the snakebite sent a search party out into the brain. It could not return until it found some way to tell the tale that gave it context, suitable villains and heroes, a sense of human place in a world still wild to the mind. The bite rendered me silent, and for some reason vigilant, expectant. It could be that I was in the middle of some cognitive dissonance about how to understand snakebites, or that I had read too much Carlos Castaneda, or that I just had a chance to frame a story that would serve me somehow.

Whatever the case, the stories that others told said more about them than about the snake. They showed fear and revulsion and fascination. They spoke to mystery and danger; they were passionate, creepy, transfixed, and certain. Also absolutely nonrational. The snake posed a physical danger, to be sure, but people face more physical danger—by driving, breathing polluted air, even eating—all the time without thinking twice about it.

The exaggerated response revealed both fascination and fear of the serpent. I was not sure what this meant, but the magnitude of the reaction surprised me.

By way of contrast, I had nothing to fill in the blank. Chatter just stopped, like a tree full of birds after the report of a rifle.

Although I did not yet know it, the bite was one of the bad ones; that is to say, it was a full shot of venom. I stood there for a second, dumbstruck as a doorknob. Did I walk into a prickly pear? Had I tangled up my ankle in barbed wire? My mind, boggled by the strange set of stimuli that did not fit any previous experience, ran a survey through stored memories and came up with nothing. There was no file to explain this in the mental hard drive.

But when I heard the rattle, I put one and one together and came up with fucking two. Bingo! and Duh! wound around each other at having answered the question of the day, but then stared into a void that revealed nothing about what to do next. The only thing I knew for certain was that it had been me and not one of my boys. I can handle pain and poison. I can be stupid and pay the price. I can take one for the team and live through it. I could not watch them in pain. I could not, then or ever, bear watching one of them taken hold of something like snake venom. Something in me said a quiet thank you and then began to settle in for a long ride into uncharted territory.

I had to appraise the moment. Square one: I had been negligent. If I were a Zen monk, the master would have come by and given me a nice whack on the back for not keeping my "lamp burning," for not staying awake and present. I was sleepwalking in bare feet through snake territory. My bad. If I were a packrat, I would soon have become snake dinner. As it was, I was just a distracted interloper coasting along in a cloud of distraction.

A cop once told me that most car accidents happen because no one is in the car. At the time he was referring to me, but I, of course, generalize this to everyone else, point the finger, include other bipeds in the observation. No one is paying attention, that is. I wasn't in the car, so to speak; I didn't have my lamp burning; I was asleep at the wheel, a dim bulb—all perfectly normal stuff.

Anyway, like most people who live in the desert, or anywhere poisonous snakes are common, I had a vague picture of what a snakebite would be like and an even vaguer plan of what I would do if bitten.

Let me say what it was not. It did not follow the scripted images from old westerns, the Hollywood version of a snakebite in which an evil, malicious rattlesnake, as thick as a good ol' boy's truck tire, locks its fangs into the flesh of the hero, only to have the hero wrestle the offending demon to the ground by breaking its neck, prying the fangs out of the arm or foot, tossing the snake aside to be skinned later and made into a belt. The hero then magically applies a tourniquet using his sweat-rotted, bloody bandana, unsheathes his hunting knife and makes two incisions on each fang mark in the shape of crosses or X's, before sucking the blood and the poison out and spitting it contemptuously onto the sand. He promptly passes out, only to wake up cured with the sunrise. He gets back on his horse and rides off into the next adventure, unchanged, the bite nothing more than a casual memory.

Nor did I follow other folk remedies. I did not decapitate a dove, then open its breast and place its body on the bite so that it might leach the poisons from my body to its body. Nor did I spread a poultice of garlic onto the wound or sing any incantations. Although I might have liked to, I did not even drown myself in whiskey with hopes of disinfecting both the bite and my brain, leaving it free of any coherent thought. Good thing too. I had some road to travel and needed every brain cell I could find, borrow, beg, or press into service for the cause. I just dodged a bullet, thank God. People die from snakebite remedies as much as get cured by them.

Nope, pretty much I was thought-less. Speechless. Tongue-tied.

I guessed that, as a minimum, I would be able to walk out of wherever I was after being bitten. I thought I would have at least that little piece of a repertoire of response.

Nope. Within seconds, I could not stand, much less walk. I could not even have ridden a bike. They aren't kidding when they say the only treatment for snakebite is car keys. And those snakebite kits? Pretty much a joke—though a mild constriction band and some suction done immediately might get about 5 percent of the venom out. No, at that moment, with no antivenin, there was nothing I or anyone there could do.

At the time, I kept hoping it would only be something of a nonevent. I thought this was a very simple, quick, surgical bite that was likely "dry," containing very little or no venom. I fully expected to go and get a shot or take a pill and be home in my bed after a brief visit to the emergency room. I would have a story to tell in the morning.

This minor hindrance was to be a blip on the radar screen of my life, a lowercase curiosity—nothing more.

Saying some things again and again will never make them so.

4 / Someone at the Door

I hopped up to the porch, because already I could not walk. I was excited but, oddly, not alarmed. It hurt, but it wasn't too bad. I kick-started my mind. OK, think for a second, sort this out. One, the actual bite had not been too painful. Two, it seemed unlikely that much venom had been injected in such a brief, inconsequential prick. The snake was simply trying to protect itself and to scare me.

And, I'm on the snake's side. I have no malice toward snakes. I understand my role in this misunderstanding, officer. I don't want to press charges. Let's just go on with our business and forget the whole thing. The snake was justified. I mean, it was humid, dark, warm—perfect time for snakes to hunt. The snake was hungry and that was not good. Because it was hunting, it likely had full sacs of venom. Given that it had rained, flooding the ground squirrel holes and packrat middens nearby, the snake, no doubt, could all but taste rodent on the warm air, and was hoping for a warm-blooded creature to come into range of the heat-sensing pits between its nostrils and eyes.

On the other hand, an adult snake often will not release all its venom to defend itself. It usually saves that for prey. I wasn't paying attention at a particularly bad time and got too close. It was a potentially deadly consequence for inattention, for which I take complete responsibility.

Three, there was some thrill in having been bitten, and I thought I would not be excited about something that was really dangerous. I didn't know anybody who had died from a snakebite. I didn't know anybody who had been crippled by a bite. I did not even know anyone who had been bitten. It couldn't be that bad. But all of my reasons for complacence faded as the swelling and pain began in earnest.

Megan, lovely, coolheaded, ever practical lover, mother of our boys, and wife, dialed 911 while I sat on the porch swing. Nonplussed, she smiled, I swear, like a Cheshire cat, and had her finger marking her page in the book *God in All Things*. She recognized the need to deal with this situation, but would return to her reading as soon as I was taken away. She reads late into the night, long after I, done in by a day of words, have expired. You can see it in her eyes. She is off somewhere, seeing past this thick world to somewhere else. I am mired in this world, and we sometimes spar about who lives in the better place. She is hot on the trail of something and, like my mother, pushes books on me. They are both women possessed, devout, zealous, utterly self-possessed. How can she be so calm, I wonder to myself.

"Here he is," she said into the phone before turning to me exactly as she would if a friend had called and wanted to gossip. A second for Megan seemed minutes for me. I sat, expecting what I did not know. Tick, tick, tick. Something was coming. I did not know what. It turned out to be the phone, and she pushed it toward me. Oh yeah, the operator. I spoke with her, fumbling answers into the mouthpiece. Yes, I was sure I had been bitten. How did I know? Well, my foot was starting to ignite and there were two rather undeniable blood spots on my white sock. They were about an inch and quarter apart. That was a big snake. Yes, I felt pain, and, uh huh, yes, my arch was beginning to swell. Would I be there when an ambulance came? Yes, I wasn't planning on going anywhere. No, I wouldn't ask anyone to go anywhere near the snake.

In general, the venoms of the rattlesnakes produce alterations in the resistances (and often integrity) of the blood vessels, changes in blood cells, and blood coagulation mechanisms, direct and indirect changes in cardiac dynamics, alterations in the nervous system, causing sensory and motor changes and depression of respiration, leading to respiratory difficulties. (Text in italics comes from Findlay Russell's excellent book *Snake Venom Poisoning*.)

I hope this doesn't sound too melodramatic, but as I sat waiting for the ambulance, the roles and titles that I thought defined who I was evaporated. In the next minutes my life as a teacher, soccer coach, runner, driver, upright pisser, runner, refrigerator door opener, burrito chef, runner, sleeper, all dissolved, and I became little more than a piece of meat that was being digested by highly toxic enzymes, a body that soon could not work or walk and that was in the first round of a fight for its life. The fibers I wove together as a kind of shield to protect myself against the pains and threats of the world, both inside and out, unraveled, leaving me holding only threads, a searing vulnerability.

The venoms of snakes contain at least 26 enzymes. . . . In the rattlesnakes we find the most highly developed venom, as well as the most highly developed delivery system. . . . All crotalid (rattlesnake) venoms examined so far appear to be rich in proteolytic enzyme activity. . . . It seems reasonable to assume that many of the deleterious effects of snake venom can be attributed to the proteolytic activity of enzymes. The damage to muscles and subcutaneous tissues has long been demonstrated. In a well-designed and well-executed group of experiments, these investigators demonstrated that when crotalus atrox *(Western Diamondback) venom was injected into subjects, it accelerated the rupture of abdominal and other organs of prey.*

As the venom spread, my foot felt like corrosive acid had been poured on living tissue. A dragon had hatched and was uncoiling under the narrow confines of my skin. As it uncoiled, its scales tore at my flesh and burned. It hurt like hell. I felt my skin could not contain such pressure and heat; I began to shake as shock set in.

They say that snakebites can be painful. I would call them unearthly agony. Flesh is digested by dynamic agents that have evolved to make you bleed to death, that attack and liquefy capillaries and nerves from the inside out. Cells hemorrhage. You cannot come up for air above the pain, pain that rolls and rakes and pummels you again and again, relentlessly, incessantly. It feels as if the venom burns the tissue, but it is the pressure from the swelling that fuels the flame.

At this point the pain was just beginning, but promised to grow from a tiny flicker to a raging fire. I leaned back against the porch swing, raised my head to look at the rough-cut rafters, and tried the techniques I use to cope with pain while running. I breathed and watched the pain rise up, tension gather, and then recede as neck, shoulders, and legs relaxed. I rocked the swing gently with my good leg, trying to focus, to stay calm. I tried to center my attention on my breath, to take refuge in my breath, and to keep my awareness on my breath instead of the foot in front of me. I sought samadhi, a state of suspended animation, slowed breathing, of disconnect from the body. I was not successful. It was a mismatched tug-of-war. All of my consciousness began to shrink onto that area around my left arch that seemed to be uncoiling beneath those two blood spots now running down my sock.

Sean, my younger son, came out of the house and sat next to me, clearly concerned. He needed me to tell him something. I told him that I loved him, that it was going to be all right, that he was great kid. Inside, however, I had some questions. I realized I had no idea what was going to happen. I wish I could say that I considered the value of my life, how I had lived, and that I vowed to live it better if I would be given the gift of survival. I wish I could say that I was able to harbor noble thoughts that one might have standing near the abyss of possible death. No, from very early on, all I could handle was surviving the pain.

I held on until the paramedics arrived and then surrendered to the shakes that had been building. They examined my foot, retrieved a gurney from the ambulance, and loaded me onto the bed. One of the paramedics captured the snake beneath a tree and bagged it for later release (I'm guessing). I saw the silhouette and judged it to be about three and a half or four feet long, and maybe as thick as my forearm at its widest girth. Probably a diamondback I said to no one in particular. Or, as an afterthought, a mojave, a big one. Then it was clipped into a metal toolbox and carried away.

The paramedics began the long process of recording the spread of pain and venom up from my arch to ankle to calf and eventually thigh, hip, and rib cage. With a permanent felt-tipped marker, they turned my leg into a kind of ruler that measured and timed the effects of venom on the tissues in my foot and ankle. The swelling took on a life of its own as it moved up my leg like a flood. It was a flood of envenomation, and proceeded up my leg about two or three inches every half hour. With the swelling came the pain. The paramedics kept asking me if I knew who I was, what year it was, who was president, where I was, how many fingers they were holding up. I felt like I was completing a survey while my house burned down around me. Rafters collapsing, beams crashing down in an array of scattered embers, exploding propane cylinders—none of it was noticed by my interviewer.

Mitchell and Reichart also demonstrated the ability of venom to produce edema, ecchymosis, necrosis, incoagulable blood, alterations in the shape and mobility of red blood cells, depression of respiration, paralysis of the respiratory centers and heart, changes in the capillary walls leading to the loss of blood, and hypotension.

I remember seeing the familiar intersections, strip malls, gas stations, and landmarks of my life go past the windows. People were going about their lives on a beautiful summer evening in August. I was in an ambulance for the first time in my life, covered with a blanket, shivering and cold. I did not know how the night would turn out, what my fortune would be, whether or not these were to be my last few hours on earth.

A cold gray cloud closed in around me. My lips began to go numb. My heart raced toward some invisible finish line. Words, still encased in embryonic impulse, wilted, died, and fell to earth like birds shot from the sky. There was no light—only darkening fog. I wondered if this was what Alzheimer's feels like, that words and awareness just slip away, leaving only a blind and mute witness to vague, dim, blunted disconnect. I was suspended in a soundless chamber of cottony dullness. She would understand this, I said to myself. Even a grown man thinks of his mother when life drains away, life the soap foam in a tub when you pull the plug.

It was then that death quietly sat down near me. I could smell it, feel it. I did not see a white tunnel, nor did I feel any warm, forgiving presence. Death was not any kind of primal home, but more like oblivion. Just oblivion. Not a big-deal, fight-to-the-end-to-resist-it kind of oblivion. Just a fact: the end, decomposition, unbecoming. My nose filled with the smell of death, and it made me want to vomit. Surprising myself, though, I did not mind. I remembered that it might not be me lying here in the ambulance. That fact changed everything. It flipped a switch that kept me from running away or looking cross-eyed at my situation. I knew that life would go on. Not my life maybe, but Life, my sons' lives. I neither ran nor fought nor clung. I wanted to live, of course, more than I have ever wanted anything, but wanting is different from grasping, needing, or demanding, like a child crossing his arms and stamping his foot. I wanted it all—the pain, the joy, the chaos, the buzzing perfection of it.

My cottony, thick-headed mind entered an immense and still place in which I could barely breathe. I felt taken over by something I could neither resist nor understand. Only the core mattered, whatever that means. Paradoxically, "outside" my senses reeled at the rising tide that threatened to extinguish my life while at the same time clinging quietly to that which remained. It was like being underwater looking up at a surface tempest, knowing that ships were being wrecked but hearing nothing except a deep hum. Yes, I can hear the incredulous among you. I know you will scoff, but what remained was enough. Anything still flickering was enough, though the world seemed to be collapsing around me. Even though a little life was all I had.

Death was not a friend, but neither was he unkind. I could sense a notion of detachment, a respect for my place in the ephemeral passing of life. I was the latest model life could take, but one that might, at any moment, go out of style in favor of the next big thing. That did not diminish my place here and now, but it did remove the illusion of seeing "me" last any longer than my allotted minutes.

I realized that despite my deepest hopes, I was expendable, part of something much bigger than my little world, and that the cycles of living and dying included me and all of us—my family, friends, and even the more "solid," enduring things like houses, cars, cities, empires. The river is always moving, and death sitting next to me simply revealed it as EMTs struggled to start an IV of something, saline solution? I knew it would go on. The EMTs looked troubled and worked at first as if I were listening, but then bent to their tasks with more urgency as if I were no longer there.

♪ / Crossing Deep Waters

On northern Vancouver Island I once took a kayak out from Telegraph Cove into the Johnstone Straits alone. When I left the cove for open water, the depth of it terrified me. Here I was alone on the rolling ocean in a flimsy plastic craft, with more water beneath me than I could imagine. I could barely move for terror, but I forced my arms to push one stroke at a time. If I survived one stroke, I would take another one, and if I needed to change course, I would adjust. The depth, the deep green inkiness of the sea, continued to tear the bottom out of my psyche. All my puny efforts to understand it drained away. I would never know these depths, would only pass over them, buoyed by mystery, always and forever mystery.

I was traveling again over deep waters. I dipped my paddle by breathing, by holding an aching heart in the cradle of my chest. When we arrived at the hospital, two more paramedics emerged from the emergency room to help lower me from the ambulance. My leg felt heavy, wooden, and looked like the thick pine post supporting a friend's ramada—pale wood, thick enough to support a castle. Already I could barely move my toes or swivel my ankle. Odd to be so immobile I thought, as glass doors whisked open with the speed of eyelids. The light of the place blinded me. I could find no shadow anywhere. They had vanquished darkness from the rooms and hallways and even from the wrinkles in the sheets. Nothing here could escape scrutiny. They wheeled me past the waiting room and directly into inner chambers of the emergency room where they continued to mark and monitor the spread of swelling and pain. White coats with clipboards arrived to determine my SSS, snakebite severity score, the assessment that would gauge the effect the bite was likely to have on me and govern what kind of a response would be best. The rate of swelling, of blood dumping into my lower leg, the early discoloration, my heart at full throttle, racing breath, and early onset of pain all added up to a high score—very severe. Oh good, some portion of my ego thought, I got a high score. If I'm going to do something, anything, I want to do it well, even if it kills me.

There could be no morphine until they checked me for allergic reactions to the antivenin, or antivenom, depending on who is talking, which had to be mixed, infused, and monitored. So we waited. Doctors came and went. Interns, emergency personnel, nurses, all came by to see the bite and its effects on this patient.

Other unfortunates moaned and cried beyond the curtains, but around me a great stillness continued to grow. So this is what it's like, I thought, to be carried, to surrender, to be consumed. I stayed away from places like this at all costs. I ran away from nursing homes, the underworld that held sick people, people who stank, who could not care for themselves. They were the harpies of my nightmares, the contents I shoved into the black bag before sealing it shut and bolting it tight. I thought of my mother, bent in her wheelchair, and imagined that she might be laughing, saying "Now you know how it is to be one of us. . . . Some of us lose our brains, some our bodies, but we all end up here sooner or later." Surprisingly, sheepishly, I said, Yup, guess I am. Oh well.

I could hear beeps, hums, intercoms, and low voices, but inside I was quiet, waiting. Pain flowed above and below me, but missed wherever it was that I had taken up residence. It was strong, but not direct, not quite hooked to me. My body had taken on a life of its own apart from my awareness and was doing what it could to survive. Somewhere out at the edges, I began to shake.

Megan arrived and helped make decisions. She and a growing team of doctors talked about the different kinds of antivenins, of risks, side effects, complications, and also of possible surgical intervention if the antivenin failed to neutralize the venom and I could not coagulate sufficiently. Megan looked worried now. She can be strong, but has a brittle strength. If a situation gets too serious, she panics. She was not panicking, but neither was she the calm, efficient persona I saw on the porch swing. Like my mother, she could handle only so much before caving in, losing it. My mother would turn off and pull away. Both were tightly wound, sensitive, standing with one foot in this world, the other in a ritualized world of spirit. They were not always equipped to manage crisis.

The doctors reviewed the options and explained that I would receive Cro-Fab, a new antivenin treatment derived from sheep plasma rather than the older horse-derived antivenin, which, in the quantities I was about to receive, would produce serious "serum sickness" and other side effects. The two antivenins are extracted from the blood of animals that developed antibodies to various kinds of snake venoms, including eastern and western diamondbacks, cottonmouths, and other pit vipers, such as copperheads.

I had heard that antivenin was scarce and that some people had to endure the effects of venom without it. The thought that I might have to do so infuriated me. I knew on some level that if I did not get some of the antivenin I would likely die. That I would do so because producers or hospitals failed to stock it sent hot indignation into my shoulders and chest.

The moments passed in utter clarity, second by second, like when you hold your breath so you can hear and feel the beating of your heart. I was holding my breath in a big way, so I could see with astonishing brilliance the passing of each second. Time took on a raw, palpable intensity from which I could not turn away. The air was ringing and the light shimmering. Now I can see why some people cling to these moments, want this kind of vitality. Words cannot capture such moments, but they can try.

All of this passed in front of a growing backdrop of pain. My fingers gripped the bed involuntarily. I was shaking so much the bed began to rattle. The light began to fade as I continued to slip into shock. I'm in here, I felt like saying to those who acted as if I was not. I wondered whether or not my mother was "in there," wherever that was, since all we could see was her dementia, her fading fire.

The significance of the fluid loss into an extremity following Crotalus *envenomation is often underestimated. I would suspect that one third of the total circulating volume of the blood may be lost into an affected extremity within several hours of a severe envenomation. Certainly, shock or near shock states could be caused by this loss in fluid volume.*

Treating rattlesnake bites is complicated business, as doctors have to take into account the amount of venom, the possibility of allergic reaction to antivenins, the severity and spread of venom, and other medical conditions. I just wanted them to get on with it, to start infusing the goods and injecting me with painkillers.

For the present it seems wisest to consider all snake venoms as complex mix-

*tures containing peptides, or polypeptides, enzymes, glycoproteins, and other
substances capable of producing several or many pharmacological activities . . .
which are deleterious to living organisms. For the physician it bears repeating
that a snake venom should never be considered solely as a "neurotoxin," "cardio-
toxin," "myotoxin," or any of the other dozens of loosely articulated symptoms,
while dismissing the overall biological activities of the whole venom.*

The test infusion of antivenin produced no allergic reactions, so they
began to inject me with morphine. I could finally come up for air above the
pain. It was not a bend-back-a-fingernail kind of pain, but instead brought
to mind the deep, abiding nausea of a broken bone, which I did know, or
what might be the concussive shock of a hot bullet. The sensations arrived
in waves, not shrill, breaking rapids, not tinny or soprano in timbre, but a
tsunamic bass note, overpowering in its low frequency. I still hurt, but the
morphine gave me the ability to study the pain rather than be consumed
by it.

The infusion of antivenin began in earnest about midnight with six vials
followed by another six to get control of the spread of venom. They had set
aside twenty-four vials, and would proceed through the next couple of days
dosing me two at a time until the venom was neutralized. I ended up using
nearly twenty vials at about two thousand dollars a vial, all but exhausting the hospital's supply. If I had not been close to a hospital, or had taken
longer to get there, I would have needed much more. The antivenin got the
jump on the damage, like smokejumpers onto a wildfire that has not yet
had a chance to consume fuel or travel on the wings of wind.

Doctors asked that Megan leave. The boys needed her at home, and they
would call when they had a better grasp on how the treatment would prog-
ress. I concurred and nodded, however vaguely. She let her hand slip out
of mine when they took me through the doors into the ICU. Alone now, I
caved in to the rolling nausea. I threw up again and again, waves of sickness
rising violently out of an already choppy sea of sensations. Death rode with
me, always quietly but determined to stay at my side. Some time in the
night, though, he moved back into the shadows as the antivenin kicked in.
Monitors kept track of my breathing, and a few times sent out shrill electronic alarms. Each time, I found air again and succeeded in triggering the
diaphragm to contract, bringing in oxygen. Each time was something of a
surprise and an "Oh, I can still do this" moment of simple satisfaction.

I did not sleep, but rested and listened to the rain on the roof and outside the walls. Monsoon storms continued to rinse the desert clean, to fill the tanks in the canyons, to bring life to the tree-lined riverbeds of the valleys.

Every other August, Hopi snake dancers invoke the Serpent Goddess to bring rain. Rattlesnakes carry their prayers out into the desert, to her, prayers born of nights of dancing, of asking for rain. The rattlesnakes had done their job I thought. They had carried our prayers.

Like the young man in another Hopi myth, I was to stay four days in the house of poisons. He stayed with Huruing Wuhti, the deity of hard substances and poisons. He then traveled with her back to the village where they began the lineage of the snake clan. I had no idea where I would be going.

Maybe it was the poison moving through my body, but whatever it was that was me began to break into pieces, to fragment, to dissolve and then float away on a flood like that running down out of the high mountains, the enormous watersheds. Whatever troubles I had been carrying broke up and were carried into an immense silence. The cool darkness of the ICU was comforting. Yes, if someone told me these things I would not believe it, but that does not make it any less so.

The marvel that is life and its fragility was a high wire that I walked all night, the most spiritually resonant night of my life. I don't doubt that dopamine linking up with pleasure receptors also played a role. It all fits together in the end.

When I told this to friends, they nodded, and added that the morphine likely helped with feeling euphoric. I would be inclined to agree, but the morphine could not account for it all. The calm would linger on for weeks. But I digress. Deep inside I was happy. Maybe I am always happy, but just forget, or lose contact. But I was excessively glad to carry this one, to die if that's what would happen. To me, there was no option, no feeling of "Why is this happening to me?" No second guessing.

The IV of saline solution filled my bladder, and I peed prodigious quantities into a plastic urinal that the nurses would measure, empty, and return, freshly washed. The waters flowed everywhere. I made it a point not to set the urinal next to my water pitcher, as the handles were very similar and I did not want to be punished again for not paying attention.

I reinhabited my body at dawn, sure that I would live. I woke. I don't know if that is the right word. I came to after a coma of years; I wheeled around the corner of darkness and reentered the world of the living. I felt I had been handed back a life and been given another chance to walk on the earth in all its wonder. Glory is not too strong a word for what I felt, and I wept in humility, gratitude, and joy.

6 / Another Chance

The storm of the venom had passed, but I still didn't know exactly what devastation it had wrought. I was content with the clear skies, the quiet after the gale. Most of me seemed fine, and parts of me seemed better than ever. I actually welcomed the morning, whatever it would bring. I felt liberated in a way, happy, accepting. I doubt I could have felt better if I were completely healthy and awakening to a day of play in paradise.

I could not eat, but the nurses brought me breakfast anyway and rubbed my back (oh my God, how good that felt), which had been resting on tubes most of the night and was bruised and sore. They drew blood every couple of hours and sent it to Poison Control and other labs. My numbers showed extraordinary amounts of venom but that I was responding well to the antivenin. I could not see the mountains or any trace of the desert. I lay in a world of white, of glass, and of steel. Time was punctuated by instruments that penetrated my skin, that kept track of the rhythms of the body. Breath, heartbeats, skin temperature, measurements of foot, ankle, knee, thigh, waist, showing in black lines. All very here and now; all very mindful. This was hard-core, inescapable meditating. The beeps, displays, and restraint would not let my mind wander. There was nowhere to go anyway.

I received no more morphine. The swelling continued but began to level off, and the damage seemed to be running in a predictable course. Pain settled into a low-frequency, swollen, constant hum. I was surprised at how clear my mind was, how light my swollen body felt. Maybe my body was so glad to be alive that it was dumping buckets of pleasure hormones into the mix, or maybe, deep down, I was just glad to be off work, but I continued to feel good, even at home, in this strange, bizarre, alien environment called an intensive care unit, where many people end up dying.

I wandered in and out of sleep, of dreams. Inside my bubble of a room, I could feel change. I am here, in some new place, but also in some new way, and I look around. I don't know this body anymore. I don't recognize this leg. I am camped temporarily on a ridge and the sun is shining, but I know I have to go down. Weather can change; storms might come. You can't stay too long in high places. The problem is, I can't leave. My leg won't move. It is numb and thick, more weight than I can carry. I cannot go back, nor can I yet proceed forward. I am stuck on a ridge well above the tree line, in limbo between the familiar and the unknown. It is lovely and wild here. No one can stay for long and live. I grasp at something solid, but can't find a grip. It is all here, but simultaneously slipping away.

The nurses came and introduced themselves as they performed their tasks—Dagmar the German princess, Pam, the girl across the street who could beat the boys at football, and the doctors: B., the beauty, L., the wise, O., the powerful, and others read the charts, drew the blood, fluffed the pillows, turned down the lights, emptied the urinal, and knew more about my physical functions and injury than I could ever guess. When they talked over my leg, they referred to the edema, possible coagulopathy, ecchymosis, and other terms I had never heard before, much less understood. When they talked directly to me, they asked me to wiggle my toes and move my foot, which I could do, but just barely. I didn't know it, but they were checking for tissue necrosis, cell death, and my toes wiggling, even slightly, meant that my tendons and muscles were still intact. A pulse in my toe meant that it was not yet a candidate for amputation, that the swelling had not yet cut off its lifeline of blood.

A dark and ruddy purple with crimson circling the toes and the bite colored a leg I did not recognize as my own, but they said that extensive tissue necrosis was unlikely because I had received the antivenin so quickly after the bite. Since the advent of modern antivenins, developed in the fifties and sixties, very few snakebite victims develop serious necrosis, provided they get treatment. Of the 12,000 or so that are bitten each year in the United States, less than 10 percent lose limbs and only about twelve die. Not so in the developing world, though. Roughly 45,000 souls die every year from various kinds of snakebites.

The window for getting antivenin, they tell me casually, is about eight hours after a bite. Time, as they say, is tissue. The greater the gap of time, the more antivenin is needed to neutralize the venom, but only up to a point. After twenty-four hours, the effectiveness is negligible.

I had no idea what my limb was doing or what it meant to me in the long run. Still, the nurses said I was one of the lucky ones. I have to sit with that. One of the lucky ones. I guess that is so, depending on how one looks at it. I was lucky that I would have to reacquaint myself with a leg gone purple on me. It didn't seem that bad if one looked past the swelling around my waist. Good thing I'd been wearing those big shorts or else they would have had to cut them off. The leg was only about as thick as my son's abdomen.

But the edema continued. From the foot the leg ballooned all the way up to my groin and would continue to swell over my left buttock before moving up to my rib cage. The leg, so strong and slim before, had become suddenly sullen, obese, and disobedient, a prodigal appendage unable to play along with the rest of me. I knew it was doing what it needed to survive, but it did seem a bit overstated, a bit theatrical.

Friday, that first day, passed in a kind of cheesecloth shimmer. Light shone from every surface. I can't explain it, but unlike my usual taciturn self, I was not afraid or reserved, and talked as openly with strangers as I would with my dearest friends. There was nothing small, even in the lucid talk with the nurses. I spent the day on my back, with no interest in food, in reading, in moving, or doing anything other than listening and observing. I had arrived somewhere that allowed me interest in everything. A bleb, a poison and blood blister, about an inch and a half in diameter began to form on the sole of my foot; another couple of them formed on my arch. Fascinating. The two fang marks dripped steady streams of blood down the side of my foot. Now look at that. Even if the swelling went down, I realized, I would not be able to walk with the blisters. Oh well . . .

This recovery would be filled with strange risks and surprises. Who ever thought of the term *bleb*? What a thing.

As I lay in bed, I overheard the nurses joking with each other and delighted in their laughter, their camaraderie. I sat back against my pillow all bloated up like Jabba the Hutt. They went about their business of tending to those in traction, fluffing the pillows of the post-ops, bending to the broken of bone. I'd say we got along famously. I felt like an accepted but temporary member of the tribe of the ICU. They did not mind my swollen, discolored limb, or my bleb, or the monitors, or my inability to do much other than be anchored by a black hole of a leg and listen. When I slept, my sleep was light, but I felt rested, awake.

I don't know why, but I was given a free ticket to a heightened state of awareness. Those who are much more spiritually evolved than I have described ecstatic states after something in them dies. What dies, they say, is craving, or grasping, or wanting things to be different than they are. Buddhists say that yogis and masters can cultivate this state. They identify with impermanence rather than with wealth or power. It is said that they live outside of time and abide in an eternal present, liberated.

I felt lost, not in a frightened sense, but in a sense of traveling through places I had never been. I felt lost in my own life, lost in time. The notion of a clock keeping time struck me as ridiculous. The idea of a day marked by hours meant nothing. I wanted for nothing—no phone, no computer, no mail. But food—now, that might soon be interesting. All this just *being* was making me hungry.

By Saturday I had tasted a few things on my tray: cookies, hospital Jello (amazing color and consistency—the same as my foot, ha! ha!), bacon, but still could not eat much. Megan brought the boys by, even though they were not old enough to be allowed in the ICU. Any illusions I had of detachment exploded when I saw them. I felt a cord tighten between my gut and their survival. My intestines gripped hard to this life, to this job I have. I wept uncontrollably at the thought of their being in my place.

While they sat, Kyle drew a picture of my room. The leg he drew took up half the page, while the rest of me barely registered. I guessed that's how it would be. My leg would take up a lot of space.

They also brought in some books, including Lance Armstrong's book, *It's Not about the Bike: My Journey Back to Life*. Not a bad subject, I thought to myself; as my students say when rating a story or essay, I could probably relate.

The books looked interesting, but again I could not partake. No written words today. I had to think, or better, to ruminate on what had just happened. I did not want to distract myself with anything beyond simply being where I was. I luxuriated in feeling the current of gratitude, of quiet acceptance running through me. I felt the fool, the town idiot, the buffoon for not seeing this sooner, this trick of seeing through the talk of discontent, to the secret that being alive is a hell of a thing. Whispering the secret energized me, almost lifted me off the sheets, and comforted me. I felt connected to something, to all things, and delighted in them being just the way they were.

Friends found their way past the staff and dropped in; one of them even dropped off a *Maxim*, a chest-thumping display of soft-core flesh, thinking it would give me some energy, a real reason to live. As good a reason as any, I thought, but I had other things on my mind, and gratefully sidestepped the usual sinkhole of fantasy.

Flowers came in, cards, more books—words, words, the cascade of words filled up the room, a rising tide of talk, drama, and transport away. Stuff started to pile up, and people spread the word about the bite. I took calls from friends all over the country who wanted the juicy details of the bite. I was not prepared to satisfy that craving or to justify vilifying the snake, of playing the role of hapless victim fallen prey to cruel, wild, predatory nature. Nurses circled the wagons and made me off-limits to all visitors excepting family. The noise banged against me, assaulted me. I was not ready yet to harden myself to the static, the bombardment of image and noise. Keep it all away, I wanted to scream.

I was grateful to my visitors, grateful to the nurses for protecting me, grateful to the universe humming to me as I lay in the sheets. I felt like I had a live feed to an energy running through all things, a direct line to some kind of peace and alertness that made everything OK, that made my joy OK, my interest in strangers OK, my acceptance of the beeping monitors, the blood draws, the pissing in bed into a plastic pitcher OK.

As I lay in my reverie, I overheard a few things about the amount of antivenin, about my hematocrit, the percentage of red blood cells in the total blood of the body being down ten points, and about possible recurrence of venom effects as the antivenins lost their potency. The swelling in the thigh had resumed, but they seemed to think it did not warrant more antivenin.

By late afternoon they were ready to move me to a regular ward. One by one, they disconnected the respiration and pulse monitors, but kept the blood pressure monitor and the antivenin IV drip and reduced the blood draws to two or three times a day. I was hoping I would be able to get to a bathroom for a toilet and a shower. My bed was a king's litter as we ranged through the corridors, IVs trailing like banners, the cargo a sinister-looking figure gone near black in the foot and hollow in the eye. As people in the hall looked, gasped, cringed, and then averted their gaze, I held a bouquet against my chest and might have looked to some like a dead man. So be it.

The burden of living according to the noisy plan had been lifted, and I was temporarily dead to the world.

I was moved to a room in a regular ward with another patient who happened to be hooked up to a lung machine. The sound was exactly that of an aquarium, a very large aquarium, one big enough for killer sharks. Howard had a collapsed lung. I had an inflated leg. I could breathe. He could walk. I lay connected to my IV poles; he dragged his life-supporting lung bubbler. The two of us made quite the pair of invalids. The room was dark, crowded, and depressing.

At first, a small part of me felt a little cheated. After all, I had lost my private room and attentive nurses and was now in this crowded, noisy environment with a stranger. Ordinarily, I would have found the surroundings aversive, something to resist, get bummed about. I would even have requested a room change, or perhaps demanded a private room. I wanted quiet more than anything in the world, quiet so that I could be with my euphoria, my intoxicating peace, my feeling of being at home somewhere other than this noisy world. I guess you could look at the new room as a test of sorts. It was a way to see if I could cultivate and sustain my peace even when conditions were less than ideal.

When invited, the strange calm and happiness resurfaced, and I really didn't care if I was in the ugliest, noisiest wing of the whole hospital. As if to reflect my mood, calls kept coming in, as did visitors. I realized my roommate was probably tired of hearing the snake story over and over and said so. Howard said he didn't mind and turned out to be a good guy—funny, deep voiced, soft spoken—and had the nurses eating out of his hand. Paige, also known as the angel, another one of the great nurses, came in at 8:00 and announced that we should all be out dancing. I imagined her and Howard in a pas de deux. Howard laughed. I felt a little sorry that he had such a serious, long-term condition. I also felt fortunate that my condition was likely so temporary, so superficial. He seemed to know more than I did, and reflected sympathy back.

As we made small talk, Howard modeled a deep patience with his illness, the prospects for surgery, and his recovery. He was in for the long haul, and I think was trying to get me to see that I was too, even if I didn't yet know it. I got to like him and even got used to his bubbler as it boiled away relentlessly into the night, the giant aerator, the exhaust vent of the

African Queen chugging its way toward some noble but impossible mission. We made an ugly couple of guys, not the kind of male ideal you would see on the morning PR releases—I mean news shows. We were not mechanized, made-up, made-over, visually enhanced, or retouched. We were real. Somehow, Howard just showed up in all his bubbling grandeur and I thanked him for that.

They moved Howard early Sunday morning and left me with the room to myself. Again, I had some space, some quiet—ideal conditions to sink into my little world of no-time and a microtaste of the big M Mind. My arms and legs practically buzzed with quiet contentment, and the most mundane objects carried in them a kind of luminescence.

I kept sleeping and waking, losing track of time. My sleep cycles stretched days into what seemed like weeks. Time didn't matter, and I didn't mind. I felt as happy and awake at two in the morning as I did at dawn. My sleep rhythms had changed, leaving me with a higher level of energy, more continually alert. A lid had opened and everything in Pandora's box had escaped. Only, the evils in my mind had not infected the world, but instead had left me relieved at not having to sit on the box or jealously guard the key. Nothing seemed so insurmountable as it had before. As long as I held the reins of staying right here, I felt I could handle anything. I told Jo Anne, one of my colleagues at work, that I would come back to orientation in my wheelchair and would present on Monday. She just laughed. I was serious. I thought about calling my brother, going back to the Midwest to visit my mother, about getting a new radiator for the Jeep, about balancing my checkbook, about cleaning out files. Having a chance to get my house in order seemed more than enough to complete the chores, if my mind would only stay quiet long enough.

My mind is an unruly critter. It likes to just jump all over the place and tip things over, act rude and impulsive. It takes one bite out of something and then leaves it sitting there. It's got mixed feelings about work: likes taking things off the to-do list, but doesn't like sticking to anything. Focusing? Forget it. That is a whole other issue. My mind doesn't like to stay on anything, except fun and grabbing goods. It definitely does not like picking up after itself. 'Tis a creature very disgusting to behold when there is work to do, and lovable, sometimes, when there isn't. Neat and clean and ordered it is not. But it does chop things into neat categories: this time bad, that time good, a nabob, as Spiro said, nattering away.

Megan arrived late Sunday morning, asked the nurses if she could move the bed so I could see out the window, and then began transferring my stuff. By afternoon, I had a view of a paloverde tree, a little piece of sky, and some appetite for food and company. Outside I could see the desert spiny lizards playing in the sultry August air, chasing each other, vying for territory. They were still there; the desert was still in the bloom of the monsoon. Rattlesnakes, spiny lizards, Colorado River toads were all still out there, looking for mates, gorging on what harvests they could find. They had a few pools of water, rapidly evaporating, and had to make hay. Tadpoles, fruits of toad breeding, would have to mature on the steep curve of shrinking puddles. The larger ones would eat the smaller ones to grow fatter faster, to become full toads before the stagnant pools disappeared. Then they too would dig into the soil and sleep the sleep of the dead until the next low-frequency drumming of summer rains on the sand awakened them, called them to the dance and the feast and the brief rituals and rites of the monsoon. Some would make it, some would not. Individuals do not matter, the species does. It was all going on out there. Even my snake was likely recharging the venom sacs, hoping to make it through the season, though his chances, if he had been moved out of his territory, were not so good.

The rains had come. Where there is water in the desert, there is life, life in all its hungry, scrambling, procreant abundance.

Life would go on where it seemed like it would end. The desert had already broken my heart, but now it had tried to smite me dead. Or it had kicked me in the butt. Or it didn't really care. Now that would make me love it all the more. I would have to love it for its outrageous and dangerous charms, accept it for the gifts, the risks, and the indifference. Loving is more important than being loved in the big scheme of things. Yes, I still loved the desert, would always love it, now to distraction, till death do us part. Would love it even from the grave.

That modest desert scene outside a hospital window might not have been many people's idea of beauty, but to me it was sublime. A view of the front range of the Rockies could not have been more beautiful or more interesting.

I read Lance Armstrong's book. Not great literature, but not so bad for a meditation on malady and healing. We'll all be broken at some point, even if we don't know it yet. To think otherwise is delusion. To run away from the fact is poison. To face a fact straight on can be medicine. I see myself obsessed with youth, vitality, beauty, the early stages of a life. Nothing wrong with those things, at their time. But life is much wider, more diverse, and much of it passes outside the limited stories we tell about it. Madison Avenue has all of us wanting to be forever young. We're poisoning ourselves no matter what you say. If it's not with substances, it's with poison ideas. We're living and bathing in a toxic cocktail. Anyway, Lance's account of recovery from cancer I found deeply moving, a perfect fit with my euphoria of still being alive. His story of transformation from self-absorbed athlete to cancer survivor defined for me a heroic change. While very different, I wondered if I could shed my old skin, unzip an old identity and step out of that suit into something much more vulnerable, fresh, and alive. I felt fresh and hungry. He is right. It's not about the bike, or just about the bike. I'll add a corollary, Lance: it's not just about the bite either.

I realized that I was beginning a long journey, and that like a run, I was in the initial adrenaline burst of the start. When it passed I would have to settle into a rhythm. My confidence rises, and I tell myself that I can do this well, that it will not hurt as much as I thought, that I might even go faster, and end with a record time, a personal best that will shatter even my views of my limitations. Maybe.

Of course, nothing ends up as easy as I imagine. Fuel runs low, inclines steepen, weather turns nasty, blisters form, people fall. Then you have to dig deep. You have to scoop up some whup-ass out of the bottom of your tank and stretch it out over the long, exhausting haul; it has to last. Before I am done, I know I will be crawling because it is the best I will be able to do. I know that I will want out of this game, whatever game this is, and that I will have to push hard against the limits of mind and body that will want to quit. Exhausted, I will get angry, desperate, and contrite, asking for help, asking that it end. And soon enough, sometimes, it does.

But for now, I was living the salad days, the halcyon season of the snakebite. For the first time in three days, I dug into my breakfast when they brought it. A man spared from oblivion is glad to eat. Only three days, but I felt like I had been fasting forever. It doesn't take much deprivation to renew a few simple pleasures. Ah, the creature comfort, the simple, sensual pleasure of food. But that was only preliminary. I thought I would melt when I sipped the cup of coffee. It was only instant, but tasted every bit of an Italian espresso brewed in the finest café in Florence. It was every cup of coffee distilled down into one, fabulously rich, orgasmic taste. The first bite of the apple in Eden must have had such a taste, the very definition of earthly delight, of knowledge of carnal pleasure. All jaded expectation washed away leaving nothing but pure, unadulterated taste—sin, atonement, confession, whatever, it spoke to and filled the curling strands of my DNA with an almost electrical intensity.

I moved back into the familiar world, bit by bit. For the first time in three days I stayed awake for most of the morning and an afternoon. I told myself again, with great hope that I was right, that I was recovering fast and would soon be able to pick up where I had left off.

OK, I said to myself, that was nice. Now I'm done with this ecstatic stuff and ready to plug back in to the noise, the crazy chaos. My little season in the wilderness is over, and I'm ready for a hot shower, some greasy food, some news about celebrities. I want to let my attention wander. And how about a night with my wife?

As I thought about these things, the curtain began to come down. My body would not move. The here and now began to feel weary and onerous. And the talk of wanting to get out of here increased in volume. I watched how, when my attention wandered on to what was wrong, away from just being glad to have what I had, I lost some of my intoxicated euphoria, some of my energy, and began to live then and there. With just a little steering, though, I could bring it back. This experience of contentment, gratitude, maybe even blessedness, the whole package, was something I could, with effort and sustained focus, modulate. That's right. I hate to say it, but it was up to me.

Now that was terrifying.

When the physical therapist came in to evaluate my leg, I told her my schedule for returning to work. I assumed that she could arrange things so that this episode could come to a close, that I could put back on my hair shirt and get on with life. She just smiled, looking at me like she would at an insane, babbling cretin with sunken eyes and drool dripping off his chin, and said, with the patience of a saint talking to a very young child, "You will not be able to walk for at least eight weeks."

What!? Eight weeks! What about running? Can I run then?

"You might not run for a year . . . or more."

That took a second, or maybe two, maybe ten, to sink in. Eight weeks!? Almost two months! A year!! So much for modulation, for acceptance, for calm, for equa-fucking-nimity. I couldn't understand it. Why so long? She explained the severity of tissue damage and other long-term effects like overall energy level. I just couldn't get it. My frame of reference for this and all other injury is strictly local. When the swelling goes down, it's over. The reality is that this injury is systemic, that it has affected my overall circulatory, nervous, lymphatic, and muscular systems. I began to realize that I had been knocked down a peg or two or three. The going just got a little tougher and I still had a long way to go.

OK, not so long ago I was dying and I was OK with that. That's something I can do. But not being able to run? Who would I become if I could not walk, could not run, could not even stand to take a piss?

Time out. I was willing to give you the notion that all of this is a dream, that this life is pretty much an illusion, and that we are part of something higher and more enduring that we cannot see. But how am I going to deal with things if I can't run? I mean, look, part of me is rotting here, right in front of us. If that goes, I won't be able to walk again, at least not on that foot. I'll be stuck. It might even be worse than losing weekends.

How fast are we moving here? Part of me thinks not fast enough, another part way too fast. The voice down there in the darkness has decided to speak up. It is the one I hear only when I am very far away from the steaming piles of hustling humanity. It says it's about time to stop and get real.

OK, I ask. What's real?

What's in front of you when you see things as they are.

But I don't want to see things as they are.

It's time. You can listen or not.

You're talking about more than just my foot, aren't you?

What do you think?

I began to see this was different from anything I had dealt with before. There was more going on than just an injury. Stories were at work. The psyche, on some level, seemed to have been enlisted in working out this particular wound.

I don't know and can't pretend to explain why my world expanded to include more than I wanted to look at.

Maybe it was the associations I had with snakes. In world cultures the systemic trauma of snakebites has engendered myths, or surrounding aggregations of stories, that define, that structure and explain, that assemble a framework to situate that which we cannot explain. A snakebite, according to some other cultural traditions, can be a gateway to transformation. The Hindus see a cobra bite as the beginning of enlightenment. Among some Native American tribes, snakebite victims spent four days in the headquarters of the snake cult with the snake, and if they survived became "rattlesnake shamans." Other cultures have synthesized snakes into a mythology consisting of no less the dark than the light. They are both death and procreation, sin and wisdom, wealth and poverty. They are circular and cyclical, the up times of plenty and the down times of weakness and loss. The Egyptian serpent deity, Mertseger, has been called the "Friend of Silence."

Our culture, my way of seeing and understanding, is no different in that it crafts stories to explain snakes. Only we tell the stories that vilify the serpent. It is evil, dark, slimy, and the root of temptation. Snakes, unless we have been taught otherwise, should be killed, captured, sold, sometimes eaten, put on display, but always pushed away. That is not the way it has to be. Snakes can represent mystery, what we don't understand, what remains unmeasured, unmapped, terra incognita.

That fits. Although I did not and still don't know what my particular story about snakes is, I felt different. I had been extracted from the world of swirling noise and allowed to temporarily abide in quiet. I did not know for sure what I was changing from or what I was becoming. I did not know what to do. It was a mess, and I felt alternately confused and content, sometimes at the same time. Something had to change. Maybe, I thought, I should quit my job. Or, maybe I should keep doing it, but do it differently. Either way, I was not in Kansas any more.

This dented vehicle of a body worked hard to repair itself. It asked to be let out of the streaming flow of rush-hour traffic, to be left alone, to be quiet, to hunker down. My leg had grown embarrassingly large, discolored, and puffy. Over and over it demanded that I sit and breathe and pump blood.

I was a servant to healing. I lay in bed and watched as my nervous, circulatory, respiratory, and musculoskeletal systems, like those in anatomy books, worked at restoring life to dead tissue. It was my job to pay attention to them, to love them, to let them do their work. The little glimmer of attention that I could muster had to return again and again to the here and now, and only here and now. I knew I must not leave it.

Nurses came in to remind me of my pulse, my breathing, the size of my swelling, the physical state of this passing, changing, healing form. In a way I was liberated to witness the functions and systems of an inner world. The knowable world kept shrinking down to this hospital, this room, this bed, this single self-contained vibrating organism. In the same way that I could not physically move because of the poisons in my system, I could not mentally wander because the body kept pulling me back, demanding that I attend to its pains, shifts, and changes. I lived in the gap, the interval, the suspension of routine, quiet, still, and alert. The days piled on top of one another, but I was not aware of their accumulation. My only perennial companion was the thin fabric of biological processes that kept me together.

Friends, hearing about the bite, spread the word and came by to see for themselves. I welcomed them and openly wept a couple of times when I again thought of Kyle or Sean being bitten and in the hospital. But there was more. I was grieving something bigger than the wound. I did not know what, but the feeling went deep. I had just touched the tip of it. The pulsing told me that something was moving that I would have little power to stop, and that I would have to follow it to the end or be made a liar by the truth of the snakebite. I felt I would suffocate; I felt the earth moving under my feet. Terror mingled with wonder. I kept returning to the same places, the same lessons, the same differences. My mood, here, no matter what the level of pain, of blood draws, of poking and monitoring by interns, was light, happy even, and I looked at friends as if seeing them for the first time and gave them all that I could and listened to them when it was their turn. I felt I saw more of their bodies, that marvel of chemical, electrical, hydraulic humming that kept them together, seeing, hearing, feeling, than I did of our talk, of shared moments past or those yet to come. I felt I should talk to their bodies, because the bodies know better. I wanted to ask them, Do you know what you are walking around in? I knew they did not, as I did not. What they did know and pay attention to were the stories trailing behind them and stretching before them, stories of likes and dislikes, goods and bads, blisses and complaints. Swamp coolers weren't working, mosquitoes were biting, grants were going to be funded, artwork might sell. Mood was conditional.

Some of my visitors were happy; some not. The wheel of fortune kept spinning. The noise of habituated living, in other words, continued without me. They felt sorry for me; "you poor dear," their looks said. I had to wonder at them. I felt like I had gotten exactly what I needed.

That sense of well-being had no place to go but into a new story, and I began to listen, to compose, to look at how I might rework a myth about fear, about healing, about darkness, or in more practical terms look at how much I resisted the fact I was getting old, that my body could not do what it used to be able to do, that I had few clues about how to be a father, that I struggled with stress and making a living, that I pushed away the sadness of a desert being scraped clean and sucked dry, that I longed for peace with my family.

Sometime late Saturday, I decided to try and get to the bathroom, noteworthy only for being a chore that now had great meaning. I had not been out of my bed for almost three days and wanted to make the long journey to the nicely tiled promised land. The best candidate for transport seemed to be a shower chair with wobbly, eccentric wheels that must resemble those on carts that carry the impenitent to hell. The things would not roll when we needed them to roll but did when we didn't. I tried to keep my leg up as four valiant women and I maneuvered almost two hundred pounds of me and my monstrous, waterlogged limb of a leg toward the bathroom. First we banged into the IV pole. Then we got stuck trying to make the corner to the bathroom. Then my leg wouldn't fit, so we had to back up and make a run for the door. I kept my leg in the position of a battering ram that would either squeeze through the space or knock out the jam. Luckily for my leg we made it. From one point of view, this could have been frustrating, maddening, and "not the right way" to go about this. From another point of view, it was amazingly resourceful, clever, and daring even. I felt that it was the latter, and took too much joy in exercising the fruits of our adventure, the simple joy of taking a shit. In the immediacy of need, nothing is more satisfying.

Even with the return of some routine, my foot throbbed with pain whenever I tried to lower it. I realized I would not be able to use crutches for a long time, so they brought in a wheelchair for me to try and move around in. Now this was a vehicle. No more wobbly-wheeled shower chair. The wheelchair was as beautiful as a hundredth-anniversary Harley in full leather dress. Now Harleys are built for Sunday morning, and I used my chair to go for a cruise, to get into the bathroom where I again, but much less eventfully, traveled to plumbing heaven. I even shaved, with my egg-plant of a blistered foot up on the sink and my face in the corner of the mirror. The foot took up most of the reflection, while my shaving-cream-covered mug smiled from the distance in the lower corner. This foot was going to take up most of my life for a while, and I would have to get used to living in its shadow, being a supporting player for a production the outcome of which I could only guess.

They kept me in the hospital until Monday evening. That made four days, the first days I had spent in a hospital since my birth. The doctors made it clear by their expressions, if not their words, that things could still go wrong, perhaps terribly wrong, and that I had to be careful. I listened with half an ear, my mind already on home.

I was released out a side door of the sprawling hospital as a light rain fell around the city. It was an anonymous baptism, a sweet wash of desert tears, rich with creosote, rotting mesquite bean, the smells of pavement baking under August skies. The monsoon desert haunts those who live here, closing in, even at night, with its oppressive presence. It's the most difficult time of year for me usually, when I give up free time for teaching. I have to make the transition to days filled with schedules, structure, teaching, stress, meetings, and continual distraction. And it's now the next stage of however long this healing will take.

I took my place in the back seat of the car, which I would not be able to drive for several months, while my two sons and wife struggled to get the wheelchair folded up and through the open hatch. I was now dead weight that they would have to carry for a while, how long I did not know. I would be served while I could not serve myself. This time was embarrassing, and somewhere, deep inside, I vowed that I would do it justice.

They finally succeeded, got in, closed the doors, rolled down the windows, and we set off into a night with no stars, rain falling. I gave in to the rain, realized that there was not a damned thing I could do about it, and let it rinse and cool the stuffy car, my hot and discolored leg; I let it run in the dark down my cheek. The boys changed the radio station to one they liked better as I tasted salt.

7 / Winding Words

Luna is ready to go out now, so I stop typing and wheel toward the door. I stand on my good leg to unlock the sliding bar at the top of the door. The French doors swing wide enough to let the chair through, and we both go outside. I find a spot to sit. Luna heads out to bark at the coyotes that have gathered in the front yard.

They scatter half-heartedly. They are hungry and want the cat or one of the quail that feed on the desiccated pyracantha berries. The lack of rain has decimated the rabbit population. No grass, no rabbits; no rabbits, no hawks, no coyotes, no bobcats, and so on.

What little wildlife remains in the area gathers around our little mesquite bosque, our little "woods" along the wash. Owls, bobcats, javelina, packrats, rattlesnakes, of course; even bear and mountain lion have passed through our yard.

What they have in common is crowding. There remains too little habitat for the animals that survive. We are surrounded by homes, strip malls, professional office suites, fast-food restaurants, grocery stores, condos, nursing homes—all new, all busy, and all sitting on top of desert that used to be home for wild creatures.

Contact with these creatures has not been easy. Our cat, Zeus, looks like a retired prizefighter with a broken nose, crushed cheek, and one eye that sits higher than the other. He was lucky. Other cats have never come home. Our neighbor's dog was mauled by javelina when he charged them while they were exploring the compost pit. Three thousand dollars worth of stitches later and he will live with hair that turned black over his wounds. And then there were the Africanized bees that moved into our bathroom. Megan used it anyway as ten thousand bees swirled around her.

I shake with the chill. The ground squirrels have estivated, a kind of desert hibernation, as have many other species—lizards, tortoises, toads, and most snakes included. Surviving in the desert requires thick skin, spines, in some cases venom, as well as space and endemic plants.

October for people is the easy time. The heat has retreated and we can sit outside and think. My foot throbs and the gauze bandage has a spot of red. I have to elevate it, so I go back in to type.

What do I see when I raise my head above the rows of days that I have been given to harvest? I look at a world much wider than I remember, when I consider something larger than surviving. I straighten my back, feel its ache, while the mind bends back on itself, a serpentine meander of self-talk.

How do I name something that refuses to be named? Old stories fall short, were woven for other times, other questions, other places. The story in which evil and inferior nature torments the dominant and innocent human is what listeners expect. Those stories of nature out there waiting to destroy the unwary traveler have grown tired. They have frayed into loose threads. So have their counterparts, the stories of nature as cute, fuzzy, eternally friendly, and beneficent. This is nature as cuddly pet, and it curdles in my gut. Nature is neither hostile nor cuddly. We are the ones who cast it that way, who paint it to fit with our limited pictures of a world according to human prejudice and ignorance. I struggle with different colors, these inchoate, fresh, delicate threads, to weave a story from the material of a night filled with cold and distant stars. I can only watch as one takes shape beneath a pen possessed.

I have been given a taste of something, just as the poor snake got a taste of me. For better or worse the snake has me to give it a voice. And so I try to remember and the story takes on a life of its own, begins winding its way through experience and reflection, outer and inner ramblings, circuitous paths to unexpected destinations. It originates in the body, in the longing of blood to absorb oxygen, only to carry it where it is most needed, then, with the same longing, like one who holds his breath too long, to release it and begin the cycle anew. The lifeblood of listening to that which cannot be named but that haunts the edges of my desire, insatiable, wanting only to find release, expression.

I listen to the snake and hear a kind of call, a call to wake up, to see that we are not separate, not outside, not distinct from nature or each other. We are the ones who have gone somewhere other than here, this glorious fact of here and now. We are in nature, even if we believe otherwise, even if we spin insane stories furiously enough to delude ourselves that we can live without it in a post-nature, virtual, imagined world.

The antidote to the poison of disconnect is care. Care about a place, about a creature, care enough to call a thing by its proper name, care for the truth spoken only from the periphery of things. That truth comes from the blood, and must be said, even if that means going beyond what people want to hear.

8 / What Remains

The Bear, my father, drove down after the bite to help out. He made the two-thousand-mile trip in a little over thirty hours, getting only one speeding ticket on the way. "Damned if I'm ever going to spend any money in that town. I was only going eighty-three," he said, with no little indignation.

You could say Bear is speed-crazy and that he passed that on to all of his six kids. He has a need to move, whether it's by car, motorcycle, bike, foot, or passing thought. It's all got to move. And moving is better than arriving; even when we get there, the first thought is, Where to next? When we traveled, his favorite answer to "How far?" was "Down the road a piece." Always on the way, just over the hill, maybe someday, moving, moving. My mother, by contrast, when she could still drive, drove with one foot on the brake, as if she could hold the speeding world at bay with her delicate left foot. Her way we never understood. For us, it was his way and the highway.

On the surface, the Bear is a handsome but coarse man, charming, profane as a sailor, imposing as a heavyweight boxer. Life has thrown a few punches of its own at him, and he carries the scars of trauma. On crutches because of a head-on collision with a drunk driver intent on killing herself, a chance meeting that left his hip shattered and left knee crushed, he hobbles through the old and smudged French doors into the living room with the same shuffle he does late at night or in the early hours when he can't sleep. In his ancient bathrobe, he wanders the halls, looking into empty bedrooms as if expecting to find someone who is missing. He has troubles. Demons circle around him, and sometimes he tries to shoo them away, like one would horseflies in summer, but they don't go away. The rest of the time he ignores them.

Yes, if you could see into his heart, you'd see the other wounds. Sometimes you get a glimpse of them in his eyes. I know the look. I know the night walks too. I have been his son for almost half a century. God knows we have been through some times.

Cripple meets cripple as I wheel up to him, my left foot raised on the padded footrest protruding like a jib forward of my wheeled sloop, almost banging the chrome spar into one of his crutches. I am still learning to use the chair.

It has been a long time. He is older than I remember him. I feel much older too. Confined to my chrome and vinyl conveyance, I have to look up at him. Part of me thinks he likes that, likes to be needed as I need him now. I am still reeling from my collision with circumstance and don't yet know how to do this, how to redefine my place, to settle into my new role as patient in the family.

He looks at my purplish, seeping, enraged foot and asks if it hurts. "Only when I dance," I tell him.

"You'll be lucky to find anyone who will dance with a foot that ugly." He shakes his head at the swollen appendage, ankle, calf, thigh, at the blebs—the enormous black blood blisters on my sole and arch—the leaking fang marks, the swollen, purple toes.

"It's worse than I thought it would be," he says. "It *is* ugly." Then he pauses for a second, trying to find something comforting to say as the conversation veers toward the quagmire of pity. "But it's yours."

He bends down to embrace me in a stiff male hug, complete with hard pats on the back, and then is back up on the crutches.

He cherishes his family, and, despite our past skirmishes between father and rebellious son, he shows up when I, or any of his children, need him.

He has brought sandwiches and explains that he felt better coming down to Arizona than he did staying in Wisconsin, wondering what was happening. I sit sideways to the table with my foot up as we settle in for lunch. I have to twist to face the table enough to eat over a plate.

"So, what do they say about it?" he asks as we dig into the Italian sausage and provolone cheese sandwiches.

I assume that "they" means the doctors and "it" refers to the poisoned limb cantilevered out from the chair. "Well, they don't really know," I volunteer, not knowing quite where to begin. Nobody knows, and not just about the foot, I elaborate silently to no one, thinking about how difficult it is to breathe sometimes, how weak my heart feels, how I cannot stand the speed of daytime, of light. Then I stop and come back.

"They say the necrosis, dying tissue, is not bad, but that it's a matter of time before they'll be able to do any kind of real assessment or prognosis."

I tell him about wanting out of the hospital, about making the case to the five doctors circled around the foot of the bed that I could just as easily sit at home as in the hospital. They looked at each other with expressions that said "I don't know. What do you think?" followed by "I don't know. What do you think?" The look and the expression spread from doctor to doctor like party gossip before they nodded, thoughtfully stroked their chins, and agreed to discharge me.

The swelling had advanced as far as my rib cage but had stopped there. It had not gone down much since, and my left bun was enormous, like that of a circus fat man. I liked that the least and was glad that it was behind me, so to speak, so less an area of conversation. One side of my body had puffed up like a balloon that refused to go down.

They told me about some of the dangers that might derail the recovery: compartment syndrome, reactivation of venom not neutralized, latent infection, connective, circulatory, and nervous tissue damage, a resurgence of swelling. I thought "resurgence?!"

But I had nodded and agreed to watch for all these things, whatever they were, to make regular visits to my primary care doctor, and to rest. Given that I was sleeping about eighteen hours a day, rest would be the least of my concerns. I agreed to get the portable commode, the wheelchair, the tape measure for the swelling, and the plastic urinal for those times when I could not get out of bed. It was a small victory to be home, and I was glad to tell it. I did not want to be stuck in a hospital bed when the Bear came to help.

The Bear nods as he works his way through the sandwich. He licks his fingers of the oil and mayonnaise, looking every bit his namesake, before wondering "What the hell?" as a stream of thick dark fluid streams down the side of my foot onto the "chuck," the plastic-covered cotton pad, on the footrest.

His tone changes, and I hear the words I've heard many times over the past two weeks. "What, did the damned thing come at you?"

He invites the story about the bite. I can tell he has his expectations, as most people do who ask. The image behind the question is one of Marlin Perkins in an old Mutual of Omaha's *Wild Kingdom* in which the aged Marlin and his assistant wrestle and eventually lose control of an anaconda.

The snake is huge, overwhelmingly powerful, and the men lose footing in the muck.

I recounted the events and more. I began to explore some of the unsettled questions, some of the confusion, some of the need to frame this time, these days. Needless to say, my story failed in some ways to fulfill his expectations.

I look at him across the table and can tell that he does not quite believe what I have told him. I have told him much more than he wanted to know, and I can tell he is overwhelmed, not so much by the injury as by my strange response to it.

Hell, I don't know what's going on. Just the same, this kind of territory is not the domain of polite male conversation. This world is more than either of us can handle. I can tell he wonders why I bring up any other worlds. Psyche schmyche. What do you mean no present and no future? We don't usually take time for this kind of talk and are not much for philosophizing.

"You know, while I was in the hospital, I felt an odd kind of quiet. And when it rained, it was like everything was going to be OK, no matter what happened." I pause, waiting to see how he will react.

The Bear looks tired and pushes his chair back from the table. He leans forward and interlaces his fingers, like he is praying. "Well, godammit. Sounds like a hell of a thing." His hands are handsome and strong. He does not know what else to say, what counsel to offer. His body says he wants to change the subject.

This is one of the places my family and I tend to part company. I break the rules against introspection and reflection. We don't go there or do that say the unwritten rules that the men, in particular, live by. I don't see this as a bad thing. I doubt my father could have survived his time fighting wars in Asia if he had given in to self-reflective ruminating. Nonetheless, I knew we, the family, were missing something. What it was I could not say, but took it upon myself to go find.

So I left brothers and sisters to find the missing family treasure and to bring it home. The prodigal wanderer, I found only words. The problem with finding what is missing from a family that prides itself on the way it is, that defines itself on the characteristics it has, is that it might not want what I brought home. Adding a new repertoire to the family identity threatens the status quo, a system that has served to get it this far. I have learned to keep musings to myself. The cross-eyed look that says "I have no idea what you are talking about" has been more than enough to shut me up.

Yet I know the Bear understands wonder. I know he understands death. I know. I see when he is least guarded. It slips out between the bars he has built to protect himself, to keep the world at bay. When he thinks he is weak, I think he is strong.

The Bear sets down his beer and crosses his arms. It is late afternoon. Telling the story has taken up all of lunch and the better part of the midday. Megan and the boys will be home soon. We'll have to clean up the table and tie up the loose ends, ones that I have not even defined for myself.

In the previous two weeks I have learned to live the life of a man exiled from his bedroom and sentenced to a rolling chair. I am surprised to find that it has not been that big a deal.

He asks about those things I can still do, those chores of hygiene and self-care that I have previously done without thinking. He then asks how he can help.

I give him the quick synopsis, the nitty-gritty of the situation. I have to use the wheelchair, but can get around for very short distances on crutches. I can't drive. The swelling has gone down from ribs to hip to upper leg, but is still puffy, still showing "pit edema," little indents in the skin after poking it with a finger. He will have to make the coffee—strong. My foot reminds me with the color and the pain that the insult lingers. He can listen; that would be the best he could do for me, though I can't bring myself to say this. I have never before asked him for this.

While it surprises me to say so, I ask that he not feel sorry for me, that this has been a physical ordeal, but more than that, the mental and psychological ordeal has not been what I expected.

The Bear looks a bit askance as I try to explain what I have no words to explain. But he listens as I fumble through my chaotic free associations. With my foot still on the table, elevated and monstrous, I tell him about something opening, something shifting, like tectonic maps of my mental landscape.

He looks at the foot and asks how much it hurts.

I answer, "Not much right now, but it has. The pain really doesn't much bother me."

He has no trouble understanding pain. He has been through plenty of it. Besides the accident, he has cared for his wife at home for years as she faded into a cloud of dementia. We gathered at his house a year ago to move her into a nursing home. The Bear found other things to do while we packed up her stuff. I guess that was too much, the undeniable statement that moving her made. He sold the house a while later and moved into a trailer. We don't talk about those things. Yes, he understands pain. But he does not quite get why I won't take more of the painkillers. It is in our bloodline to medicate.

"Doesn't it keep you up at night?" he asks.

"I don't get as much sleep as I might," I respond, reminding him that I spend most of the day prone, leg up on couch cushions and pillows, body on the floor of the living room, snoozing away. I try to tell him that when I'm not asleep, I still feel the glow of something that took root while I was hospitalized, that I got a taste of a heightened intensity of being alive, and that in some ways the physical pain in my foot reminds me of that. I don't want to lose it. I guess I'm superstitious and think that painkillers will break that connection to whatever it was.

"If I got any more rest, I'd never wake up," I say, apropos of nothing.

The pain, I go on, cautiously, redundantly, trying to say it in a way that he will grasp, that I will resonate with, is not something to avoid, but is my cue to stay experientially awake, to tap into giving all the attention I can to this moment. As I say these things I am aware of how hokey they sound, how inadequate words are for conveying what I have felt.

He brings the conversation back to what is tangible, the bloated appendage on the table. He wants to know how I feel about losing the ability to walk, of being physically unable to lift my swollen butt off the chair, of sleeping alone on the floor in the living room.

"I have to admit that I'm scared," I tell him. And that is true. Like anyone, I worry about my leg and wonder how it will heal. I don't know how deep the desires to move reach. I haven't even thought about the little stuff. I still want to run. I say it again. I want to . . . scratch that—need to—run. Up until now, I have taken refuge in running, in moving, in defining myself as a runner, as a physically formidable man. I want to play soccer in the adult leagues again, to lace up my cleats, to feel the ground beneath my feet, the faint jiggle of the bulk of a forty-year-old man taking the shock of a full sprint, of the primitive satisfaction of a touch of the ball, the ancient drive to chase after attackers. Part of me is not ready to toss in the towel, to leave the pitch, to hang up the running shoes.

What would I say if I could tell him more? I hope the recovery will be complete, but getting "back to normal" is not the point, nor is it my hope or expectation. I want both. I want to regain strength and motion and I want peace. Returning to moving is important, but I am still intoxicated by slowness, by simple delight in just hanging out. I am not fit for human company any more than a person hallucinating should be taking a standardized test or controlling air traffic.

This I cannot yet say to my father: I do hope to grow from this, to hang onto it, to sustain contact with the magic of the here and now, to become capable of sidestepping distracting self-talk, to walk a razor's edge of presence, of getting past all the old shit that seems so important when life is just jack. I met death, and this time it left me, temporarily. I don't have much time. I respect death, but for some reason do not fear it. That changes things.

I am glad to be alive, to be back in familiar surroundings, and in some ways my life feels the same. But in other ways, ways I cannot even imagine, everything has changed. The reasons for my thinking and acting the way I have for as long as I can remember have, in some ways, evaporated. Without the fear of death to run from, I no longer find the truth of my life something I should run from or cover up.

Pain has woken me up. Pain strips away everything that is superfluous, everything that is illusory, and reveals the most basic needs we must fulfill to stay alive. Recovery is the counterpart of pain. If I stay quiet and receptive, my attitude toward my days is one that is more reflective, conscious, slowed-down, able to listen and to respond rather than react. I felt good in the hospital, different somehow, grateful, uncomplaining, compliant to my destiny, whatever that would be. I had no control and had to surrender to the care given by others, to let them literally carry me through this incident, this crisis. Doing so, utterly, completely, allowed me to let them give, allowed me to receive.

I feel that in accepting this moment as inevitable, in flooding my body with the consciousness of this moment, this place, whatever it contains, I get a taste of eternity, of a sweet mystery that runs through all things, living or not, and that now runs through me like the venom of the snake. Only it is not poison anymore, not something to compulsively avoid. The snake venom has been neutralized by antibodies; they are now medicine. Attending to this moment is the antidote to toxic talk, to habitual harangues about what's wrong with my life.

All of this leads me to the fact that I know I am dying, that my mother, his wife, is dying, that I have been a fool to think I could be happy by running from the facts. I wish we would stop tearing up the desert, stop tearing at each other, and face the real fact that it is fear that drives us to violence of all kinds. I want to tell him that it is my role to end my part in this crazy, self-perpetuating cycle of victims and executioners. That might mean I look to some like a pussy or some cactus-hugging lunatic, or just a man in mourning. So be it.

I wonder what has happened to me. I sound to myself like some crackpot mystic who has lost all sense of irony, of discretion, of polite distance.

While these thoughts run through my head, we change the subjects to other things: the new car he drives, my brothers back in Wisconsin, his brothers who live in Arizona, how good his new cell phone coverage is. We pass some time doing not much of anything, and leave the crumbled wrappers of our now devoured sandwiches on the table, evidence of food shared, of bread broken, of two guys trying to figure out what to do next.

Before we finish cleaning up, Megan and the boys walk in, flush from a full day of school and work.

9 / Cocktails

I did not know anything about snake venom before. Even though I live in the desert and see rattlesnakes often on the trails and in the mountains and canyons around the valley, I did not know what venom can do to a body. There is a price sometimes for not knowing; it can make you lazy, complacent, and sleepy when you should be awake, or maybe terribly afraid. What I know now scares me straight and silly with alertness. There are some things that are good to know, even if they are scary.

Venom is a poison that one animal generates so that it can inject it into another animal, either to eat the other animal or to defend itself. People mainly inject each other, or themselves, with poisonous talk and harmful gossip or self-destructive stories, but that is another discussion. Poison is a broader term than venom and describes any harmful substance that disrupts healthy processing, irritates tissue, or kills. Snake venom is a complex, concentrated form of poison. It is also a form of saliva that has evolved to first immobilize and then begin digesting prey. The delivery system and chemical makeup of rattlesnake venom make rattlers the most evolved of the reptiles.

Chemist friends tell me venom consists mostly of water, but also contains proteins, proteolytic enzymes, polypeptides, glycoproteins, and other molecular compounds. My eyes glaze over when I hear the words, words that hammer at the edges of my brain, failing to sink in; but I have to admit it sounds like quite a cocktail. These compounds are all mixed together to create multiple toxic effects that include hemotoxicity, which is an attack on blood cells; neurotoxicity, which is attack and paralysis of the heart and lungs; and myotoxicity, which is digestion and breakdown of muscle tissue. The exact makeup of venom varies not only from species to species, but also among individuals of the same species.

The different components of venom target different types of tissue and have a molecular signature and structure that allows them to "attach" to different kinds of proteins or cells. Once attached to these specific receptors, the venom then begins to break down and weaken the molecular bonds of chemical compounds and living tissue.

It's like a jigsaw puzzle on the molecular level. When a "fit" is found, though, proteins on the wall of a cell or necessary compound will break down and split up or die. Enzymes, in particular, digest tissue on the molecular level. Blood flows out of opened veins, nerves cease to carry signals, muscle tissue ruptures. Imagine a kind of guided missile mayhem, an attack on many fronts. Pumping stations shut down; transformers explode; streets are turned to rubble and goo; electrical circuits fizzle; buildings crumble.

Of course, the body can counterattack. It has defenses. Bodies are continually exposed to toxins, poisons, and antigens. These things come after us every day. Viruses, bacteria, allergens—all have to be neutralized or dealt with. If an antigen bad guy is new or arrives in large quantities, though, look out. The body can't mount a defense unless it has the molecular structure of the marauders stored in memory cells or in the hypothalamus gland.

Bodies fight toxins by generating antibodies that mimic the molecular makeup of target cells, matching the molecular structure of the toxins. The toxins bond with the antibodies and are neutralized before they are escorted from the body by white blood cells. After that, they are filtered out or eliminated.

There is no way my hypothalamus gland could have generated enough antibodies to neutralize all the venom in my system, so I had to get help. Help came in the form of a serum taken from sheep that had developed antibodies after long and gradual exposure to pit viper venom. Historically, horses have been injected with near lethal doses of rattlesnake or coral snake venom until they developed immunity, or a cadre of antibodies. Their blood is then drawn and processed in a way that concentrates the antibodies into a powder or a solution that becomes the antivenin.

The immune systems of the animals had done the work, and now their antibodies were "hooking up" with the chemical compounds in the venom from my snakebite. Once the antibodies neutralized the venom compounds, those molecules could no longer bond with and then break down the tissues in my foot or, more systemically, my lungs, heart, and nervous system.

I have no illusions that I somehow "beat" the effects of the snake venom. Without the antivenin I would have had a much more serious injury, one that threatened, as they say, life and limb. If you ask me what would have happened without it, I would have to answer, with no melodrama intended, that I would be dead. Even with the antivenin, one of the doctors did write off my big toe. On a chart, he noted simply, concisely, "Dead big toe."

Before the antivenin, I was being eaten alive. It was not the first time, nor would it be the last. In South America, I had been the host of giardia, amoeba, various bacterial and fungal infections, and other parasites too gruesome for polite conversation, but all had been resisted, thrown back behind the perimeter, temporarily. Something—cancer, disease, infection—will get me someday. This time the balance tipped back toward my survival after help, after the antivenin kicked in—antibodies quietly linking up with enzymes and proteins that were bent on disrupting, digesting, and destroying my circulatory system, my nerve endings, my connective tissue, and respiration.

Because the production of antivenin is complicated, antivenins are expensive. They are also sometimes scarce, and Tucson has suffered from antivenin shortages. Antivenin is the only antidote to snake venom. There is no other treatment.

Even though they are the best hope in the event of a bite, antivenins are not without risk or consequences. The earlier horse-derived antivenin often caused severe allergic reactions, even death. "Serum sickness" happens less frequently with the new sheep serum, but can happen.

If I were to be bitten again, I could not receive antivenin. Once exposed to the animal antibodies, the body can develop a hypersensitivity to them and may go into severe allergic shock if exposed a second time. What saved me once could kill me a second time.

I have generated some of my own antibodies, but not enough to handle a severe envenomation. I am not a doctor, but now I know some of what snake venom can do and how important it is to stay away from poisons of all kinds. It is a good thing to know when I feel the slide into complacency as I'm moving through snake territory in snake season. "No second chances" should be written on a card that you get when you are born. Take one time to learn, then accept the responsibility to wake up or to endure the consequences of poison, of whatever kind.

It is here, in the domain of the details, in the smallest of actions, that my attention rests. I can watch thoughts—some of which I would call "toxic"—turn into emotions, then ratchet up into full-blown attitude at the slightest stimulus. What strikes me as strange is that I don't feel the need to play along, to believe the stream of associations. My antivenin is a calm witnessing that transmutes what used to seem so real into just another passing train of distraction.

10 / Momentum

The long-nosed snake sees me before I see him, immediately hightailing it to the edge of the trail. He takes cover on the sloping riprap of stones that lines the geometrically perfect wall running along the perimeter of a new subdivision down by the big wash with the little name, the Rillito. There are miles of these developments now that the river has been tamed and the seal of flood-proof approval stamped on the real-estate brochures. Now that he is in the rocks, he blends in. I doubt I would have seen him if he hadn't caught my eye with his dash to safety.

Exquisite, as a term, does not approach describing this snake. Red bands cross his back in brilliant contrast to shining black rectangles along the spine that transition to gray and yellow on either side of his flanks. Thin lines of yellow divide the black and red pattern running the length of his body. His scales are smooth and catch the last rays of the setting sun. I am smitten just watching him.

His errand is folly. There is no forage in the rocks that he explores, and he will never get over the ten-foot cinderblock wall at the top of the slope. The wall stretches perhaps a quarter of a mile both east and west.

Last year, this was open desert scrub, full of wood rat middens and ground squirrel towns. Now I can smell barbecue wafting over the wall and hear the shrieks of children fighting over toys.

I stand and watch the snake as he relaxes and continues his search in a wasteland of imported stone. A man comes up behind me, walking on the trail. I assume he will stop, ask me what I am looking at, or merely look himself. But he doesn't. He keeps walking, an island unto himself. No "hello," no eye contact, just mechanical motion. He is one of the new ones.

Satellite dishes sprout from houses that have sprouted from the ridges like mushrooms after a heavy rain. They go up fast, almost overnight, and are built to look stronger than they are, with "sticks and mud," wood frame and stucco rather than adobe. They are not built to last in a desert rife with termites and heat. They look massive, but are lightweights.

They look down on us. Their guard dogs bark at us from behind pool fences. I never see anyone outside. They have tinted their windows, giving the effect of mirrored sunglasses, of self-importance traveling incognito.

Once in a while I hear them tinkering with motors before they try to drive down the wash. In sand rails, dune buggies, and ATVs with polished chrome they come, squeezing into a wash that cannot accommodate them. Their clothes are bright, new. When I tell them they cannot drive in the wash, they look angry.

I look past them, over them, through them, to a peak in the distance, Boboquivari, the center of the universe to the Tohono O' Odham. I can see it across the city and across the valley. Only high-tension power lines cut the vista.

The hum of cars on the highway, of electrical currents feeding appliances, the radiation of radio waves is everywhere around us. We swim in humming, buzzing, siren songs of our making.

It will be like this for a while, until things again fall apart.

In the meantime, this lovely red-banded, long-nosed snake will likely lose a bet in a game he did not agree to play.

The Sonoran Desert, minus people, is a slow, quiet, empty place. Oh, there are moments of dramatic displays of speed and noise, such as summer monsoons, and the place is defined by some sensual extremes—heat, clarity of air, light—but it consists mainly of quiet and space.

Living in the desert, for most of us, however, is an urban experience. The desert serves as a backdrop for lives run by speed, distraction, and anxiety. And it is getting worse. Winding one-lane dirt roads become two-lane paved roads that become straightened four-lane highways, like the one that runs behind our house. Between the quiet periods of night, motorcycles race up and down the freshly paved and straightened stretch of highway.

When I was born in 1956, about 87,000 souls inhabited Tucson, and the town took up a little over seventeen square miles. Between 1955 and 1956 the population of Tucson grew 45.5 percent. In one year. But the population density for the same period actually decreased. That is, more people were coming in, and each of them, on average, was taking up more space. Even so, at that time, the town's heart was where the action was. Theaters and department stores dominated the downtown scene. The place had not yet begun to sprawl. Ninety percent of Tucson's current population has been added since the mid-1950s.

Development began to explode around the edges of the city, and Tucson, like other cities of the west, began to take up more space, a bigger footprint, with more land given over, on average, to each new resident. The city spread out from the center of a large valley toward the surrounding mountains. It continues to expand. Every day in 2004, another twelve acres of desert is consumed for new housing. Tucson is like an expanding donut of development. Its heart is the hole and the desert the edge. This donut eats rather than being eaten.

In 2000, the population of the Tucson metropolitan area was pushing 850,000 and took up almost seven hundred square miles. The populations of the northwest and southeast corners of the area grew at astonishing rates between 1990 and 2000. Marana, a town on the northwest border of the Tucson metro area, for example, grew 520 percent in ten years. There are plans for homes that will house hundreds of thousands more people over the coming years. Arizona grew faster than every state in the union except Nevada in the same time frame, and the Southwest has the fastest growing population in the country. The Tucson area alone increases by 20,000 inhabitants a year. Tucson will more than double the area it occupies by 2020 if current trends persist.

The heart of Tucson all but languished in the eighties and nineties because the periphery was growing so fast. Buildings that could serve as businesses or houses or storage stood empty while virgin desert was carved up for the same businesses, houses, and storage, all miles away from basic services. Almost all of these developments push higher into the mountains and deeper into canyons that surround the city. The developments usurp wildlife habitat, and people come into contact and conflict with animals.

The Sonoran Desert is the most biologically diverse desert in the world. Between the cacti, trees, reptiles, and mammals, the place is a xeric garden. And people want to live next to it. They want the canyons, the mountains, the sweeping vistas and sunsets. And they want it as far as possible from the nearest neighbor. The only problem is that the desert has never been able to support many people. It is a place of space, emptiness, limited by heat and water.

There is a price to pay for growth, or, as Edward Abbey put it, "Growth for the sake of itself is the ideology of the cancer cell." The price in the desert is steep: water is limited, land is fragile and does not recover easily, animals live in delicate balance with each other and habitat, and we lose the quiet that we came to enjoy. Like the cancer cell, growth that is unrestrained destroys its host.

As people come in and housing densities drop, wildlife adapts or dies. In short, the situation becomes a crisis. Crisis, as the saying goes, is both danger and opportunity. The danger is clear enough: we destroy by loving the desert to death, by importing every vice, bad habit, noxious, allergen-producing plant species, and criminal behavior we want to leave behind in those places from which we run. The opportunity: we can begin to examine how to live sustainably in a delicate ecosystem, to examine our relationship (or lack thereof) with our desert setting.

The opportunity will require that we get out of the car, take off the earphones, unplug the TV, loosen the grip on the credit card, and sit down. Knowing the desert presupposes attending to it, quieting down enough to really see it, hear it, witness it. Connecting with the desert requires actively attending to it, waking up to it.

That's where snakes come in.

If the snakes—and other potentially dangerous animals—are extirpated or removed from the desert we inhabit, there is less incentive to pay attention. Snakes do not just range freely, eating whatever they encounter as they travel randomly and viciously over the desert. They live in a home range and migrate with the season. They move from rocky outcrops where they winter to lower, warmer streambeds in the summer. If moved, they most likely will perish. Our crowding the desert crowds them.

Streams of images and sounds scream for attention while dry riverbeds wait for rain. Rivers used to run through Tucson, but excessive pumping has lowered the water table. Other rivers are in peril—the San Pedro, east of Tucson, in particular. By looking at the dead riverbeds of California, where hulks of cottonwoods stand gaunt, dead, and broken against the sky, we can glimpse our future. We are bleeding the desert dry even as the streams in our heads rise and breech the levees of attention. We're wired, even when camping, as state parks begin to offer Internet connection while we try to connect with nature. The stream is rising and taking our minds with it. A war for our attention is being waged quietly and ubiquitously. We can play DVDs in monster SUVs as we all speed toward a distant vanishing point as the desert vanishes beneath the bulldozer's blade.

And the desert is only part of a larger, global crisis brewing out of our hunger for distraction, for oil, for sunlit, dry places that have too little water. At current rates of growth and consumption, our unsustainable, car-crazy, sprawling lifestyle will collide with a lack of supporting resources within twenty-five years. No rates of production, whether it be steel, grain, oil, coal, or wood, can keep up with demands. In short, we are maxed out, and the world's most populous countries are just getting a taste of what we have enjoyed.

And, although this lifestyle doesn't work, the rest of the world wants it. By 2031 China alone will consume more oil than the world currently produces, according to Lester Brown at the Earth Policy Institute. India will want the same piece of the American Dream, and its population will be even larger than China's. Imagine billions driven by the same story that we have lived by: that resources are inexhaustible, that water can be wasted on whatever we want to waste it on, that forests can be felled, that species can be driven to extinction without consequence. The old story no longer answers the questions that need answers.

Something's gotta give.

11 / Carried

For the next two weeks, the Bear, this as yet unbeatified saint of a father, takes kids to school, picks them up for soccer practice, for tae kwon do, for tennis and jazz band. He drives me to doctor appointments, to get a handicapped parking permit for the Jeep, to get groceries, to pick up prescriptions. We work out a system for loading the chair and me: he parks, pops the trunk, opens the door. I grab the roof in one hand, the door in the other, and swing my leg into the space in front of the seat before twisting and lowering my butt and then swiveling in my good leg. He then folds up the chair like a card table, tilts it onto its rear wheels, scoots it back to the trunk, and lifts it in. He shuts the trunk lid, wipes his hands, and then limps to his door where he takes the wheel like he used to grab the controls in the cockpit of his helicopter.

It is not my father's nature to be a nurse. I see him grimace when I ask him to empty the plastic urinal, to help cook, or to get some cheese out of the fridge. He limps and shuffles between these chores, part of him grumbling, part of him doing the service he has to do. It is hard, too, for me to ask him for help, but I have no choice but to be grateful, humble, and allow myself to be served.

I tell him that classes start the day after tomorrow and that I have to get a copy of my syllabus down to the university to be photocopied. He looks at me with some puzzled reluctance but then settles into the persistence that kept him alive in Korea and Vietnam. We load up my book bags and head down to the crowded campus where I have my computer and the files I need to print to meet the demands of making a living.

The streets are choked with students returning to campus after a summer off, or showing up green and new, right out of high school. The Bear finds the traffic maddening, the young women distracting.

We get to my office, practice the wheelchair unloading sequence, and then the Bear goes to try to find parking. Heat rises off the sidewalks, the streets, the roofs, and all but robs us of air. My foot feels like it will explode when it is exposed to full sun. As if on cue, the fang marks begin to bleed, leaving red trails down my arch and over the swollen bleb before pooling on the vinyl padded footrest.

I search through the labyrinth of my files for the syllabus that I wrote months before and promptly misplaced. After a long, circuitous search through the catacombs of my hard drive, I find it accidentally, just as the Bear swings open the door of the office.

I print the file and call the Writing Program office to let them know I am coming. They are appalled that I have come to campus, and one of them leaves the office to walk the two blocks to meet me. Both the Bear and I leave, I in the wheelchair for the first time in real traffic, the syllabus on my lap, he on crutches, following behind.

I wheel down the sidewalk, to the crosswalk and to the long descent to the English department offices. Gravity tugs hard on the wheelchair and my hands begin to burn with friction from braking on the wheels. I need to get some gloves I note somewhere in my growing mental list of things to remember.

I gain speed and the braking becomes more difficult. I have to dodge pedestrians who share the sidewalk with my careening chair. Most don't notice, but a few are obviously annoyed—my first taste of the discrimination against the handicapped.

Ahead of me and closing in, I see Penny, the office boss, concerned and disapproving. When she knows I can hear her, she lays into me. "What *are* your doing here? You look terrible." I realize that I have something of a fever and say "Thanks, you don't look so bad yourself."

She smiles a weak but conspiratorial smile, takes a look at my bleeding foot, and lifts the file folder from my lap. "You go home. We'll take care of this," she says with finality, before I redirect her attention to the Bear.

I introduce them and she tells him quietly to take care of me, because they don't want to lose me yet.

I could have kissed her. Some secret place in me still hopes that my father will see me as worthy in ways I don't feel worthy. Strange, old emotions.

I am flushed from the effort, the heat, the rush of people intent on things bigger than simply healing. I can't wait to leave.

How strange it is to be the son again taken care of by the father. How many times has he rescued me? In 1969, swept up in the heat of adolescence and the overpowering confusion surrounding the Vietnam War, I turned against him and all he stood for. I wanted out of my life and used anything I could to cover churning emotions I could not comprehend.

After a particularly successful, and especially toxic, party when I was in eighth grade, my friends dropped me off, shit-faced drunk, at my parents' back door. Partying was where "it" was at. I mean I felt like I had to believe in something, and feeling good came easy with enough drinks.

Some friends stole a few bottles of brandy from their parents' liquor cabinet, and we did our best to drink it all one night. They left me in a passed-out heap at the base of the stairway going down to our basement. I woke up in the concrete pit, jacket soaked with vomit. Somehow I made it to bed.

The Bear woke me to deliver the *Washington Post* Sunday paper, the thick chore I did every weekend at four in the morning. I was still so drunk and sleepy that I couldn't even tie my shoes. I sat on the edge of my bed, stooped over, struggling to see my shoes, to get my fingers to move. My rebellion and flying-fuck-you had run out of gas, and I was busted, broken, and under guard.

He didn't say anything but drove me around as we assembled the various sections and delivered the thick papers to slumbering doorsteps.

"I don't know what you were on last night," he said when we finally returned home, paper route done, Sunday morning routine just beginning, "but you aren't going to do that and live in this house." That was all he said.

We went to church like we usually did. My brothers and sisters did not notice how tense their father seemed to me. His jaw was set harder than usual, and his eyes had a sharper edge to them, a honed steel I did not want to test. We came home and had an uneventful brunch. Then, with no ceremony, he took me back to the bathroom where we did the usual haircuts and shaved my thirteen-year-old head.

Fury mixed with shame as I roamed the middle school hallways, the definition of freak and pariah.

That punishment was what he knew, the army colonel's response to insubordination.

He did not say much about it, but grounded me for a couple of solitary months. I did not know it then, but now I think I was secretly relieved. He cared enough to intervene then and is no different now. Only the poisons have changed.

That time presented a different poison than the one I deal with now, with dangers that I had to meet later in life to understand. I sought that one out to medicate pain that never really went away. This one has found me, and perhaps has medicinal qualities I have yet to comprehend.

Some days now, between necessary errands that he carries out with only a little complaint, he goes out, leaving me to sit on the porch swing to write and to watch summer work out the last of its storms, heat, and humidity. The clouds build around the mountains and come boiling down the canyons, whipping the house with wind, rain, and hail. With heavy rains, the wash runs with a foaming stream of thick silt and debris. I have to put on a jacket and hope the wheelchair does not get struck by lightning.

I split my time between reveling in the quiet and dabbling in the electronic noise of work that spills down on me out of the computer.

I watch the shadows shorten and then extend as the days pass. I have to rest every couple of hours. Then I tap into the drama and the noise of work and notice how it grates on my sensibility. It is like the background traffic noise of the highway up behind the house and the algebraic homework my middle school sons bring home. I can feel the stress, the anxiety, the "hurry sickness" begin to germinate again deep down in a deeply rich, silent, pulsing core of my being.

Yes, that silent war fought over attention is being conducted somewhere in my mind. The battlefront moves and shifts as one side gains the advantage over the other. I try to ally my sensibility with the forces of quiet, of calm, of presence, but don't always do a very good job.

Sitting on the porch one morning, the Bear asks me why I leave sections of hoses in the yard. I see amazement spread over his face when he realizes the shape is alive, a king snake making its way down a ground squirrel hole.

He does not like snakes, hates them in fact. In that, he is a good Norseman. As a Lutheran and Norwegian, he sees snakes with the double stigma of tempter and monster. Norse mythology has Thor trying to kill Midgard, a serpent capable of becoming more powerful than the gods, and failing. The huge snake still lives in the depths of the seas and our minds.

I saw it in the white face of my nephew when we startled a rattlesnake while hiking years before. I see it in the faces of brothers, uncles, even strangers. The fear is alive, but fears, like great stones, can be worn down and reworked.

As I said, we sit together almost daily as the sun comes up, he, the purist, with his hot water; I, the sensualist, with my strong coffee. We sit in silence. Yes, silence. We see wondrous things. Like a rabbit that climbs into the mesquite tree to reach green leaves it cannot reach from the ground.

We see a tarantula hawk that lands by the garden. This wasp's impossibly iridescent indigo abdomen, as sharp and lustrous as a fighter jet's, rises and falls as it skitters over the hot sand, tangerine wings signaling poison to any who might interfere with its errand. Beware unlucky tarantula. Should she find you crouching in your lair or wandering overland in search of a mate, your chances of escaping will be slim. She will first paralyze you with a sting that, to humans, is one of the most painful of the insect world, before laying an egg in your fleshy belly. That egg will hatch while you are still alive and will eat its way out. The unlucky tarantula midwife will then expire as the next generation of hawk is born.

We see Gambel's quail, cardinals, gold finches, listen to mockingbirds, trace the speedy courses of Sonoran whiptails and zebra-tail lizards as they wind around the trunk of the paloverde trees. A night-blooming cereus wilts as the first rays of the sun strike its delicate petals.

We watch. We see another king snake come up around the corner of the porch and glide right past us. We are glad to see it. King snakes can eat rattlers. We see coyotes, bobcats, and a troop of javelina that chew up the quail block. There is an owl that wants the cat and a vulture that watches the road. Hummingbirds have a tiny nest at the end of a pyracantha branch.

But most of all, it is quiet inside and out, and that quiet speaks to the surprise and mystery I feel about living. I can't speak for the Bear, but I feel awe when I consider the possibilities. There is nowhere to go and nothing to do if I would get there. Erasing options has a way of inscribing necessity. Might as well just hang here and enjoy what I've got.

I learn, gradually, to function on one leg for short trips to the bathroom or the kitchen or even out to the edge of the wash. When I hop out to the porch, and we mobilize for a foray into the sun, we three—father, son, and dog—form a parade of three all hobbling on good right limbs while the left either limps, drags, or is held suspended. I can almost hear the coyotes and quail laughing at us from the cover of the wash.

My leg slims down over the passing weeks, and I can flex my calf, painfully, though there is less muscle than before. My foot stubbornly retains its reddish thickness and stays hot to the touch. It is hard as cardboard, dry as dust, and looks leprous. The doctors we see aren't sure how the recovery should go, so I stay on antibiotics and keep the foot elevated as much as possible. It is red, and the giant, black blebs refuse to go down. Pain keeps me awake, and I spend my nights tossing and turning, trying to get comfortable. During the day I either lie on the floor and exercise my good leg or sit on the porch.

One afternoon, the Bear and I sit on the front porch as rain falls in drops so big they kick up clouds of dust before bouncing back into the air like wet fireworks. The sun is shining, and the stronger it shines the harder the rain falls. Impact craters form in the loose soil. We look at each other, aware of the magic of this moment, of the deep opposites enhancing each other, a rare display of elemental tension: fire and water duking it out.

"Mom would like this," I say, apropos of nothing.

After a pause, a deep breath, a crossing of the arms, and a determined lean back against the porch swing, he sighs. "Oh, she always did like rain in the desert," the Bear says, as if remembering a dream. It is one he does not much like. It is one he pushes away with the same steady intransigence that closes his gaze to snakes. He is quiet for a few seconds and then continues: "She loved it here and wanted to move back to Arizona . . . ever since you were a kid . . . she was happy before we moved to . . ." he again pauses, as if he is not sure he should say more, and then, "up north . . . to Alaska." I can tell he wants the moment to turn and slide away under the woodpile. But it stays where he conjured it, and he looks at it for a moment and then lets it go. It is glad to return to the shadows, to a narrow cool place where it can wait until dreams rule the porch.

My mother hated Alaska. When she got the phone call that the Bear, the lieutenant colonel, was being transferred there, she cried. I can remember her sitting on a stool in the living room in our Arizona house, the one that looked out over the Huachuca Mountains, the one that invited the sunrise on one side and let you watch the sunset behind the mountains on the other.

Anyway, she started crying, and my two sisters and I, we must have been about eight, seven, and five years old, watched her for a second and then joined her, all of us bawling. We kids leaned up against her lap and asked what was wrong. She said, "We're moving to Alaska."

We cried harder until one of us broke in between sobs to ask, "What's Alaska?"

With that, Mom cried harder but did not answer the question.

Once we got there, the Bear loved Alaska, as did the rest of us kids. But I don't think I forgot that my mother loved the desert above all places and would hold every other place up for comparison with the desert knowing it would never be a contest. She made it a point, in Alaska, Minnesota, Missouri, Virginia, and Wisconsin, to let us know how much those places did not measure up.

Yes, she would have liked that rain now, if someone with advanced Alzheimer's can like the weather.

So, we watched the rain give way back to sunshine as we sat on the swing, my leg up high enough to keep the blood from rushing painfully down to the foot.

I think the Bear liked being in Arizona. In some ways, it might have reminded him of things my mother loved.

I had to wonder how much of my mother's desire ran beneath my migrating back to the desert, back to something lost and hoping blindly to win back.

I debate whether or not to tell him all I feel about death, about the accompanying quiet, about how I would like to talk about him and my mother, about things we fear and push back into the dark, out of sight. The "other" gains power there in the dark. It can haunt us in the day as well as the night. The dying mother and wife, the hated creatures, the dark aliens wanting in across our borders, none of them goes away because they are pushed out of sight.

We don't usually discuss such things. It is not part of the family code of conduct, especially among the men. Stories for us are more like scenes followed by a lesson of how men live or a punch line delivered as an arrow of how they shouldn't. Digressive, exploratory speculation is taboo, as is any subject deemed hoity-toity or the subjects interesting only to some hated aristocracy. It is not our place to tell personal stories. That is for the idle rich, the celebrity, or the insane. The town drunk has earned the right to ruminate. Yes, we are taciturn and stoic until the conversations turn to cars or sports. But the Bear has changed, has been beaten down a bit by life, and, as a result, has risen in my eyes. He has become more generous, more able to reflect. I think that, as an aging man, now he might be willing to listen, maybe even to understand. And it is here, in the quiet, unhurried moments when we have the chance. Chances don't come often; they are opportunities that can be lost.

The moment passes and we don't talk.

He stays to help until I can use crutches reasonably well to get into the bathroom and back to the bedroom. I am simultaneously delighted to be able to move, sad to see him leave, and frustrated and edgy at being crippled.

The Bear leaves me to work it out and heads back home.

12 / The Plumed Serpent

On the side of the Temple of Kukulkan, a pyramid in the Yucatán Peninsula, the setting sun zigzags down the wall supporting the stairs, suggesting a serpent's shadow. The pyramid was dedicated to the plumed serpent, Quetzalcoatl, the serpent who blends heaven and earth. The winged serpent's image pervades Mexico and Central America and symbolizes birth, renewal, spiritual opening, and is seen as inspiring the written word.

At Chichén Itzá, the shadow moves with the rotation of the earth, winds slowly along the edge of the great pyramid, visibly animate, even to this modern eye when I saw it on the autumnal equinox. Seeing this, I envied those who had created such a reminder of their connection to this heartbreaking, solid, living earth. It struck me, like rolling thunder, that there are other *maneras de ser*, ways to be, ways to see one's place in this world. The shadow descends the staircase of the pyramid if you watch it closely, patiently, as testimony and persuasive case for the power of forces we sense but do not understand.

Of all of the longing, the hunger, and yearning in my bundle of desires, the one that is carried by blood, bone, and nerve, one of the most unspeakable and profound is that for contact with the sustaining garden of wild places and animals. I pursue, hoping to earn and realize, an undeniable, unceasing awareness of membership and interdependence with a living, breathing, wild nature.

There was a time in Guatemala when I heard a reminder, was witness to a way of seeing that generated a connection between people and place, between flesh and spirit. I took a walk into the forest up the side of a mountain and listened to a Mayan guide's stories.

The pistol rested inside his pack, an ambiguous lump beneath faded canvas, an incongruous modern reminder that the world is not to be trusted. The pack blended in with the other bundles of crops and firewood in the back of the tiny pickup truck as it bounced along the dirt highway following the shore of Lake Atitlàn. I was seated on the wheel well of the truck, and my guide, Bernardo, sat next to his pack, raising his eyes from time to time with a look that sought to appraise our destination.

Bernardo leaned over into the wind to say something I didn't catch to the driver. They both laughed. The driver shot me an expression that sought to verify whatever Bernardo had said. He kept smiling, but not at me.

It was almost dawn, and the volcano we were about to climb loomed across the smooth and impossibly blue waters of the lake.

Light shone high on the ragged crown of the otherwise perfect cone, but had not yet reached the patchwork of milpas, or family croplands, below. The dark green of a cloud forest extended down the steep sides of the volcano into shadow, giving the mountain the illusion of ancient, undisturbed wilderness.

Steep channels have cut and eroded the volcano into distinct and precipitous canyons, like pleats in a skirt. At one time, millions of years ago, its sides were smooth and unwrinkled, but the scars of age now run deep. From where I sat in the back of the truck, the volcano looked wild and impenetrable, dangerous and exotic.

"Es para proteccion," said Benardo when he saw me looking at the pack.

Protection from what, I wondered. All of the large animals, jaguars among them, were long ago extirpated or perished for lack of territory. Maybe it was something else—*bandidos* or Guatemala's own soldiers. I didn't know.

I stopped for a minute to wonder about this: a long climb up a large mountain, unpredictable weather, the wrong equipment, and now armed protection. As an aging gringo in mediocre condition I had to think twice; I barely slept for all my doubts the night before. Here I was, an outsider, in this strange, lush, and fabulously beautiful, tightly woven tapestry of Mayan land and culture, fascinated by the "otherness" of the people, the soil, the food, the language, the ways of being. They: short, dark, hardened by fieldwork and sun, wearing clothes crafted on their own looms, eating food grown from family land. I: a product of industrialized culture, surviving in climate-controlled classrooms and automobiles, meeting my and family's travel needs with the power of money and American political clout.

Generations had passed since my clan had to earn its living by working the land. We had gained wealth and mobility, dropping a direct connection to the earth like a hot, shameful, poison potato. But we had lost something in the trade, and I was out looking for it. You could say we had tamed just about every square inch of the North American continent and there was no place to call wild. Between the culture and the land, I was hoping to taste something of that here. Yet part of me felt like a greedy voyeur looking in from a safe distance on a people still drawing their lives from the land and the stories that grew out of their love of the land. For that I was hungry.

Yes, I was hungry, but there was more. Dreams lingered at the edges of my awareness, out of sight, in the background. Sometimes, waking early, I caught a glimpse of them. Often there was a mountain. Something told me it was this mountain. Coming to Santiago del Atitlán had felt like coming home, like some other places, other mountains, had felt like coming home, but this place had something else, promised something else. Permanence? Redemption? Unbroken connection with something lost to me long ago? I couldn't tell, but felt compelled to meet it, not to conquer it, but to honor it in some way.

There was no doubt that I would go to the mountain if I had the chance. I was here to get something that I had given up, or so the instincts said. Like other mountains, this one asked me to get outside the inertia, transience, and grind of daily life and to step onto something other, something solid, something lasting—something requiring immense focus and exertion, something that offered a tangible beyond walls of limitation and exhaustion. This mountain felt like a pilgrimage and something more that I could not put my finger on.

We passed a hacienda. One of the gardeners was already up trimming the grass with his machete. He knelt down and swung the blade in a low, fast, arcing swipe. Tiny shreds of grass leapt and fell in a neat wave in the wake of passing steel. The result was the same as a power mower, giving the thick green hair of grass a military crew cut. He did not look up as we passed but bent even deeper to his task, intent on the even precision of his stroke, the clean edge of his blade.

We traveled along a dusty, dirt-lined defile that ran between the villages on this side of Lake Atitlán. Lake smells mingled with those of cow manure and soap from women washing their clothes along the shore. The detritus of snack culture littered the ditch along the road: chip bags, cigarette butts and packages, bottle caps, along with the organic discards such as banana peels, mango pits, corncobs. The ditch made walking precarious as there was little space between the path of traffic and the loose slopes.

I sat in the windy bed of the *picop* with the other passengers—a woman in full traditional dress of *huipil*—embroidered with a dazzling display of roses set over a pattern of colored squares set on a diagonal that reminded me of the patterns on the back of a diamondback rattlesnake—a wrapped skirt, and braided hair, carrying a basket full of bananas; a hollow-cheeked peasant farmer who had to be in his late sixties carrying an adze; and a young guy wearing western clothes and a "No Fear" cap. I nodded and tried to shake off the stares as I rested my elbows on the rim of the bed. The truck could haul people, animals, firewood, crops, or whatever else would fit in the bed and between the walls of the rack.

I had ridden in the bed of pickup trucks before as a farmworker in the Midwest and as a hitchhiker between backpacking trips into the Rockies, the Tetons in particular. Happy days of clear light and tired body, they carry a beauty I find painful to remember. I was so sure back then—confident, trusting, sure of the permanence of nature and of wild places.

Now Bernardo again leaned around the cab and said something to the driver, who accelerated, spinning his wheels and throwing me back toward the tailgate. I tightened my grip as I caught a glimpse of the old man chuckling to the woman who settled down onto the spare tire, smiling as they chatted away in Tzutujil, one of Guatemala's indigenous languages.

The morning promised a cool day—good for climbing. Bernardo said we would be ascending most of the morning and asked if I had brought any water or food. He seemed relieved when I said I had. He looked at my shoes, some stiff sneakers, and asked to see the tread. I thought the lugs were thick for running shoes, but Bernardo winced a little before agreeing that they were probably sufficient.

We slid past ranches with elaborate gates, walls topped with broken glass embedded in concrete, and muddy, rock-strewn main streets with *tiendas* proclaiming the virtues of Crush and Pepsi. A soccer field tilted wildly toward the lake in a way that would give a great advantage to the team trying to score downhill. Pigs and dogs roamed the streets freely, but bothered no one, having learned how to survive traffic and stay out of people's way. The truck lurched along the rutted road that climbed past the town toward the mountain. Women walked on the side of the road, carrying baskets on their heads, whistling and flirting with the driver as he passed. They laughed hard and deeply, unafraid. I was alert and on edge as we neared the trailhead.

Bernardo's calm reassured me. I would never have guessed the contents of his pack, and his appearance was startlingly standard. His T-shirt was worn but clean. It had a Nike swoosh that covered most of his broad chest. He was a compact man and looked like he could climb forever. He had the hook nose and the smooth, beardless face of a Mayan warrior. His eyes were clear and looked at things patiently. His hands had thick calluses, like a cowboy. I had seen those hands on men who worked with tools and tractors. I had seen them often, crumbling dirt between the fingers and thumb, testing the soil, savoring and revering ingredients of the land. He saw me looking and remarked that a drought had dried up much of the land around the lake, that times were going to be very hard, that the dust would likely deepen before rains returned. I nodded. He said nothing else. I wondered if he felt he had given away too much or had not spoken appropriately to a client.

One by one the others climbed down when they came to their destinations until Bernardo and I were the only ones left in the back of the truck. I was about to start up some small talk, but we rounded a corner that exposed us fully to the wind off the lake. It struck us hard and cold and carried so much dust that I had to lower my eyes and cinch down my hat. Bernardo just looked at me and said quietly "*mucho aire,*" lots of wind, and then pointed up to the volcano now looming above us.

The truck pulled off on a shoulder, and Bernardo signaled me to climb down and stand to the side while he paid the driver. He kept his body between me and the cab, shielding me from the view of the driver. After the truck sped off, trailing behind it a choking haze of fumes and fine dust, Bernardo seemed relieved, more at home in the trees than on the road.

We left the road and the shore of the lake. Lake Atitlán is about a mile high, and we had another vertical mile to climb to reach the crater and summit.

Bernardo stopped when the trees closed around us and asked that I wait while he said a prayer asking the mountain for permission to climb. I waited, not knowing exactly what to do, a little intrigued and a little uncomfortable with such a display of reverence. When he looked up, he nodded and said it was a good time to go and that we should start before it got too light.

The path followed a steep, cobbled road through vestiges of cane fields, the cash crop before coffee, and then we entered the *cafetales*, coffee fields that grew in closer to the road as we climbed. Soon the road petered out and a trail wound through the rows of coffee plants. I knew that pickers earned less than two dollars pay for a fifteen-hour day, and I thought about the times I had spent more than that for a cup.

That seemed like another time and other life ago as we picked up speed and I began to sweat. Rotting avocados lay pecked over in the dust in the shade of the bushes. Bernardo passed easily beneath the branches through a tunnel that was about his height. I either stooped or swung my elbows to clear away the bean-laden branches. Here the earth was brown, dry, friable—easygoing. We climbed steadily as the flank of the mountain grew steeper up the slopes of its perfect, rising arc.

Coffee plants gave way to groves of avocado, then maize. The contours of the mountain were traced by corn rows held in place by stakes. Stalks from previous crops were buried in the soil, reinforcing the loose soil into neat terraces. Some of them formed a solid stairway up the side of slopes so steep that they would never have been farmed in the States. This incline and remoteness was a blessing of sorts. Big multinational corporate farms were not interested in this land and farmed instead the flat stretch of land between the highlands and the coast. Easy to run a tractor down there. And the gringos had taken the level land around the lake for airstrips, tennis courts, and hotels. One had even exhumed graves to build a luxury resort. The Indians farmed, and sometimes died, in the hills.

Not long ago, guerilla fighters hid in these same forests and mountains. They covered the same ground I would cover, but they went barefoot, with little food or water, carrying weapons, sometimes running for their lives. The army had been brutal here. Fully a fifth of the village of Santiago had been either executed or "disappeared." They were fighting for their way of life, for this mountain. The ground held their blood.

Between fields the trees grew taller and closer. The woods were dense with fruit and nut trees—*zapote*, oak, *semilla de marañon* (cashew); thick undergrowth wound its way up the trunks of trees. The strangler fig had a way of using a host tree for support as it sucked the life out it with a seemingly passionate entwining. Healthy figs grew over gray, dried hulks of larger host trees, reminding me of the perils of love turned to obsession, or desire for comfort to greed, lust, the hunger for raw experience—anything to escape the boredom or fear of dying. Epiphytes and bromeliads punctuated the heights with fantastic displays of flower, leaf, and root high in the upper stories of the canopy.

The climbing grew steeper as the earth grew darker. Deep, rich, black soil had been cut into steps that became the regular trail now, switchbacking through the forest with unrelenting incline. Breathe, breathe, breathe, step I told myself over and over. Bernardo stopped just ahead and listened, always keeping me in sight two or three switchbacks above.

The hours passed and still we moved through high, cultivated fields. Bernardo said that these fields were owned by the poorer families who could not afford land farther down the mountain, so they carried tools, seeds, food, even water up to the fields and then hauled the harvest out on their backs. I thought about transport, the cost of *elote*, corn still on the cob, and it just didn't add up. But then I looked at the view of the village and the lake, imagining what it must be like to work the fields by day and sleep beneath the stars above the lights of the town, and I wondered if on another scale the work wasn't worth it, at least from the romantic perspective of a nature-hungry gringo. I saw the vestiges of the crater rim of the most recent caldera that formed Atitlán, this place they call the umbilical connection between the material and the spiritual. These volcanoes are young, only about eighty thousand years old. Only Atitlán, across the bay from us, is still active. The volcanoes provided the raw materials, while the lichens and algae did the work of making it usable. The volcanoes had built the land up. Erosion and biological breakdown were leveling them out, slowly, so slowly that it seemed they would last forever. For my purposes, they will. Volcanic rock has broken down into rich soil that gets darker as we ascend.

After the last of the milpas the climbing got dirty. Or rather I got dirty. We were moving up slopes held together by moist, loose, black soil that provided little purchase for the lugs on my sneakers and left a telling smudge on whatever touched it. I touched it with knees, hands, elbows, hips. I touched it by falling, leaning, losing my balance, and just scrambling. I grabbed branches of roots whenever I could to help offset my sliding back after hard-won gain. I crawled on my belly beneath roots as the cloud forest became thicker. Eighty-foot oak trees shot up to the sky and caught some of the wind that was blowing over the summit. Clouds cut off our view of the sky as we moved in a muted rhythm through a narrow world of fog and ghostly tree trunks.

Bernardo pointed to footprints in the trail. Someone had been here before us today. He said we were above the fields, so he doubted that it was someone who came up the mountain to work. We had entered old-growth forest and saw a wild turkey take wing and roost right in front of us. Like a messenger from a lost era, it sat and preened itself, watching, wondering perhaps what we were doing there. Deer, squirrel, spider monkey are all gone, Bernardo explained. The islands of cloud forest are too small and the pressure to farm too high for them to live here. Natural habitat exists only on the unfarmable slopes of the volcanoes and the deep canyons. Shrinking wild lands and native ways, I think to myself. Here I am sure that the thread has been broken, that people who still have a connection to place are destined for extinction. I remember something vaguely, like a scent I used to know but have not smelled for a long time. It swirls over and through me and I relax. I am glad to be here in this strange yet familiar place that is so threatened, yet so enduring.

It's a good place to take a break, I said to Bernardo. He agreed.

My forearms, wrists, knees, fingernails were all stained deep black. Bernardo had some dirt on his shoes. He was too dignified to note the distinction. I gratefully took a pull on my water bottle and got out a Clif Bar. Bernardo unwrapped a roll soaked through with honey. He asked how much my bar was. It was as much as a nice breakfast out would have been and could have bought almost twenty of his honey-soaked rolls I told him. He asked how my legs were. Only then did I notice that they felt tight and hot. I asked how far to the top. He said another hour. I didn't like the sound of that. The steepest was still to come.

I noticed the yawning distance between us. We found some common ground in Spanish, a second language for each of us. He asked if I had children. I said two sons, but no more. I have made sure of that I told him, holding my fingers up to indicate scissors clipping. I wondered how he would react to this, being a member of a Catholic country opposed to birth control. He said he had three but will have no more and has made sure of that, making a similar gesture. "The church tells us not to interfere, but we are beginning to find our own ways. There's too many people and too few jobs to have any more kids," he said.

Uh oh, I thought. Here come the questions about the United States and about life there and how much money can be made, cable TV, celebrity worship, how much people look to "El Norte" and consumer culture as the best way to live. But nothing. Bernardo kept musing silently as he chewed his honey bread and took long draws on his water bottle.

"I used to work as a guide doing horse tours," he said out of nowhere. "I worked from six in the morning, getting the horses ready, until seven at night, leading the tours, cooking, cleaning up. The people who took those tours paid fifty dollars each, sometimes eight, ten, twelve people. I made two dollars. In your opinion, don't you think fifty dollars is too much for a horse tour around the base of the mountain?"

"That does seem pretty expensive," I answered. That seemed to satisfy him and closed the discussion.

"Don't you sometimes want to leave here and travel?" I asked anyway.

"No. My family is here. My father, mother, brothers, sister, all generations, all here. Together we can take care of each other, of our milpas, even if someone gets sick. My life is here. My life comes from the food grown on these hills, my water from the lake. This place is me and I am this place. Why would I want to go anywhere else?"

"Do you want to do anything else? Go to school? Have a profession?" I heard myself asking, somewhat incredulously and surprising even myself.

For a long time he was silent. Then he said that many of his friends had either been killed or had disappeared during the civil war. "I wanted things for myself when I was younger. I gave them up. I am part of my village now. The village is my life. . . . It was God's will that I live," he said, "and when it's God's will for me to do something else I will. Right now I just want to stay here. I have plenty to do between my family and my brotherhood, the men of my village, the elders." Then he surprised and angered me. "We wonder why you gringos come here. You all seem to be looking for something. You leave your families, your villages, your work, and you wander around like lost burros." He didn't say so, but the next line could have been "We think you are insane." It was the first and only judgment I heard from him. The rest seemed description, neutrality in the cultural exchange. After I measured my defense to such a comment, I had to confess I thought he was on to something.

I wondered if I could live so humbly, so simply. Working long days with no hope of anything better. But then I began to think about things I wanted: more connection to nature, better ties with community, fewer distractions, meaningful work, care for my family, and realized that Bernardo had all this in a simpler form than I was used to seeing.

When we continued the climb, Bernardo became more animated and pointed to a plant he said was good for a headache, another whose root was good for a toothache, a bark that when boiled made a tea good for skin infections. I tried to memorize them, to listen, but my legs were shot through with fatigue. I feared that I would pull a muscle or worse on the loose soil and rocks as the trail continued to steepen. Breathe in. Breathe out. Rest. Climb. Breathe in. Breathe out. The blood in my ears, hydraulic blips pulsating through my arms and legs and brain, and the breath—these things I know. I know them now above all things. The talk has been drowned out by breath and blood. I can see. I can see this place for what it is, see it now, before the avalanche of talk again takes over.

Miraculously the trail leveled out and we were on the summit, looking into a knot of trees, vines, bushes, and snags that filled the deep crater in front of us. We worked our way around to a rocky outcrop that afforded us a view of the lake and of the village below. The wind whipped at us, carrying fingers of icy cloud and fog that brightened or darkened depending on the thickness of the vapor. Bernardo watched the trail closely and found the footprints that went on past the summit and down the other side. They went only one way. Again he relaxed in this place so familiar yet so contested, so rife with magic and envy. Bernardo seemed at home with it all, content that he would survive, adapt, hang on, hunker down.

Here where we were too high to stay for long, we could see far across the lake. Tiny cities hugged the hospitable places, wanting to be more, bigger, better, richer, I thought. The wind sung in the branches as I tried to decipher its message. Was it warning or mourning or just moving? I couldn't tell.

I put on my Gore-Tex jacket. Bernardo threw on an old sweatshirt. We found a place on the rocks and watched the clouds come and go above the lake, above the village, above our families far below. Some of the clouds scuttled by like ships below us, and I remembered the stories of Atitlán, mother lake, edge of dreams, belly button of the world, source and destination of "the people," the Tzutujil. Natives believe they are blessed if born on the shore of Atitlán, for it is heaven on earth, the highest plane a person can achieve. There is no word in the language for people to leave, for each step away is the first step toward return.

For a fleeting second, in the clarity born of exhaustion, I thought I saw what they meant by the lake being a passage to a world we visitors know only in fragments. The village passing in and out of sight, the lake shining like a living jewel, the unbroken line of indigenous life and its contrast with my own. This could be the center, I thought, and there is no need to go anywhere else. In the color-drained mist I could see the village standing its ground of contentment in a swirling sea of urge and distraction and a need to be and to do something else—my world, a world in which I stand with both feet. Why do I want so much and what am I afraid will happen if I don't get it? The mountain and lake stand in contrast to my fleeting need to have before it's all gone. They last. They abide. It is this fear of passing, of impermanence, of dying too soon that drives me to drink more than I can hold, to devour the thrill and danger of other places. Here, there was no fear of impermanence. I held both the fear and the peace of just being in the clouds on the mountain in my mouth, like marbles that could never melt together.

Metallic, if not acrid, the taste was not pleasant. This was not a fair exchange of values, no even contest of cultures. I could see how we outsiders cling to our lives and our money in fear they will be taken away, that we will be taken away, that there will then be . . . what? Nothing? And I saw the beauty of the men and women of the highlands, their sense of place, of sacred relation to each other and the land, the dependence on each other for survival. I wanted to taste more of that, to sustain contact with a world so different I could only imagine it; but I knew I could never possess that world or take up residence in it. To do so would be yet another act based on greed for experience. Yet, it was not enough, would never be enough. To want more was nothing better than petulant greed. I did not want to become one of the gringos gone native I saw selling jewelry in Panajachel.

Bernardo was patient. The cold got into my bones and I wanted to leave. He reluctantly stood, stretched, and said the descent would be tricky. A gringo had tripped over a root not long ago and broken a leg. Bernardo had to fashion a kind of travois to get him out far enough for a rescue team to help.

We retraced our steps, threading through roots and around switch-backs, hanging on to trees when possible. I slipped and skidded on my butt down some of the more difficult sections. Bernardo seemed to listen for my sliding before resuming, waiting, I could tell, just out of sight.

As the trail evened out into a steep set of switchbacks with a surface of packed dirt, Bernardo started to trot. He took small steps and held his shoulders smooth, his arms loose, elbows tight in. It was the same stride I had seen old men doing when they were in a hurry, carrying heavy loads of firewood. I decided I would follow. I imitated his smooth gait, letting my arms swing loosely, cutting my stride to tight staccato steps that ate through the curves and cut stairs on the steeper stretches. It felt good for a while, maybe even an hour, and soon we passed the first of the milpas.

Farther down, my legs turned to rubber, then to lead, then to noodles. I kept going by limping and swinging them like prosthetic dead weight, care-ful not to repeat the fate of my gringo precursor.

I asked Bernardo for a rest break. One look at me and he knew. "How are the legs?"

"Pretty tired," I confessed. Something about the shared exertion, com-bined with the mountain, the forest, the work going on, seemed to open him up. His expression stopped being guarded. I could almost hear barriers lowered, a clunk as they locked open, a relieved air moving freely between spaces recently divided.

"Let's drink some water. We need it and it will mean less weight."

I sat and drank.

"Why the pistol?"

Bernardo looked at me with a new expression. "You never know what you will find on the mountain," he said. "Men with machetes are sometimes angry. They want more than they have. They see the mountain as giving many things in many ways. It's not always safe."

Then he asked: "You have *serpientes* where you live?"

"Yes," I answered, *"viboras de cascabel."* *"Muy peligorosos.* People kill them, or sometimes capture them."

He stared at me in disbelief. "To kill a *serpiente* is a misdeed. We don't kill them. We try to learn from them. . . . I have spoken with them," he said, looking surprised by his admission or confession. "Some of the priests and the *evangelicos* say the *serpiente* is evil, but I don't think so. We tell a different story, one much bigger, much older."

He gauged my reaction, looking to see if I followed his drift. Or was it an appraisal of some kind?

"Time is a circle," he said, "like the snake. It is like the star Venus that sometimes appears as the Morning Star, just like the serpent loses its skin and becomes new. We used to count the years by the star's patterns."

I thought of El Caracol observatory at Chichén Itzá and its spiral construction. The spiral also accompanied images of Quetzalcoatl on glyphs at various structures. I remembered that the shells were both spirals and suggestive of water, the serpent as river, as cycles of inhale and exhale, and that the serpent, like water and breath, is tied to regeneration and renewal, constant change and transformation.

"We tell a story," he continued, "of Quetzalcoatl. It means many things, depending how you listen to it, when you hear it. We use the stories to teach."

Teach what, I asked myself. He looked at me like I sometimes look at my students when I talk slowly to convey a complex point.

"It is a story, but it is also *una manera de ser*, a way of being. We talk of the serpent, but also of the cycles of the stars, of the rising and falling, of dying and being born. We are part of the circle, and the story teaches that." He let that sink in.

I studied Bernardo's face. He struck me as a man possessed by himself, complete in himself. He seemed to radiate something and smiled a quiet, patient smile. I thought I could see something of plumes rising from him, a kind of crown, but shook that off.

"We don't see ourselves as separate," he went on, letting his momentum carry him through to the finish. "Do you know that you can hear breath in the conch shell?" he asked, apropos of nothing. "We are all made of breath, even the serpents."

This was more than I could digest and he knew it.

He looked at me a little suspiciously and then, apparently satisfied, decided to continue. "Sometimes Quetzalcoatl can even take the shape of a man, so you have to be careful what you think of people." He waited again. "Serpents are especially powerful. They can even control the weather. Be careful and listen." Then he was silent.

I tell him that there were once grizzly bears where I was from, a desert place called Arizona. That there were even creatures called wolverines. But they are gone now and live only in the highest mountains far north of my territory. "But we still have snakes," I say, hoping to gain at least some credibility for my home territory. He nods approvingly.

"I guess our mountain is not high enough for the big animals, like the jaguar," he said, looking back over his shoulder.

I thought about losing the jaguar, what that might mean. How balance gets tipped when there is no wild place, only pale memories where great talking cats once reminded people of their place in a great and wild web.

"Aren't you afraid of the *serpientes*, the *jaguares*?" I asked him.

"Not as afraid as I am of some other things. Men who forget their place in the world turn on each other. That is not the way of the jaguar or the serpents. The wheel keeps turning. We were here before the Españoles, before *los gringos*, and we will still be here when you are gone. I never felt the need *antes*—in the old days—to haul *una pistola* in my *mochila*. Sometime I won't again."

His look told me he would say no more.

I looked down at the lake and realized we still had a long way to go. The thought sent a crippling cramp through my thigh and I groaned.

Bernardo helped me up and told me to keep walking and to keep drinking.

Breathe. Breathe. Breathe. Step. Limp. Step. Watch out for that rock. Don't snag your foot on that root or roll your ankle in this narrow rut of a trail.

I dug deep for a story that might sustain me, might help me lift my exhausted feet over interminable traps and obstacles, but found only traces of something dimly remembered. I see only the end. I don't see a new beginning. Our heroes go off into the sunset and don't return. Nature is a threat that must be subdued. It's all about me. Me above everyone else. It is so lonely here with such stories.

One hour. Two. The trail leveled out just as I felt I could not take another step. The dusty road was a relief from the terrible downward tug of the trail. Bernardo had me sit on a rock while he flagged a *picop*.

Once again he negotiated, and we hitched a ride back to the *posada*. The truck was crowded, and this time the other riders paid me very little attention. They seemed aloof, perhaps even jaded, but giggled when I had my back to them. We made our way around the bay, leaving a rooster tail of dust in our wake.

I could barely climb out of the rattling, wrinkled, rusted, glorious chariot of a *picop* when it stopped at the posada. I had overdone it and would feel the topography of the climb between the torn fibers of muscle for a long time. I was glad though. I wanted to take a little of the mountain with me.

"How are the legs?" Bernardo asked.

"Me duelen mucho," I replied. They hurt—a lot.

"They will hurt more tomorrow," he said. I knew he was right.

I got out my wallet and paid him. It felt good to give him the money. "I really wanted to go to the mountain," I told him. "I don't quite know why."

He looked at me squarely. "We all have strong wants. The gifts we get should be appreciated. I hope you get what you want from your trip. Next time, bring boots. There is still more to know. Not far from here, in the higher mountains, many *serpientes*, some say they have seen a jaguar. If you are strong enough, I could take you."

I didn't know whether to hope or to resign myself to wanting the impossible.

"If we are both strong enough," I say with a weak laugh.

With that I offered my hand, and this time he took it. Then he turned and walked—bowlegged, with a light step—down the cobble drive to the dirt road where men bent beneath weight of firewood they had cut and were now hauling to town. He rejoined them in their long walk, through the dust, above the lake, beneath the volcano. I turned too and walked up the drive, sore, spent, trying to hang on to something that kept slipping from my grasp.

13 / Enemies and Brothers

As long as my brother KC and I shared the same enemies, we got along fine. But somewhere we split, I to the city and university, he to an early marriage and life in a small midwestern town. He has come back to me now; I can hear him, see him, feel him in the shadows. He came to me in a dream last night and made it very clear that he did not approve of my staying at home, even if I was working some online, writing, and living a few days free from the clock. I could hear the contempt in his voice, the tone that whispered "weirdo/enviro/teacher" who bench-presses only half of what he can.

His is the voice in my head that struggles with accepting my crippled state. It speaks from a need to get up and go back to work. Move. Toughen up. Beat down whatever gets in your way. Much of who I think I am is tied up with some of that story. If I am doing nothing, I am nothing, or so the story goes. He goes on with a litany of disapproval even as I try to mollify his venomous assault with appeals to some of the things we used to share. "Why you live in that desert wasteland, I'll never know," I can hear him saying when I ask him to come down sometime, come down and see the desert from the seat of his new Harley.

Maybe he is always there, covered by the noise of day-to-day juggling and householding, the busyness of my life. The voice is not KC, of course, but a tyrant at work in my head. It's my inner redneck you could say. I hate this voice, just like I hate the dually wheeled pickup trucks that run whole groups of cyclists off the road when we ride into the hardcore cowboy country on the other side of the Tucson Mountains. There, out by Picture Rocks, where the road is still narrow and tortured, on Sundays when cowboys want to get to town traveling back over the pass we have just traversed, they cut it close, sometimes clipping, even killing, cyclists or walkers or any creature unlucky enough to be in their path. Yahoos, with their rifles blowing the life out of lizards, birds, rabbits, javelina, deer, snakes, coyotes, anything they see that moves out in the desert, off the four-wheel-drive tracks, tear down the road leaving clouds of diesel fumes. They have pointed their guns at me from trucks and off-highway quad-runners when I have asked them what they are doing after bullets fly over our heads.

I have learned to wear fluorescent colors when out running or hiking, a survival strategy as well as a fashion statement. They are rigid in their defense of guns, sticking to them, you might say, when asked to justify lazy, outdated thinking. It's a story worth dying for, going down in blazing gunfire and a rain of bullets.

"They" are in me. They are a voice that runs below the normal frequencies of audible sound. They are a color outside the visual spectrum. Those voices are pissed at having to live in the dark bag of my mind and come out from the shadows to snipe in the quiet. They are old patterns of talk and ways of seeing that reemerge and have begun to colonize my quiet, my calm.

I am getting more impatient with each passing minute. Those old stories are at the root of my anxiety and together form a tyrant that reigns in darkness.

Mine is a scared, hungry tyrant who wants to squeeze every last drop out of the planet before changing his ways or giving up the ideal that nature is here to make me happy as it writhes beneath the heel of my boot.

I hear them in KC's voice when we talked during a recent phone conversation. When I told him about the snakebite, he was suspicious and not impressed that I did not personally kill the snake. He flatly asked, "Did you at least skin the thing and make a belt out of it for putting you through all this trouble?" The line went quiet for a moment as I thought of how to respond.

"No, the fire department took care of the snake," I told him.

"Well I hope *they* killed the thing," was all he said to that, indignant, implying, to my way of hearing, that I did not have the guts to do so.

His disapproval is like a wound that will not heal but that festers, and the venom of it coils inside of me, poison I have yet to neutralize. He was the last of my family, even of many friends and some strangers, to call and check in. I doubt that I can live up to his expectations of what a snakebite should be like, how a man should respond to one. We have deep rifts that run between us, and that distance disturbs me when I have time to think, time to browse through the unfinished business on my psychic desk. But all I have is time, time and new roles I get to play.

When I look at him and what he evokes in me, I see it is really fear of the unknown, of the different. My fear is not about KC the person. He is not some slack-jawed, interbred dimwit who thrives on the pain of other creatures. He is a hunter, as I once was. He also loves to stomp around the woods as much as I do. No, it's not about him, even if he does fear snakes. It's about that part of me I fear becoming, the part that is still disconnected from the desert, from anything that I react to in excess, with a knee-jerk reflex to kill or own. The repulsive voice in me comes from the throat of a redneck cracker with a sharpened shovel aimed at the neck of anything that challenges me, the way I do things, or any aspect of my little tight, controlled world. He is me that I run from.

For most of my adult life I have run away from this fearsome part of myself. At one time, I had the guns, the pickup truck, the twelve-packs of beer around a campfire. I saw what I was becoming, saw that another part of me was starting to die, and I ran like hell. I ran toward the light, toward logic, toward reason, and toward a kind of smug superiority of mind. I have found it a dry but sterile place to hide out.

Carl Jung claims that humans carry within them all possible characteristics, but that, as we are acculturated, we force some of them into "shadow," out of sight, as we shape our "appropriate" personalities. He also claims that the energy we use keeping those characteristics in check saps life energy. If life feels flat and empty, it is likely that too much energy is used up keeping these disowned characteristics under wraps. He thinks that vitality is restored when we embrace that which has been lost, disowned. "We do not become enlightened by imagining figures of light," he writes, "but by making the darkness conscious."

That doesn't mean I have to go out and kill rattlesnakes because my shadow tells me to. It does mean that I need to reclaim that part of me that is capable of doing so. By empathizing with those I oppose, I stand a better chance of reaching them, of hearing their story, of affirming it in order to change it. It means that to fight for what I want, I need that redneck, or something like him. Right now I'm too soft, too passive, too resigned, too out of balance. No brag, just fact.

KC, Bear, and my brothers remind me of where I come from: Scandinavian peasant stock. My ancestors were the unemployed of the nineteenth century, the marginalized hicks and hillbillies of the fjords. The stigma attached to this has been strong, so strong that my grandfather "forgot" his Norwegian as soon as he was able to get a job collecting trash in town in northern Minnesota. That is another story.

Still, my uncles and brothers liked to go into the woods to hunt. In some ways, they were wildlife managers, using their taste for venison to keep populations in check. They did some good. Continue to do so, but I can't see it. All I hear is the disapproval, the disconnection, the shame of running and denying.

I know there is something I've got to remember before it's too late, even if it is too late.

14 / Measuring Zero at the Bone

But never met this fellow
Attended, or alone
Without a tighter breathing
And Zero at the Bone
Emily Dickinson ("A narrow Fellow in the Grass")

One Saturday almost four decades ago, some grade school friends and I were playing in the tumbled truck-sized boulders of Cochise Stronghold in southern Arizona. Between killing and playing dead in some kind of war game and scrambling over the rounded granite ledges, cliffs, and spires, one of us spotted a blacktail rattlesnake.

We might as well have seen a blasting cap live-wired to a few sticks of dynamite. Fear and primal fascination combined to hold us spellbound, or maybe snake-bound. All of my disparate senses suddenly focused on a point of tight, coherent, blisteringly bright awareness. I magnified my attention onto that snake, compelled by the supreme importance of paying attention to it and to all the immediate sights, smells, sounds, and escape routes.

That visceral awakening was my first taste of the impact a live snake can have on one's psyche. I had dreamed of snakes before and had been vaguely aware of them in some abstract sense, but I had never really felt the grip a snake can have on one's attention. Mythological imagination suddenly materialized there in front of my distractible friends and myself; more than just a snake, the creature evoked submerged archetypal memory, generations of hardwired conditioning. On some level, I knew more about this snake than I should. I "knew" the snake could kill me. I "knew" that shape, the consequences of not attending to it, a caring about every move I made. The undeniable fact of the snake brought the present moment into stark, brilliant clarity. It was my first realization that I was not invulnerable, and a veil fell away, leaving an unbearable intensity of sensation in its place.

Peril and fascination supercharged those moments, closing down whatever portal had opened the morning to imaginary play. Here was something real, something that evoked an almost unbearable state of elevated consciousness.

The snake was not a large one, but its effect on me could not have been greater. I felt simultaneously drawn to the mottled markings and gripped by a reflex to flee.

As we watched it, the snake calmly tasted the air with its tongue, and seemed alert but not hostile. We stared silently for several moments, unable to do more than just breathe. Then Lyle or Seth, one of us, poked a stick at it, bringing it into action, complete with a buzzing from the tail and a tightening of the coil, an S to the upper body, and a lift of the wide head to striking readiness. That sound and shape went straight to some genetically programmed part of the brain that began to pump what felt like buckets of adrenaline through our bodies. Its rattling tail left no doubt it wanted us to leave.

Not unlike spotting a dragon, it lit into our fear, sending us running out of the rocks, back to the hiking trail and then down off the mountain, back down to the picnic area.

Another time, more recently, some friends and I were mountain biking on the Arizona Trail near Oracle, Arizona. The single-track trail climbed and wound through scrub oak, mesquite, rangeland, and canyons. We had all but exhausted ourselves for several hours and were closing the gap on the cars, food, water, a few laughs, and rest before we drove back to the comforts of home in Tucson.

I could see the others ahead of me, their bright jerseys winding through the low trees and over the ridges of the next rise. I was hanging back and in a pensive mood. The trail traversed a steep, rocky section that was peppered with cacti that discouraged leaving the trail for any reason.

My trail buddies had passed here just moments before, and I knew I could catch them if I wanted to do so.

As I turned a corner, lifting the front of the bike over a small ledge of rock, I saw a rattler extended across the trail, sunning itself. I had no choice but to stop and wait. The snake looked straight at me, calmly tasted the air with a curve of its forked tongue, which shone in the light. It darted in and out neatly through an opening just the right size to let it pass.

The eyes looked wise to me, but what do I know of reptilian wisdom? I have no doubt that he was studying me, though, maybe even mildly curious. We sat with each other for about ten minutes. I talked to him some, though I don't remember what I said.

I have the habit of talking to animals, both wild and domesticated, and have had some success, I think, communicating with them. Coyotes, for example, seem to stay out of the front yard of our house after I met them in the wash in front of our house and listed my demands. They stood a safe distance away, some looking at me through the cover of low-hanging branches of a mesquite tree, as I made my request. I asked that they recognize our front yard as our territory, and that, in return, Luna would surrender the wash. They looked at me with wild green eyes, listening, maybe. I pleaded my case as the plaintiff, the yellow lab, stood behind me, but not too close or obsequious. Our session yielded the desired results, for the most part.

The outcomes of this case I could not discern. I did notice the ridgelines of hills to the east, toward the Galiuro Mountains, and the sloping alluvial skirts of the Catalinas rising steeply into the southern sky. I also noticed the blue underside of a yucca leaf and some ivy winding up the willowy, spine-encrusted ocotillo. The moment was one that situated us into the bigger scene, the one that I could not see while negotiating the tricky sections of the trail. Small talk. Big horizons.

After listening politely and studying me with no trace of self-consciousness or embarrassment, the snake moved off the trail quickly when we heard a hiker coming from the other direction. I remounted and continued on to meet my friends.

When they asked me what had taken me so long, I told them I stopped for the rattlesnake in the trail that they must have seen beside it. They said they had seen no rattlesnake, though they had passed less than a minute or so before I had.

And another time in Sabino Canyon I all but stepped on a torpid mojave that blended in with the leaves, and walked past a rock rattler coiled on a ledge when we entered Onyx Cave. I have seen a rattler strike at a friend's bicycle and watched my sister leap from her bike when the front tire rolled over a large diamondback.

We have also had several snakes in our front yard, and each time we see one it triggers stories people have to tell about snakes. One visitor, a wealthy, well-known Tucson businessman, told me he saw a rattlesnake that was twelve feet long and that its enormous head was the size of a garden shovel. He said it took two blasts from a shotgun to subdue it. When I pressed him about the particulars, he stood his ground with real fervor, swearing that every measure of his tale was true.

Yes, we have met before. The ornate patterned scales that serve the twin opposing purposes of camouflage and warning leave me awestruck and puzzled. The shape and design serve as a signal, a cipher, an omen, the meaning of which escapes me, stops me in my tracks, forbidding any movement beyond this moment. Our contact has been enigmatic, opening a gap filled with questions.

About ten species of rattlesnakes live in Arizona. I say "about" because herpetologists disagree. Some say eight, others go as high as eleven. I have seen blacktail rattlers, a sidewinder, a tiger rattler, several mojaves, several dozen western diamondbacks, a rock rattler, and what I think was a pygmy rattler. I have also seen one coral snake.

Snake scales are smooth and dry. Snakes are cool to the touch, but shimmer in the light.

Rattlers can live up to twenty-five years, but do not add a rattle a year. The largest western diamondbacks rarely reach six feet, but an exceedingly rare specimen can approach seven feet. They eat rodents, birds, lizards, frogs, and even other snakes. They are prey to roadrunners, raptors, badgers, and king snakes. The king snake is immune to the bites of rattlers and can eat one almost as long as itself.

Rattlesnake exuviation, or shedding, is dependent more on food, moisture, and general health than on any rigid pattern or season. Snakes show up with a new body, free from scars, parasites, and disease, every time they shed the old skin. In some ways, snakes renew themselves, become young again, reclaim original luster.

Snakes have no legs, nor do they sport hair or fur. They never blink because the "lid" over the eye is a specialized scale.

Radio telemetry has shown that rattlesnakes are neither aggressive nor ravenous. One study in the Chiricahua Mountains in southeastern Arizona has estimated that snakes strike prey perhaps three times a year. During a twenty-year life span a snake spends about a minute fulfilling the famous curriculum we ascribe to it. They eat only a few times a year. They spend the rest of their time waiting, finding the right temperatures, gestating, defending territory, or just hanging out.

The life and perceptive capacity of the rattlesnake is about as different from ours as a life can be. They have an organ, called Jacobson's organ, that interprets microscopic particles picked up by the tongue; it is thousands of times more sensitive than the human tongue. A rattlesnake is acutely sensitive to sound, scent, heat, and image. In the sensory deprivation that is the desert, they find rich trails of stimuli, and have evolved to read the slightest signals. They are literate to the signs we can't even detect.

By contrast, we are hugely untutored in the ways of reading the desert. We miss most of what is there. We see emptiness, hear silence, smell only the most pungent of scents. Snakes live by being able to detect the footfall of a mouse and the molecular scent trails of prey and other snakes in the breeding season. And by avoiding the clumsiness of people.

They are, in other words, much more sensitive than we, infinitely more tuned in to their surroundings. Yet we see them as cold and unfeeling. We also see them as vicious, hostile, always on the make. We think they are like us.

In terms of mythology, they suggest the famous Freudian phallus and appear often in dreams. During human history, they have been associated with sexual power, healing, fertility, intelligence, and mystery. They represent, as much as any animal can, all that we do not understand. Even the ways they live are foreign to us.

Yes, snakes are different. They are hard to understand. When we fail to understand snakes, we fear them. People tend to fear what they do not understand. We react to our fear of the other, of "them," usually either by trying to kill them or capture them. Rattlesnake roundups, like those in west Texas, vilify snakes and kill hundreds yearly. Yet behind this killing lies a fascination. It is this fascination with mystery that is the gift from snakes to us. Even if we do not understand, we need to respect, even revere, the others in nature.

Right now we just remove them or kill them.

Both lead to removing snakes from their habitat, and that creates an opening in the ecosystem. An opening in the ecosystem leads to imbalance. If we remove a predator, prey populations will increase.

We are getting rid of snakes and breeding rats. We are the ones who will determine what creatures remain and flourish on the planet, and if we keep going it will be cockroaches and rats, the camp followers of humanity.

We do know some things about snakes, but not everything. We don't know what roles they might play in any ecosystem, nor do we completely understand how we might need them, how their presence serves us in some way.

The Tohono O' Odham tribe west of Tucson, for example, has always revered its creatures. The Gila monster, for one, has begun to reward that reverence. The tribe suffers from a high rate of diabetes, and it turns out that Gila monsters produce a substance in their saliva that might cure the disease. It seems that a compound, exenatide, in the saliva of Gila monsters controls blood sugar and decreases appetite. Some of the people who will most benefit from the drug are those who have best cared for the lizard that produces it. Who would have thunk it?

We just don't know what rattlesnakes might end up meaning to us, either biologically, psychologically, or spiritually. We do have some things to learn, some new attitudes to cultivate. One is a healthy respect for mystery, of opening up to things we just don't understand and never will. I want to make room for mystery in life, to take responsibility for caring for it, for giving it a place in my awareness. I am lucky that rattlesnakes have done that by being both dangerous and iconic.

When we walk in the desert identified with the streams of talk in our heads, we put both our mindfulness and our bodies in jeopardy. Fear of snakes, in part, is fear of waking, of disengaging from the ongoing flow of talk that debases direct experience of anything. We live in a tyranny of talk that snakes, as one of the few existing alarms left remaining in the psyche, can disrupt. When snakes are nearby, we have to focus, look where we place a foot or a hand, listen for warnings, tune in to the senses. Snakes embody and model a meditative state of awareness that we have forgotten and resist cultivating, and if we could see them for what they offer, we might better coexist, or maybe even get along, even if we don't quite understand each other.

Until we learn to live with rattlesnakes as one of the prime "others" in nature, we will keep missing part of the experience of nature. We need to broaden our definition of life to what lies beyond our perception. The benefit of learning to love what we cannot understand in nature is that we may begin to love that which we cannot understand in each other or in ourselves.

15 / Patterns

In wildness is the preservation of the world.
Henry David Thoreau

"Here is where we do the surgeries," says Matt Goode, a researcher special-izing in radio telemetry to help study rattlesnakes. I've come to talk to him, to find out more about snakes. He points at a table that looks like nothing special, except for a stack of plastic tubs and microscope. His large, strong hands look steady enough to be a surgeon's, and his short stubble of hair adds to the clean, surgical look.

Matt is a big and friendly guy who talks easily about his work. He's good at what he does and gets grant money where others only dream of it. Part of his success comes from his ability to write. He earned a master's degree in English while at the University of Wyoming. It shows in the elegance of his reports.

The wood floors creak as he shows me around his office and lab. I hear cars, trucks, and the occasional siren on Speedway Boulevard, just in front of the house. Inside the house, it is Speedway that feels out of context. Matt's lab and office are housed in a restored old stone mansion, built when the university was surrounded by rangeland. The wainscoting around the doorjambs and the floorboards echoes the anachronism of wood floors and windows raised and lowered with the counterbalance of sash weights.

It seemed to fit that rattlesnakes were brought to such a place to have radio transmitters implanted beneath their scales.

Matt shows me his library—philosophy and field studies, hardcovers and paperbacks, freshly minted pieces and old standards. He pulls a thick volume off the shelf and hands it to me. I read *Biophilia*, and see that it was written by E. O. Wilson. Matt says the guy is one of the great thinkers about human relationships with nature in general and those with rattlesnakes in particular.

"We need to reconfigure the stories we tell about snakes," he said, looking at me with some expectation. "The ones we have just don't work when it comes time to share the desert. People think snakes are out to get them, that they are vicious, aggressive creatures. . . . Of course Eve's encounter with a snake in the Bible doesn't help much."

I take some notes and start to wonder what kinds of stories we might begin to tell, stories that might work better for the desert we live in now, where we see things differently than cowboys did a century ago. The hard-wiring at work behind the rush of fear and adrenaline that accompany seeing a snake is not going to go away until we evolve out of it, but the story we tell about that rush might be malleable.

Matt has models of snakes, pictures of snakes, screen savers of snakes, fecal samples from snakes, semen samples, and a head filled with snake stories. This guy knows snakes.

Matt explains that development is putting people into contact with snakes. As we expand the boundaries of the city farther and farther up into the canyons, we will likely have more contact with snakes, with mountain lions, with all of the creatures that inhabit the desert.

A researcher at the University of Arizona, Matt studies this contact, calling his project "Snakes in the Neighborhood." He has shown that development near the Saguaro National Park has invited contact with snakes by building in a snake migratory path. Tiger rattlers move from winter territory in the rocky ledges above homes and a resort and migrate down to the lower washes in the summer to mate and to hunt. They have to pass right through the development.

In other words, we, people, have put ourselves in harm's way if you look at it from the perspective of who was there first. The snakes do what they have done for perhaps millions of years, and we cry foul when they cross the yard, and then we call in the fire department.

So what? you might be saying. What difference does it make to relocate a couple of rattlesnakes? Well, for one, doing so likely kills the snake. Relocated snakes tend to overextend themselves trying to return to their home ranges, and they even seem to stop eating, committing a form of reptilian suicide. For another, moving snakes is just one more step toward sanitizing nature to keep it "safe" and under control. Part of why people live in these places, on the boundaries of a city, next to a large national park, is to be close to nature, even if nature poses some danger.

As Thoreau said, "In wildness is the preservation of the world," but he could have gone on to include contact, connection, peace, mindfulness, attention, imminent possibility of death, membership in life, the cycles of being. In other words, we need wildness to remind us that we are living here, living now. Wildness requires that we pay attention, that we be care-ful, full of care, that we attend to our surroundings and appreciate our place in them. That comes with a cost, and that cost is some potential risk. A risk-free world is not a wild one. It is an amusement park, a construct, a managed reality. It is in some ways what we call civilization.

But civilization has not served to make us more civil. It has served to speed us up, to disconnect us, to weave a reality based on a bombardment of images, soundtracks, more drama and stories in a week than some people fifty years ago got to see in a lifetime. In civilization is disconnect, noise, distraction, anxiety, misery, suffering, dis-ease, the belief or hope that we will somehow be free from death. Civilization plays to our desires to be somewhere else, to be continually striving, to stampede toward something better, scrambling over each other leaving a trail of extinctions and casualties in our wake.

16 / Just Enough

It is my first day back at work after the snakebite and I am able to hobble around campus on crutches. Hallelujah! and Oh shit! It is mid-September and still hot, one of the last really hot days before fall overtakes the fading but persistent heat of summer in the Southwest.

One of the ubiquitous fighter jets that circle the valley passes overhead, putting conversations on hold, splitting the air, and all but deafening anyone walking between classes. Now those things are dangerous, I think to myself, remembering how much fear I see in the eyes of those who know why I am on crutches. In the late sixties, one of the jets crashed on the southern border of the university, narrowly missing a middle school, killing one person. As soon as one passes now, its engines fading as it closes in on the air force base, another takes its place. As loud as they are, it is as if we don't hear them; they don't seem to exist. We are selective in what we pay attention to, and it is only because I have been gone that I notice them at all.

Teachers pause in midsentence; students hold pens at the ready as they take a break, and I wonder what it is we are so afraid of that we need weapons circling overhead, reminding us that we can strike first, fast, and lethally.

I have wrapped the foot in an Ace bandage and squeezed it into the leg of an unhappily stretched baggy pair of jeans. They are the first long pants I have worn since the bite. I feel anything but normal: excited—despite going back to work—and anxious to see the students that have begun without me, but not normal. Chris Hamel, friend and master teacher, has taken the class while I was out. I am a little concerned about how the students will feel about changing horses in midstream, but press on into the heat of the morning, crutches swinging, book bag slung over my shoulder.

I get a head start on the crowds of the passing period, but get caught in the rising tide of students in spite of my hopes to beat the rush. Sweat runs into my eyes and soaks my shirt. I am a hindrance to the stream, a boulder that students must go around as they rush in a flow of our own making. I am a hobbling bottleneck in traffic, a struggling obstacle to sidestep and then leave in their slipstream.

Students walk the sidewalks dressed for the beach—boys in their droopy-drawer trunks that hang below their knees and girls in bikini tops and shorts that reveal the delicate ridge of the pelvis, the dimples of the lower back. They are postcard perfect, these undergraduates raised on the milk of glossy advertising. I am struck again at how elite universities have become. The children of the affluent show us the newest and the best of casual and provocative Sun Belt school fashion. Most are shod in flip-flops. Hawaiian prints and surfer logos add to the beach feel, despite being land-locked deep in the Sonoran Desert. They wear cell phones close to their ears, as intimately as the way they talk to friends with whom they chat unself-consciously. Only the backpacks betray the true nature of their errands as they pass between classes. Why are we so eager to suggest other places, other times, the vacation vision? Because we can. Doing so has become another national pastime.

I feel stodgy in my jeans and button-down shirt, sweat running into my eyes, my graying temples plastered to my scalp. Yes, I am older than they, but I am here, feeling the heat, the brilliance of the sun, and don't much care that I am flawed, wounded, hobbled. In fact I like it, and feel just a little proud to serve as evidence of the inevitable demise waiting somewhere in every life. My book bag reminds me of the tasks that await me, but for now I just limp and swing past the student union, the desert gardens, the blunt and imposing metal sculptures. I am immersed in the three-dimensional play, and it scares me to be so vulnerable, so ephemeral. But the weight of my bag counters that passing with the substance of struggle to teach and to make a living.

Part of me knows how lucky I am to be here, and I surprise myself to find the path to class as enjoyable as a hike to a secret waterfall deep in an Arizona canyon.

I slowly make my way step by step up two flights of stairs, crutches holding the weight as I swing the bad leg, and I am there, outside the classroom door. I listen for just a moment to the chatter coming through the door. They know I am coming and are probably more than a bit anxious. Then I push the door open. The class goes silent; heads turn. I make my way through a narrow passage of desks to the front of the class. A few of the students smile and offer a friendly hello. The air is thick with novelty, tension, and excitement.

I turn to face them and say "Hello, guys. I hope you've had a good couple of weeks because the honeymoon is over." I am joking, but a few of them squirm involuntarily.

I take a seat and wipe the sweat from my forehead with a bandana. We begin with an open session of questions before they report on what they have worked on so far in the semester. It will take a while to get acquainted.

I squint hard with the effort to focus and to better remember faces. There is a Brian and a Mia. David has done some good work preparing for a presentation he makes, as scheduled. They have been pushed well by Chris and are more than a little suspicious that their work might be in vain, thinking, like most students do, that English teachers are capricious, arbitrary, and rigid with their grading. The atmosphere is imbued with a sense of fear, of a future that threatens them. Like a cloud of doom gathering above their heads, the thoughts and self-talk of what might happen keep them from attending to the work that will earn them the grade they want. If they would only put more attention into the doing, I think to myself, the results, the fruits of that work, will likely have the quality they are seeking.

Their anxiety charges the air with an almost palpable scent of fear. They have set their sights on the end of the semester, putting the grade before the work, the cart before the horse, fretting over the results of effort that has not been expended. They are smart kids who have learned their lessons well. I listen to them, trying to settle some of the nervousness. We are going to attend to language and to look closely at some stories, maybe composing a few of our own. I will be surprised if they can bring their attention back to what we are doing at that moment, rather than spinning out worst-case scenarios.

I am talking, of course, to myself as much as anyone. How true it is that we want to teach what we most need to learn.

The class is over before I know it, and I am again the crippled tortoise gimping back across campus to the English office. Once I am out of the building and back in the sun, I swoon and have to rest.

I did not realize how tired I am, how taxing it was to be out in the heat, going up and down stairs, back to work. Megan had argued against my going back so soon. I wanted to prove her wrong, wanted to show her I could handle the resumed stresses of work.

When I arrive at the English office, I am pale, clammy, and all but exhausted. Chris and Stephanie gang up on me and order me home. I rest there for a bit, and slowly make my way back to my cubicle, the car, and then home.

I chalk my exhaustion up to lack of rest, to having to climb the stairs, and to meeting my students.

Back at home, I remove the bandage and notice a faint stream of yellow fluid out of one of the fang punctures. I say to no one in particular, "That doesn't look good," before forgetting about it and finishing the evening helping with dinner and homework.

The following morning I feel more tired than usual and am back in bed after the rest of the family has left for school. I am home for the day and have a doctor's appointment that afternoon, so plan to catch up on e-mails and student questions.

I sleep until noon, when I awake in a cold sweat shaking with chills. I try to stand and fall back on the bed, struggle up again and crawl to the bathroom where I throw up again and again until nothing is left. I black out, curl into a fetal position next to the toilet.

Well, I think to myself when I come to, I guess I won't be driving to the doctor's office. I chuckle at my joke before crawling to the phone to call a neighbor. Kind and generous Harriet answers and agrees to give my sorry sack of a body a lift to the doctor's. After she agrees I fall back into a swoon of sweat and chills. She wakes me hours later out of a deep delirium. I shake off my weakness enough to get out of bed and try to think. I must have serum sickness I tell myself. Anitvenins often have serious side effects, sometimes profound allergic reactions, and I am convinced I am in the middle of one.

I am sorry to find out that I am again wrong. I am getting used to misreading just about everything. It is not an allergic reaction, I soon discover, but something called sepsis, the body's response to a severe infection.

I have never heard of sepsis or a septic infection. I know we have a septic tank and that I use antiseptic soap sometimes, but sepsis—widespread, systemic reaction to an infection of the body? Never. Not a clue.

And so the sequel is acted out with almost the same dramas: near death shock, ambulance ride, emergency room discussions, doctors, but this time with a trembling, baffled, scared patient.

I guess I did not learn what I needed to learn the first time around, so get to take another tour with my dark companion and his chilling presence. Only this time I tighten my collar, button my pajamas, and tell him once is enough and that I am not going peacefully.

17 / In Bad Taste

The shakes, chills, delirium, the being crippled by a toxic, swollen foot, the trip to the emergency room with the flashing lights and IV hookup were all replayed, despite my disbelief and embarrassment. I realize that repeating many of the characteristics of the previous trauma of the snakebite was in bad taste, but I guess I still had something to learn that required repetition.

One of the fang marks had become infected, formed an abscess, and bloomed into systemic collapse. Sepsis had spread ten days after finishing the course of antibiotics. In the space of three hours, I went from feeling fairly healthy and enjoying a normal day to spiking a 104-degree fever, shaking uncontrollably, and vomiting the dregs of my digestive tract into the sink at the doctor's office. My blood pressure dropped to eighty over forty and lower. The EMTs said that dehydration was causing my blood vessels to collapse and to begin leaking.

So here I am, again on a gurney, waiting in the emergency room, hooked up to an IV. Megan has come in and taken over as I have taken over for her when she has collapsed. She had her own "snakebite" a few years ago, and I played the nurse. Now she is here, returning the favor, again, a little surprised by the redundancy. Kyle is with her, and he gives me a blasé look and "hey Pops" over the top of his homework as if nothing is out of the ordinary. I feel a fixture in the emergency room, that my being here is right as rain.

What is up with this? I ask myself. I just don't get it. Megan has again brought me books to help me figure it out. The answer to everything can be found if you do enough reading. I sigh as she stacks them next to the bed. I can't sit up.

My condition posed a series of problems that had to be solved. Doctors had to decide what to do with the abscess and how to treat the infection. Orthopedic surgeons collaborated with infectious disease specialists to find the simplest but most effective way to head off the raging growth of bacteria that was spreading through my body.

One of the first steps was to identify the "bug," the type of bacteria. In order to do that, the doctors would have to get a sample and do a culture. A blood culture had been taken in the ER, but would take seventy-two hours to grow, and blood cultures often did not succeed in catching the offending bacteria. Another, more effective way to get a sample would be to get a swab directly into the abscess, and that could only be done surgically.

The possible surgical interventions ranged from minor lancing and draining the abscess, which could be done at the bedside, to formal debridement, or cutting and removing dead or dying tissue, which would be full-on surgery, complete with general anesthesia. Two surgeons and the infectious disease doctor considered the options.

Why all the medical details? one might ask here. Good question, another might answer. The response doctors arrived at when confronted with evidence of a swelling abscess and a system gone hot with infection was not, "Well I'd rather not consider that today. Let's just pretend it doesn't exist and schedule that foursome for this afternoon." In an easy-to-imagine universe that might be an appropriate response, but in this one I can see that the body is something worth monitoring and caring for. If someone is bleeding, I would apply pressure and some kind of bandage because that is the right thing to do. I act to heal, even if acting hurts.

If evidence suggests an ailing spirit or weak link in an ecosystem, however, most of us will look the other way. We say we can function temporarily without a happy heart or an intact, balanced desert, but we won't live long losing blood. That is true. We can function, but can we feel awe?

"Your foot has been colonized by a form of bacteria," the infectious disease specialist said, "that got in there when you were bitten by the snake. Snake fangs are very dirty because their prey defecate on the way down and those bacteria collect on the fangs." He went on to explain that the infection had probably been growing since the bite, despite the oral antibiotics I had taken after being bitten. He said he hoped that the bug at work was sensitive to antibiotics. Some that he had found lately were not, and required more aggressive forms of intervention and heavier doses of super antibiotics over a longer time.

Damn. From poison to bacteria, the world is having its way with me. Little critters have taken the place of nasty molecules, but the effects are the same, my curriculum of healing prolonged.

When I asked how long I would have to be treated, he told me he didn't know and that for the time being it was better that I not worry about it. Some antibiotic-resistant bacteria had been found in the hospital and in the city at large. Some of it was the "flesh eating" kind and had developed, in part, because of our misuse and overuse of antibiotics and other resistance-creating influences like antibacterial soaps. Fear leading to overreaction that leads to greater problems and more overreactions—sounds familiar somehow. Those infections required the most powerful antibiotics made, he said. He then gave me a worried look. I thought of friends, two of them, who had been infected with such bacteria. They knew what he was speaking about. Every move creates a countermove.

It appeared that the infection ran very deep into the foot because of the redness, the swelling, the heat of the foot, and type of edema. When poked with a finger, the depression left by the pressure remained, indicating a lack of circulation.

If the infection was deep enough, "very deep" to be medically precise, bones might be infected. If bones were infected, the intervention and antibiotics would be more invasive, more intense. The doctors decided to do X rays and an MRI to determine if or how much the bones had been infected. Determining whether the bones had been infected would help decide on the type of surgery. If they were not involved, the surgery could be as minor as lancing and draining the pus. If they were infected, the surgery would have to be deep in order to clean the infected tissue away from the bones.

All this was being decided as I lay in the hospital bed, IV antibiotics going, foot throbbing, head swimming in feverish delirium. The surgeons squeezed my foot hard, poked at it, felt its heat, lifted it to examine it from other vantage points. Hmmm, this looks like a good foot. Ripe. Firm. Nice color, temperature, bouquet, texture. We have to get rid of that black skin, though, a very unbecoming blemish. I think it's ready . . . perfect. Let's hack it up.

I did not mind the prospect of having to stay on intravenous antibiotics, but the thought of having my foot cut, the muscles being opened to get at the infection, scared me. Ahead would lay months of recovery with no running, little walking, stitches, pain, and a big wad of gauze. Healing can be downright unpleasant, if not comically melodramatic. I mean, really, I went to work yesterday. This has to be a mistake, or someone else's turn. I'm willing to forgo the attention, the expense; no, you really don't need to . . .

I wanted to take the path of least intervention that would still beat the infection. That meant doing the lancing, the draining, getting a sample of pus for the culture, and cleaning the abscess somehow with other methods, like a whirlpool or other means. I struggled to get the questions straight, to sort them out. The real issues, I repeated to myself, that had to be decided were avoiding surgery if possible, beating the infection, finding the right antibiotic, culturing the bacteria, getting my butt out of the hospital. OK, I consoled myself, it was a case of simple problem solving. Buckle down and do it.

Three doctors, two surgeons, and an infectious disease specialist, stood at the foot of my bed discussing the matter with me. The general surgeon felt the infection was too deep to do a simple incision-and-draining procedure. The infectious disease specialist, Dr. N., agreed, but wanted a sample of pus to culture, soon, like within ten minutes. He kept looking out the window and muttered something about having to leave the hospital. A third doctor, Dr. G., wanted to know what I thought. I told him I wanted to do the least intervention.

That meant opening the abscess to see how deep it was and to get a pus sample. The decision gelled even as we spoke, and the doctors left to get supplies.

They regrouped with swabs, scalpels, syringes of linocaine, gauze bandages, "chucks" (waterproof incontinence pads), hemostats, sterile gloves, face masks, and plastic goggles. Once again, G. took a solid hold of my foot and squeezed around the head of the abscess. Until then, I had no idea what the goggles might be for, but N. winced, covered his face, and leaned back as if expecting the volcano on my foot to erupt. G. then swabbed the foot with Betadine before taking one of the enormous syringes and plunging it into my foot near the head of the abscess. The sting was almost paralyzing, but my curiosity kept me looking as he worked the needle, rotating it as if he were stirring cake batter, to numb my arch.

When they did the initial lancing, a fountain of pus rose in a fine arc, about two or three feet above my foot at a forty-five-degree angle. It held the tightness of a stream, much like the jet from a squirt gun. It reminded me of a scene in the film *M*A*S*H*, where a wounded soldier squirts a powerful stream of blood from his jugular vein before Hawkeye promptly plugs it with his finger. In our little scene, N., the infectious disease guy, had to duck and dodge to avoid taking a shot of pus to his left shoulder and very nicely pressed shirt. After the surprise fountain lost pressure, attention went back to the abscess.

The nurse, Pam, tried to keep up with the surgeons and was injecting me with morphine as they began to make the incision. It seemed a little late, but fit right in with the impulsive chaos of the moment.

Dr. G. relished going after the abscess, so much so that he forgot I was there watching. Yes, I was there watching as he practiced a cut and then made the real move. I have heard that some doctors are like that, that patients present problems that doctors have to solve, but that we are more the problem than the person with the problem. They seem to forget that, being caught up as they are in the need to solve the problem.

So, that's how it is done. Just grab the bull by the horns and jump in. If you have the tools and the materials, it's messy, painful, and sometimes uncomfortably gross, but productive.

I had almost no painkiller in me as he cut, squeezed, swabbed, and dug. He and the others were eager and were just doing their jobs. They had asked me what I wanted to do, which was to pursue the least invasive path that would still do the job of overcoming the infection, so I was an accomplice in moving ahead, fast. And moving ahead meant popping open the head of that puppy to get an idea of what was beneath it.

They went to their work like miners at the exposed tip of the mother lode. Dr. G. worked the scalpel while Dr. N. worked the swabs, delighted, finally, to have his sample to start the culture. He wanted to go home and was impatient to get the sample to the lab before it closed. G. seemed to just love what he was doing but looked at my foot too much like a practice cadaver rather than a living, sentient husk of a redneck Norwegian gone soft with the sloth of convalescence sitting in his bed watching the procedure through the fog of fever. These guys were good. By opening the hemostat, he spread the rim of skin wide to make room for the swabs and, later, the packing tape. Yeeeouch! I about leaped out of the bed in pain of both the spreading and the tape being shoved so aggressively into the small cavern on the side of my foot.

Before I could really be overwhelmed by the pain, however, it was over. It had not been as bad as the bite, but my tolerance for pain had been stripped away and was still very low. My foot hurt, but G. was lifting it gently and wrapping it expertly in gauze. He set the foot down on a pillow and smiled at me confidently before saying something like "That should feel better."

I don't know if it did or not, but we were on the first step toward determining whether or not I would need further surgery and had made another step into unknown territory of how we would beat the infection. And it had to be beaten back to the last bacterium and then a few steps more, because even one organism could grow back into another infection, abscess, and possible system-wide infection.

The incision and draining went so fast, I could hardly react to it, but the dressing changes . . . they have to "unpack" the material from the open hole, clean out the hole with swabs that go deep to the bottom of the pocket of the abscess (about an inch and a quarter below my skin), and then "repack" it, stuff the packing back in with a hemostat. It was very hard for me to watch and even harder for me to remember and recount.

This is the part in most stories, after all, that is left to the imagination. A door closes and the next thing you know the patient emerges. Simple as that: sterile, clean, in no way threatening to applecart of romantic or adventure narrative. I feel the same squeamishness looking at blood that I do hearing people cry or raise voices in anger. I turn them off, tuck them away, erase the hard drive. Here, I made it a practice to watch everything. It was an experiment. What did I have to lose, or to gain?

The next morning I was taken to the whirlpool, where they cleaned out the pocket where the abscess had been before putting my foot into the warm swirling water. The whirlpool room was on the other end of the hospital in the physical therapy section, on the far side of the pool past the gym. It was a dank, sultry, musty, rusted place full of stainless steel tubs with pumps, motors, gauges, hoses, and various lifting apparatuses. It reminded me of the engine room of a steamship: the glistening, oily churning of pistons, driveshafts, the humid bowels below the deck of the *Titanic*. I was wheeled in and placed on a steel chair with arms that locked around me. The chair could roll and was capable of hydraulic lift and lowering. As I rose in the air, I marveled at the power, the commitment, the intention, and the know-how behind medicine. We really do want to heal, to be healthy, within certain limits.

The physical therapist, Cindy, unwrapped the gauze bandage, plucked the squares of gauze off the top of the abscess, and then extracted the tape that had been packed into the hole. It amazed me how much tape fit into that dark, moist cavity on the side of my foot. She then raised my steel chair and maneuvered me over one of the tanks. She filled it with water and turned on the pump before lowering me and my foot into the swirling mix. The pain wasn't bad, and I doubted it was doing much good since the deep cleaning force of the currents did not penetrate the open, empty abscess. But it was nice to sit up there so high and watch my thoughts swirl around like the water. I just wanted to sit still and close my eyes. The morphine and double dose of Percocet was overkill, but the euphoria was a nice break from the edgy surrealism of being back in the hospital.

The painkillers allowed me to watch with less pain, but it still hurt like dancing on the tines of the gates of hell. Cindy swabbed the wound before refilling it with packing tape. She did a slow, deliberate, mindful job and kept her materials in neat order on a stainless steel table: gauze, swabs, ruler to measure the depth of the wound, sterile gloves, alcohol wipes. She was a kind reminder that I was still a patient, if not patient. Oh yeah, right. I remember that one. I'm supposed to be learning from this ordeal. Breathe. Breathe. Slow down. Even if it doesn't work, keep practicing. Watch not being a good patient and you will do a better job. That is a start. You will find someplace to be, to stand and observe while this is going on soon enough.

Drs. N. and G. entered the room in tandem with the flair of celebrities on the red carpet of a premiere and announced that the cultures were growing well—a form of staph along with a strain of strep—and seemed like they would be sensitive to readily available antibiotics. Yee haaw. Now we know what's wrong. Step one, naming the problem, done. Check. He also said he wanted to do an MRI to get a better sense of the degree of infection of the bone. He made some quick notes on the chart after taking a look at the abscess. The chart was filling up with lab results, doctors' orders, records of treatment. I had to admire the coordination necessary to treat even simple but serious infection.

When I got back to the room, Beth, the adult soccer team manager, came by to visit. She brought flowers and a card from the team. I didn't know if I would ever play again, but I liked how it felt to be acknowledged by the group. I had missed being able to do only a few things, but not being able to run, to play, to move, carried special poignancy. I knew that pining away for that which I could not do was not helpful, but nostalgia overwhelmed me, still does when I am tired. I sat and wept in self-pity. Beth patted my back as I felt the fool who just couldn't help it. She didn't mind.

I have always been a runner. Not a trained runner, but an under-the-radar, impulsive, study-the-pain-on-your-own kind of runner. I had some talent and could have raced, but seldom did. I was the fastest kid in my grade school, even beat the gym teacher in a fifty-yard race. And when we did conditioning runs for wrestling in high school, I set the pace. I ran a half marathon once in my forties in less than an hour and a half, with almost no training. Before the bite I ran with those half my age and held my own. But times and speed never really mattered much. I liked the long, slow burn of extended exertion, of stepping along the knife's edge, of "blowing up," of "bonking," of filling with lactic acid and losing the capacity to chemically process oxygen. Paradoxically, I ran in physical pain in order to ease emotional pain, or maybe to substitute physical pain for emotional, to stay with the one I could handle. Running also became a metaphor for staying with something, even when it became painful, difficult, boring. My motto doing the PhD program was "Too damned dumb to quit." It helped me get through rough times in my marriage, the long nights with infants. Running taught me how to live with overwhelm and pain.

Of course, if there were no pleasure, only a Lutheran would run. I also ran for the hit of endorphins, or whatever it is that causes runner's high. While running, I have felt good, happy, and at home in the world during long, lonely periods of my life. It is the constant; it has sustained me better than anything else could.

"Being" a runner, in other words, is a story that defines me, is an important thread of my identity. I can see from where I am now that this is a fiction: "I" am not my ability to run. That aspect of my identity has dropped away, probably temporarily. I think that is part of why I feel so happy, in spite of the pain, the setting, the physical confinement.

There is nothing wrong with living a story of being a runner. We have to tell stories. Storytelling, identity making, defining the world, and then identifying with a particular set of stories is a hardwired part of being human. It goes with the territory, like standing on two feet and needing to be right.

Problems begin when we forget that our identity—personal or national—is just one possible story, that there are other stories out there just as valid. When I make the error of believing that my story is the only way to be, that it is True, that others are false, then I get into trouble. Contradict someone's story, or challenge it, and watch the fists come out.

If I believe that I am my ability to run, and I then lose that ability, it follows that I am then worthless. If I am not conscious that my identity is a story, one that now needs to be revised, I get depressed, angry at God for making me a cripple, and do anything possible to change the facts of my life. In short, I suffer.

I don't know why, but right now I can see all this. For some reason I am not bothered by being a temporary cripple. Maybe that's why I hang onto the probability that not being able to run is temporary. Only in letting go have I been able to see.

But there is something else. I have temporarily been given the gift of detachment, of being able to sit back, if just for a moment, and play the role of witness and observer of my chatter and see it as just that.

I am also aware of the paradox at work here. Yes, the stories that define me, that make up every characteristic of who I am, are just talk, but, and here is the rub, talk matters. It is all we have. Like I said, I see now that it goes with the territory, so I'm stuck with it. The question then becomes, which talk will I listen to? Which talk is healing? Which talk is in my long-term best interest? And what does it take to let go of the old, toxic talk that I identify with to keep me unhappy, depressed, suffering? What does it take to dis-identify with calcified stories, stories that run deep into the psyche, that have roots wrapped around old pain and ancient needs?

18 / Seeing Inside

Right after lunch I was taken to another lab for an MRI. What a place. Deep in the labyrinth of the hospital, past the X rays, radiology, biopsy rooms, there were the secret chambers of the MRI. I am sure someone could locate it on a map, but for me it will forever be shrouded in fog, on the other side of a raised drawbridge, surrounded by a moat full of piranha and poison sea monsters. There lies the golden goose, the singing harp, the eye that knows all, reveals all, no matter how well hidden.

The chamber holding the MRI is not unlike the bridge of the starship *Enterprise*. There is no shadow, no room for darkness or blemish, only bright, white light. Nor is there any dust. The machine shines with the promise of a highly technological and very expensive future.

I am not an MRI person. MRI people can be still in a confined, narrow space, can relax, maybe even enjoy lying motionless on a flat slab. They can focus, can put their minds into a narrow point of concentration and sustain their gaze for as long as necessary.

Everything about me says space, chaos, rambling, free association. My mind is a drifty, impulsive creature that is loathe to stay anywhere longer than a casual visit. It likes passing through town, stopping at the saloon, maybe taking in a card game before remounting and moving on. No strings, no accountability.

MRI people balance their checkbooks, join the school board, clean up toxic waste dumps, and pay taxes early. They drive new cars and agonize over decorating decisions.

I avoid organizing my life the ways I would like it to be organized. I have files that I need to go through, a desk piled high with papers that only sees light at the ends of semesters. My tool bench is littered with half-done projects, assorted debris left over or dumped when one of us moves on to something else; my closets are bulging with ancient threadbare T-shirts; my drawers are full of broken sunglasses that I can't bear to throw away or afford to fix. The house is a mirror that reflects back to me all the work I have left undone, the things I can't let go of.

No, I am not an MRI person. And what I fear most about the MRI is the scrutiny, being under the all-seeing eye of the imager. I am afraid to be found out. That thing will see into my skull and locate the exact places of dysfunction, will see the secrets, the cordoned-off areas of the living cerebellum. Would they find the seeds of dementia, knowing that I am my mother's son? I am not an open book.

And what if it can see into my heart, into the broken places? There are some disasters that are not meant to be screened or viewed, no matter how medicinal the intentions. I can remember.

I am filled with foreboding sitting here, half naked, patient smock revealing more of me than the world wants to see, waiting for them to roll me into the next level of surveillance. I am a little worried at what they will find, worried that somehow all my methods of encryption, all the years of forming scar tissue over old wounds, will be undone. Why did that snake pick me to subject to these procedures?

Then they came for me. I was put on a backboard-like stretcher and slid into a cylinder inside a giant, space-aged, bright white plastic doughnut. I thought it would be silent, but it was not. A low frequency, a rumbling, a seismic roar filled the chamber when the MRI was working at full power. It built an image of my foot using radio waves. Of course, I listened to the radio through earphones they gave me to escape the noise while the radio waves took pictures of me—Johnny Cash, Dwight Yoakum, and some others I don't remember. I made pictures in my head from the music while the MRI made pictures of me. All this happening as I lay still as death, images flying in the ethers of my brain while others traveled through cables and by invisible waves into the processors of computers. At the end of it all, my bones would be found to have only minimal infection, and that pockets of infection had gathered around them, deep in the steamy, previously inaccessible tissues of my foot. The healing waters and radio waves fill around me. I am learning, slowly, to soak them in.

What would we see, I wonder, if we put the earth into an MRI? Would we see the cavities created by pumping water out of the aquifer beneath Tucson? Would cities look like tumors that debilitate the host organism by poisoning it? What if the earth were slid into an MRI? What stories would we tell about such a thing? What would we be willing to give, to sacrifice for the earth in crisis, in grave danger? If the earth could fit into an MRI, could we tune the dials so that the micro-organisms necessary for systemic, mythic, or physical health would show up as a color in peril, a part of the spectrum about to fade away? Would we then stand back enough to see the earth for the wonder it is as we travel on this watery globe through the dark, cold, silent stretches of space?

After the MRI, I was taken back to the room where the PICC (peripherally inserted central catheter) nurse was waiting to install a PICC line, or a durable IV access, that I will use for the duration of the antibiotics. It is kind of like a hose that you can put into a river to pump water out or in. It's a direct line of fluid sharing between my heart and the outside world. The personal is political, and inner health does depend on outer actions. I can see the slender tunnel between the two worlds. Gates open and close, but what's out here can go in there, so I have to be careful what I put into the pipeline.

She slid a catheter into a vein in my arm that eventually led to the superior vena cava, where antibiotics could most efficiently mix with the blood. The plastic tube runs directly into my vein and is sutured there with four stitches. It has a clamp that keeps it airtight when it's not in use for an infusion and a special port for running IVs.

The best part, though, is that it's covered with a fishnet bandage. I wanted pink, but all they had was white. Now this I could get behind. Megan, though, would not be impressed. If I have to be wired for IVs, at least I am styling. To make sure the line is correctly placed, they brought in a mobile X-ray machine. It looked like a backhoe that got lost on the way to the construction site, or a square-headed dinosaur made of steel and glass. They fired the blast directly at my chest to the film on the other side. I hope I didn't blink.

The PICC line essentially has crippled my left arm. I can't lift more than five pounds and cannot extend it or put weight on it. That means I can't use crutches, push uphill in the wheelchair, or lean forward on a stationary bike. Between it and my left foot I am immobilized, except for what I can do at home in the wheelchair.

As I suspected, the whirlpool did not sufficiently clean the wound, so Cindy and other physical therapists decided to use a kind of power washer called a "pulse lavage."

Michelle, one of the physical therapists, a member of the small army pressed into service to do battle with the infection, came in and put on a waterproof smock before lifting the tub with the pulse lavage and other supplies from the top shelf. She busied herself preparing the pistol grip sprayer for deep wounds. She cut a hard rubber tube at a forty-five-degree angle and said "this should get in there deeper," "there" being the hole in my foot, "with a little more power." The water would come out in a stiffer, higher-pressure stream into the abscess on the side of my foot, would clean out the dead tissue, and would burn and sting so much that my heart would race, adrenaline would pump, teeth would clench, and breath would be labored.

Even fifteen minutes later, I knew the ache would still throb.

So she hooked the hoses up to the suction, covered the bed with the "chucks," the waterproof incontinence pads, positioned my foot over the bedpan that would catch the runoff water, and then raised the bed to get the best line on my open abscess. She took a look at me and asked if I was ready, then lowered her safety glasses. I gripped the top of the bed and arched my back in pain when the jet of sterile water hit the wound. I kept breathing and counted off the breaths. It reminded me of running four-hundred-meter intervals and wanting to die about two-thirds of the way through but looking at the finish line and pushing through the pain that was saying "Quit! Quit!", going anaerobic and running anyway. Man, could she get after those bad guys. I hope I am never in her sights.

I looked up at the sterile bag. It was about half done. I was on breath twenty-eight.

Michelle stopped and switched to the other suction head, one that did not hurt as much, but also did not clean as well. "We'll finish with this one," she said mercifully.

My heart was still pounding, the adrenaline pulsing through me, but my jaws relaxed. I knew the worst was still to come.

She finished the pulse cleaning and removed the bedpan from beneath my foot. It held almost a liter of water contaminated by the infection and dead tissue from the abscess. She carried it to the toilet and emptied it. She then brought out the swabs, cut the packing tape—the narrow ribbon of sterile cloth—and stacked up the bandages she would use after cleaning out the wound.

I watched as the swab again disappeared into the side of my foot and then winced as it reached the bottom of the pit. Michelle didn't balk, but nudged and spun the head of the swab against the bottom of the abscess. I again arched, grimaced, clenched, and began counting. She went through one swab, then a second, and a third. The swabs were red, but nowhere near as saturated or as stringy with tissue as they were the first times. "It's looking good," she said, "cleaned up compared to before."

She then poked at the tape and tamped it down to the bottom of the wound, like a soldier packing her muzzleloader with powder, and fed the band of tape into the wound, folding and layering as she went. A deep burn and long sting shot up through my leg and again tightened my back and grip on the rail. Packing the wound kept it from closing, allowing both air to circulate and drainage to continue. It had to go deep and wide to fill the space of the abscess, and that meant it had to hurt in order to be effective.

She then cut the tail; I was again relieved and relaxed back into the bed, more than able to handle the dull ache of the wound held open against its will, against its cellular programming, to close, to cover, to protect. In this case, though, that would mean a return to the infection and likely reformation of the abscess. Some things are best opened, even when it hurts.

19 / Resonance

When it is dark enough, you can see the stars.
Ralph Waldo Emerson

I have begun to wake before the sun rises and just sit in the darkness. I will continue to do so for years, if not the rest of my life. When I return home, my eyes will have gotten used to the dark and I will move like a blind man through the familiar arrangements of furniture, my only guides the LEDs of the stereo equipment, the computer, the DVD player.

Awakening while it is still dark is new and is not a choice. Something inside compels me to rise, to sit, to listen, and to follow.

I could feel the PICC line in my shoulder last night, and the foot shot pain through my leg like a bullet when I put pressure on it in early hours. Today I need to learn about this IV catheter and how to care for it, so that in using it I don't accidentally inject air into my veins and stop my heart. Right now, it is a tool to deliver the antibiotics, a necessary link to the medicine that will kill the infection.

In a few weeks, the bacteria will be out of my body and I will be again in the world of the healthy, but now I am tied to a pole and dressed over an open hole, dependent as a newborn kitten on the hospital for care. That is my reality, and no amount of wishful thinking will make it different or shorten the time between now and the day I get to extract the line.

I eat my entire breakfast—gooey scrambled eggs, tart juice, and Jello (again?!)—and have no fever. My thoughts turn again toward the future. Soon the antibiotic will match the bug. When the hole begins to heal from the bottom up, I will be able to leave. The healing then will be only a matter of days. I will reenter my life and resume my role at work, at home, and in the community at large. I know that it will be difficult to remember what I have learned as the stresses again wash over the walls that are my ability to contain them. Until then I will prepare.

This past week was another round of wake-up calls and destabilization, of reconstruction, all set in the routines of hospital life. Inside, I've lost my bearings; outside the nurses come every four hours for blood draws or just to fluff the pillows. I am forced to sit without distraction, to be quiet. I am confined to this bed with only my words and the sensations of my body for company, diversion, and salvation. Like lovers who find each other years after separating because of a petty fight, they are glad and grateful to again spend time together, now more mature, more vulnerable, seasoned, weathered, and deep-running. I hope to sustain this connection between them and the other various parts of me. It's what's for breakfast, and lunch, and dinner. It's what I do now.

The best words are good and offer reminders: you are made of blood, bones, and gristle; you breathe; it is best to move slowly, to pay more attention, to watch the talk and don't let it take you places you don't want to go. I have to learn not to link up with the chain of incessant distraction that supplants my awareness of the present. It starts with caffeine, complaint, hurry, distraction, sugar, and conflict. It becomes the tightened neck and the shallow breathing.

I know I don't have to be in conflict. I'm learning to accept what is, even if that includes pain. I want to let the pain teach me. I hope it has tempered, strengthened, and rooted my experience undeniably in a witnessing presence. It will be the thread that I cannot drop as I move back into the rent-extracting world of loss and gain, of success and failure, of winner and loser, of either and or. I will wear it as one wears gray hair for having aged. Cuanto me costaria? I wonder though how much it will cost me.

20 / Infusion

Devoted father, the Bear has again made the two-thousand-mile trip from Wisconsin to Arizona. He has resumed his uncomfortable role as nurse to a convalescing son. He even helped me set up the easel so that I can paint while sitting in the wheelchair. He does not understand why I paint. (Nor do I.) But he did ask if I would do one for him sometime. I said I would.

He is here because I need him again. This time, though, we must fulfill the sometimes complex intravenous infusions of antibiotics.

My mother was a reader, a feisty devotee of beauty, and a nurse. We, the Bear and I, are not nurses and mainly admire beauty when it takes a female form. We are wimps when it comes to attending to the details, the meticulous procedures, the boring thoroughness of caretaking. The inferential leap between our discomfort with having to administer the infusions and the discomfort of thinking about, or even talking about, my mother is not a long one. The associations are clear, and we approach our medical tasks with the same enthusiasm we bring to the topics of death, debt, and dental work.

Six hours have passed since the last infusion, and Megan cannot leave work to come home and set up the next one, due now. We two are all I've got. Megan, bless her organized heart, has left a detailed sequence, all typed out and with a sheet-protector cover on it, for us to follow. We look at it like it is written in hieroglyphs. It looks back at us in its shining, organized smugness and sneers. Bear adjusts his glasses; I fidget and hope something interesting will happen outside.

Even with the typed guide, I struggle to remember the sequence: Unclamp and then uncap the PICC line? Then wash with antiseptic, flush line with saline, no, heparin, or . . . ; connect IV line after puncturing antibiotic bag, then drain out air, and on and on.

We assemble the goods on the table—IV bag, tube, shutoff valve, syringe, sterile wipes. They might as well be pig tripe for how eager we are to handle them.

"You have to take off the cap and then use that syringe with the Heparin to flush the line," I say, not so sure.

I can't work with any of the sterile threaded contacts because one needs two hands to tighten them. I can't reach the PICC end with my left hand, it being at the crook in my elbow. Bear has to do it.

He unthreads the cap. So far, so good.

He then removes the cap on the syringe to reveal the sterile end and begins to thread it on. He is about to depress the plunger when I notice that we have not purged the air out of the syringe; if he presses it, he will send several cc's of air through the line and into my heart, likely stopping it.

"No! Stop! We have to evacuate the air out of the syringe!"

The Bear freezes.

"Goddammit! And I'm a fucking pilot. Can't even follow a pissant checklist!"

He unthreads the syringes, holds the tip up, and depresses the plunger, forcing a thin stream of heparin through the orifice at the end of the syringe. He looks at me with tired, apologetic eyes. Then he continues his tasks. His thick arms and large hands dwarf the tools he uses. He fumbles with the delicate instruments. They look like doll accessories that he tries to make work in a life-sized world.

"Damn near killed you."

He is embarrassed, upset. We are both frustrated with these procedures, this need to pay attention to—I hate to say it—women's work, or more precisely, mother and wife's work. We are both happier when Megan is at home. She has stepped into being the nurse like she was born to it. Her response to the entire ordeal has been graceful, direct, helpful, and efficiently detached. I am sure that the spirit of my mother is standing here somewhere as well, at least in the shadows of our strained psyches. We are both aware of, and assiduously avoiding, Marlene, my mother. She looms so large that neither of us can comprehend what she means to us. How does one come to terms with such things? I can feel her in my paintings that hang on the walls of my homespun, funky, adobe decor. She is in the bookcase. And she is in my being pissed off at a world that does not conform to what I want it to be. It does not answer to my desires, and my rage has taken root in my mind and body. I feel wronged and righteously indignant. I could pluck the cords of my neck and play banjo tunes.

This thing that goes unnamed grows and fills the room, leaving us very little space to breathe.

The situation suggests my mother, whispers my mother, and it makes us uncomfortable. Wife and mother take over when caretaking barges into the room. The Bear and I tell ourselves that we can't do it, that they know we can't do it, and so become accomplices in our own failure. We, the army colonel and the English PhD, fumble with the slightest complexity and balk at the array of bandages, different-colored caps, IV lines, shutoff valves, pack of gauze, syringes that look like bullets strung together. It is not just the complexity; there is something more.

The two of us, at home in the light and rested awareness of midday, can barely stand the thought of having to set out the equipment, much less plug in the meds. We are again father and son, upset in each other's presence with the added tension of unspoken grief, not knowing what to say to ourselves or each other. It is a place we know well, but are both flushed with the shame of it. We can't help it.

"OK, what comes next?" he asks, this time getting me to confirm the next step.

"We're ready for the IV," I say.

This time we work the air out of the line, get a smooth hookup, open the gates, and let the meds rip. I lie down to get the best flow and look up past the pole to see my dad looking down at me. His face is drawn, old, worried. He moves a pillow under my foot, and we raise the puffy, bandaged appendage high enough that it won't drain too much into the gauze. I lie on the floor and look at the skylight, noticing the stain from leaking rainwater. It looks like desert varnish. I smell the oil paints. I feel like painting some of the places to which I can no longer travel. They will have to come to life on canvas now. The Bear sits back and crosses his arms. He looks like he will take a nap in the light pouring onto both of us. I tell him thanks.

He waves it off, but I can tell he feels proud.

Again the Bear stays as long as he is needed, and then makes the long drive back up north, to home. An itinerant outpatient nurse has taken his place. There was very little room anyway. The Bear now passes his days mostly alone, you could say holed-up, in his anonymous trailer, but close to my mother, my brothers, their sons, daughters, and familiar haunts.

He can handle it that way. I don't blame him. It's not my place anymore to look to him for ways to be a father or husband. It's time for me to heal, to stand up, to give back. Soon enough it will be my turn to help, to go home.

Zeus, the cat of the broken nose, and Luna, the limping yellow lab, both welcome the nurse, who has come to help with the dressing change. For some reason, they seem to like hanging around when we do the IVs or clean the wound. They watch from a distance, but with considerable focus. Marilyn, the nurse, noticing them watch, inquires which it will be today, the lab test or the CAT scan. Zeus got it. Luna just shook her head, trying to dislodge a bug from her ear.

It is still strange to be at home living a life that revolves around a schedule of IV infusions and wound-dressing changes. A Styrofoam cooler full of IV supplies sits in the middle of the living room where my recliner used to be: Ziploc bags loaded with syringes preloaded with five cc's of saline solution or heparin, rubber gloves, alcohol wipes, red caps to keep IV connections sterile, IV hoses, sets, shutoff valves, and the first-aid stuff.

This morning, doing the dressing change, we could see a tendon. It was a pearlescent color and was soft, a little giving to the touch. I'm glad I did not try to pull it out last night, thinking it was a piece of leftover packing tape. As we pulled back the bandage and dabbed at the bashful skin, it tingled. The gauze revealed the soft new skin growing beneath the old. My foot itched like crazy and skin sloughed off in sheets. Marilyn just scrubbed away with the gauze, the way a woodworker would use coarse grit sandpaper, almost amused at my surprise that I could lose so much of what used to be me. The old, dead skin just gave up and fell away, like the skin of a king snake I found not long ago. The six-foot-long skin was perfect, only recently shed, complete even to the tiny eyeholes, and was lying on the ground, a ghost of a snake capable of devouring the snake that bit me. The metaphor of finding a remnant of something capable of digesting that which once digested part of me is not lost.

As I sit here watching the healed skin rise up from beneath the dried outer layers, watching the healing proceed from the inside out, I know, deep down, that the king snake is somewhere near, hunting, awake, wild, just outside the house, its fresh skin trim and new, shining, indigo black in the morning sun.

21 / Unwinding Narrative

The rattlesnake bite and the ordeal of healing that followed transformed me into something of a local flash-in-the-pan celebrity. Tom Beal, a friend and city editor of the *Arizona Daily Star* helped me to craft an account of the bite for the paper, mostly to educate people about how to avoid being bitten. It came out on a Sunday; my foot was on the front page. The piece took on a life of its own, a story that catalyzed some inert substance of collective memory, and created a reaction that connected me to people's fears. "Oh, my God," people would ask when they recognized my notorious foot, "you were walking in your *front yard*?"

I became a lightning rod for snakebite stories. Casual conversations turned into hoary accounts of close calls, and we communed on things dangerous that wait for us in the dark. One woman, Anne Tillman, a feisty ranch wife now in her eighties, called long distance to let me know she had been bitten on her left foot. I had been bitten on the left foot. She was forty-seven years old when bitten. I was forty-seven years old. Her children had been standing nearby. My children had been standing nearby. She had not seen the snake. You get the idea.

"For three years I felt sick from that bite," she wanted me to know. "Even my scalp turned black and my hair fell out when I was in the hospital," she continued. Hemorrhaging caused by the venom traveled up the left side of her body, over her head and down the other side. Her story humbled me and mine. "Now, one of the things you have to remember if you want to heal is to slow down and not rush things. You take the time you need to get your life back together. Do it the way you need to."

We talked for over an hour, during which she had to repeatedly shush her husband. He had business, but she was having none of it. Not a character to mess with, Ms. Tillman threatened to do me bodily harm if she heard that I was rushing things.

A hand-typed copy of the article arrived in the mail along with a query about whether or not I believed in divine providence. The writer wanted me to join him in condemning evolution. Several people wrote letters with rattlesnake stories of their own. One of them came from the East Coast. One woman swore to me that her bite was more painful than labor. Another lost her pinky to necrosis. A man died from a bite a month after I was bitten. A second-grade class sent me letters inquiring whether I had been bitten by a python or a king cobra. My favorite read "Dear Mr. Toso: I don't know you, but I love you." Several teachers reported that students who normally had great difficulty sustaining a focus while reading had been riveted by the article.

The subject, predictably, tapped a primal fascination with snakes, with danger and mortality. I was not up to the task of providing wise counsel for those who asked for it, but part of me knew there was more of the story to tell that I was not yet ready for.

The healing was going far beyond the physical recovery from the bite. Something else was at work. Something had happened, and the line of this narrative began to wind and coil into places I had not imagined.

Like a river that runs red when it floods, the speed of my life carried a kind of sediment that kept me from seeing my days, from appreciating the sensual delights offered up by the earth every moment of our lives.

A circuitous, serpentine structure of healing that progressed from the inside out began to thread its way through my days. The line ran through various and disparate areas of my experience, including memories of family and desert dreams as much as physical tissue. No, the meander did not proceed in a linear trajectory, nor did it always move forward. It took on a life of its own, a slow, deliberate life. It is that pace and that unwinding, living path that has sustained me since. When I lose the thread and begin to speed up, I feel toxins again begin to percolate.

Slowing down and finding the right words, I am convinced, can transmute poison to medicine. Locating the quiet line within the speeding stream of noise in my mind and following it with sacred attention has become a private, sustaining curriculum. Things that seemed "bad" have become beneficial, and for those things that I commonly called "good" I lost some of my obsessive attachment. I am reluctant to let the story follow its serpentine path, because I don't know where it leads, what it will ask of me, what price I will have to pay to arrive at some unforeseen destination. Images lead to hunches under which emotions lie. Together they weave a truth both new and connected, like the rattle a snake adds every time it sheds its skin.

I don't understand this process, can't "think it through," and it doesn't fit or follow the typical conventions of a story about snakes or about the desert or about an injury. The meander has veered, turned downward, and I have to duck my head as it takes me into yet more uncharted territory. Although uncomfortable, I stay with a story that is going after something, something I fail to decipher or comprehend. This state of being is as exotic and foreign to me as snakes are "other" to mammalian life. This experience is new and fragile and I still have much to learn.

Somewhere I adopted the mistaken notion that if I was miserable enough, I would get what I wanted. But as Melville said, "There is a woe that is wisdom, a woe that is madness." Now, my woe, my misery, has not been real misery, the kind of misery that grows out of gnawing hunger or grief over dead loved ones. Mine is a neurotic misery, a cultivated misery, one that I developed like a bad habit. Feeling miserable was a substitute for fearing death, a way to run away from death, and I am hardwired for it. If I was miserable, the thinking must have gone when I learned to put this together, time will slow down, and I will get what I want—to live forever, or at least longer. I guess too, that when I was miserable, my mother must have rewarded me for it. I learned that being unhappy was a way to get what you want.

What I didn't know was that being unhappy in an indifferent universe just made sure that I spent what little time I had unhappy. The supreme arrogance in being unhappy was that I thought it would stop time. Being unhappy was my weapon in the fight against time. If I was unhappy enough, the story went, surely time would stop and I would get what I wanted, maybe even turn it back on itself to a healthy mother, to a place where it might still all happen, whatever "it" was. Right now, it cannot. I am mad. I am terrified.

The facts of my life stare me down. The desert is going under the blade; no dance that I can perform will impress my family, make them see me; I will never win the race for money.

And I will do anything to run from the fact that my mother is dying a slow death from Alzheimer's. This is real emotion, real pain, real grief. One that I don't want, but that death will not let me forget. The smell of death whispers this fact again and again into my ears. I cannot stand it. I need to find some way to ease the pain, to terminate the anguish. The more neurotically miserable I am, the less I have to look the fact straight in the face and let it sink into my bones where the real hungry ghosts of hysterical attachments wait like harpies to rise up and wail. Death opens the doors and lets the light in, and that light reveals all that has been hidden and denied and avoided by neurotic anxiety. The desert is too much when shown to me by death; the moon is too cruel in its beauty, the sky too brilliant to be real. I want to, but cannot avert my gaze.

22 / Beneath the New Moon

One Saturday a little before I would be able to return to work, I decided to clean out a packrat nest. The packrats had taken over a small abandoned chicken coop in the backyard and filled it with spiny branches of cholla, prickly pears, and, their favorite delicacy, mesquite beans. The pile was almost three feet high and filled two fifty-gallon garbage cans.

Now cleaning out a packrat midden is not only unpleasant because of all the spines that penetrate the thickest of work gloves and the acrid stench of rat urine, but is dangerous. Rat middens attract mice, and mouse feces can carry hantavirus, a potentially fatal flulike respiratory infection. The dust from the rat turds rose from the cavity of the garbage can after I emptied each shovelful.

I had put it off too long and decided to take my chances. I wore a dust mask, long sleeves, and heavy boots. I spent the morning shoveling, hauling, sweeping, lining the shed with hardware cloth, and setting traps. This was war.

Packrats can get into cars and eat the insulation off wires. In fact, they can even get into your dreams. In houses, they can do serious damage to electrical systems, insulation, clothes closets, boot barns, recliners, TVs, swamp coolers, cordless tools, corded tools, sex toys, and masonry. If you have it, they will get it, and either take it, pee on it, or wreck it. If you don't hate pack rats, or wood rats, or trader rats, or rats by any number of aliases by now, you are probably dead or living in a bubble at the bottom of the ocean. They had already eaten the wiring out of the dryer, meaning I had to disassemble it to trace and splice the stub of brown wire with the other end of the brown wire, the white with the white, the blue with the blue, and so on, all the while sprawled out on a carpet of pencil cholla branches and other spines that the rats had hoarded and stacked as a protective barrier. They glued the whole mess together with urine. It was nasty work, for which there will be no forgiveness.

A repair service guy refused to even consider the job, citing reasons I have already mentioned plus a heart condition that forbade him from secondhand talk about the evil creatures.

That night, my first night out in months, Megan and I went to a party and stayed late. She wore some sexy sequins, I tight pants and a bola tie, official neckware of all Arizonan cripples. It was my debutant ball, after all, and I was to debut with style, now that de butt had gone down a bit. I had not been out after ten o'clock since August, a full three months. Wine, bright lights, music, and feisty conversation had all helped distract me from the pain in my foot. The women, they were gallant, chivalrous, and witty. The men, lovely and polite. When we returned and were walking from the car to the house along our desert path, I looked at the moon and thought unspeakably lust-filled thoughts. Megan, being more the practical type, had remembered the flashlight, and had given it to me so that I could scan the ground in front us, making it safe for innocent pedestrians, hapless partygoers.

It was a cool night and, to my mind, well past rattlesnake season. Plus there were no packrats now; I thought snakes would be out where the action was. By now they should have at least found a den and, after a final meal of evicted pack rat, bunked down with a mate or small group of snakes for the winter; so I wasn't watching as much as one might expect me to watch.

With a jerk, Megan grabbed my elbow, gasped, and pointed at a rattlesnake curled up on one side of the trail. It blended in with the ground and had settled itself into a circle of mounded sand. It looked comfortable, harmless, benign.

I wanted to talk to the snake, to direct it to the backyard where my nemeses were regrouping for a counterassault. I wanted to give it half the backyard and draw a line in the sand that it could not cross under any circumstances. I wanted to lead it to the promised land, where pack rats flowed like honey. Of course I could do no such thing.

I collected my garbage can and snake tongs and captured the snake after calling the fire department to come pick it up. Reaching for the snake forced me to overcome some pretty fierce visceral memory, but the snake did not struggle. Instead it looked straight at me, wondering why I was disturbing it, flicking its delicate tongue, catching the scent of Red Tail ale mixed with human fear and regret. It was time to rest, to sleep, not struggle or hunt.

That snake could have lived with me if I had no children, had no obligation to remove all unnecessary risk to their well-being. If I lived alone, I would make a pact with the snake to be constantly aware, to step lightly, to join forces against the rats.

It wasn't going to happen tonight, though. Instead of rattlesnakes, we will have rats. Humans are selecting out those species we fear and creating habitat for those that they hunt. We are moving toward a world of rats and away from a world of rattlesnakes, mountain lions, bears, bighorn sheep, pinacate beetles, spadefoot toads, and even the poster-child creatures like native songbirds and Arizona sycamore. We have messed things up big time. All this made picking up the snake that much harder. I wish it was simpler. Nothing is simple.

I thought my heart was going to break as I stood in the parking lot waiting for Rural Metro to come and haul the snake to an almost certain death in a new territory at such a sensitive time of year.

The lights of the large truck bent around the curve, tracing the contour of our driveway before swinging toward me, headlights growing as they shone straight into my eyes. From behind the blinding glare, the driver emerged from the big diesel rig. He left it running as he stepped down, grabbed his snake box, a small tackle box, his snake tongs, and stepped forward into the light.

As he approached, he looked at me with some recognition.

"Aren't you the guy?"

"Yup."

"Man, I've been an EMT for over twelve years and I was here that night. Worst bite I've ever seen."

I just nodded.

"So you've got another one," he asked, looking into the shadowy void of the drum.

I nodded again with some resignation.

"You must hate these things," he went on, aiming his flashlight into the can before grabbing the snake hard with his tongs and thrusting it into the small tackle box. He surprised me by slamming the lid shut before the snake's tail was fully inside. I think I saw the tail get pinched by the lid, but I wasn't sure.

"No, not really. I think about them a lot though."

He looked at me for a second like I was the strangest man on earth, and then turned back to the truck, throwing the box and tongs onto the passenger seat. "Well, you take care now," he said as he climbed in, his mind already on something else.

He backed the big truck into a Y turn and then sped up the grade back to the road. The lights dropped over the ridge, and the engine's clacking valves and low rumble faded into the distance. I was left standing there in the dark, snake tongs in one hand, fifty-gallon plastic garbage can in the other, breathing in the dispersing fumes left by the big diesel.

I limped back toward the house, pulling my jacket tight across my shoulders, a cold and unforgiving loneliness blowing through my soul.

My hands still smell of death. The smell gets into my clothes and lingers, a stinking cloud from which I cannot escape. No one else seems to notice. I search their eyes for signs when they are close to me. Even my wife detects nothing, she of the discerning sniffer.

I am the reaper who hauls the pack rats to the wash where I bury them. Coyotes watch from the bushes; their keen noses tell them I am coming. When I have finished mounding the sand over the tiny graves and turn toward the house, they emerge from hiding to harvest the prizes I have trapped.

I take the place of the snakes I have displaced. Their ghosts wander through the summer vapors, tracking the scent of pack rats, now hungry spirits whose territory has been usurped by me and other humans. I do their work and carry their smell, a heavy burden.

In a way the snakes have cursed me, have made me take up where they had to leave off. Instead of cleaning the stables, as Hercules had to, I wander the middens, traps in hand. And there is plenty of work to do to bring things into some kind of balance.

But there is more. The snakes have blessed me too. They remind me of those things I run from, the inevitabilities. They brought death into my life, and remind me of the sharpness of life that living near death presents. The smell of death tells me life is passing, that I run from it. Until I turn to face it, and in so doing embrace my life the way it is, death will follow me, will stink up the place.

John Van Dyke, a Sonoran and Colorado Desert traveler of the late nineteenth and early twentieth century, described the light of those deserts with scientific precision and romantic passion. He was struck by the beauty, the purity, the clarity, and the searing intensity of the light. His descriptions took on the intoxicated longing of a lover. Of color he writes:

> All color—local, reflected, translucent, complementary—is of course, made possible by light and has no existence apart from it. Through the long desert day the sunbeams are weaving skeins of color across the sands, along the sides of canyons, and about the tops of mountains. They stain the ledges of copper with turquoise, they burn the buttes to a terra-cotta red, they paint the sands with rose and violet, and they key the air to the hue of opal. The reek of color that splashes the western sky at sunset is but the climax of the sun's endeavor. If there are clouds stretched across the west, the ending is usually one of exceptional brilliancy. The reds are all scarlet, the yellows are like burnished brass, the oranges like shining gold.

Reek of color indeed. My days are scented with the assault of color that accompanies autumn in the desert. The light, now softened by the lower ecliptic of the sun, defines and reveals the depth and contours of the ranges around the city. It is like an accordion opening, displaying pleats of canyons where before one could see only a flat surface. In the case of the mountains, the summer heat and high noon light straight above compressed and flattened the multitude of ranges into a single ridge; during the summer, the deep ranges of mountains had appeared two-dimensional, having no visible depth.

The light follows me to work and turns the university buildings to warm, glowing complements to the green of the palm, now stirring with cool breeze.

The sky, clouds, mountains, all display the rich amalgamation of subtle blues alongside buffed rose. The colors act on the mind like fine food, stirring sensory wonder if not outright disbelief.

I become a dangerous driver, trying to fix the colors in my memory to better pay tribute to them with oils.

I fill canvas after canvas with the riot of light and color that I see radiating from the desert and mountains. Something is running through me that turns into paint at the end of a brush. My skills are no match for the flow of energy, but for once it doesn't matter. Red clouds drift over purple mountains lit with brilliant amber. Cerulean blue flashes and dances behind raw sienna, yellow ochre, and burnt sienna. Earth and sky, Heaven and soil. The canvases soon total ten and fill the living room with the smells of oil paints and linseed oil. They are stacked on the chairs and leaning against the walls. My clothes are a stained mosaic and my eyes burn in their deep sockets. I give the paintings to anyone who lights up looking at one.

The clichés of the desert being a spiritual hot spot and mountains being a metaphor for wisdom seem suddenly real. They are for me a conduit to something I cannot understand but feel in my present in my arms, my legs, my foot. They tingle.

The spaces between atoms seem less filled in. As physicists tell us, we are mostly space, but I don't usually feel that way.

I know that it is melodramatic, a righteous celebration devoid of limit and skepticism, but I have to channel what I feel into something. I grieve and I paint. Slightly terrible pictures, overdone with the colors I see, like some childish hyperbole. Impossible colors, but true to my sight; I see magic where others see only blight. I am crazy, a lunatic, stung and smitten by the moon with no defenses. I weep for no reason and am excused for it because I am crippled, bandaged, poisoned, slipped free from the tracks of habit and convention.

When I can't paint anymore for all the aches in the back and neck and the throbbing in my foot, I reach for the laptop and continue to empty the energy spilling out of my heart.

My words are a conduit for the overflow of emotion pumping through the viscera and ephemera called my body. I sit with the keys and let words run through my fingers like water. Sometimes they feel like sacred words, incantations, healing words, words that want out. The power of them pushes my censor far into the background of my psyche. He doesn't mind, but lets the Dionysian carnival run its course. There will be time, he says.

They say carnival is a time of spirit, "*carne no vale*," the flesh doesn't matter, but I see it the other way. Flesh is everything when I am in my body. It contains the mystery and sacred processes of life. I love it to distraction. But it is also finite, passing, impermanent. I know I will have to let it go, let it go. It is this odd paradox of love and release that feeds this fire I feel burning behind my eyelids, in the flesh beneath my skin.

Whatever this "I" is, inhabiting this body, it is delighted to abide in the living tissues, and it draws nectar from the folds and tubes and sheets of flesh. It is not "mine," but neither is it divorced from me. It abides within me, in fact, is the only direct experience of spirit that I have.

Running has been magical thinking in motion for me. If I ran hard enough, somehow, it would work out. Now that I can't run, the world has taken to swirling around me. I don't know if I am moving from something or to something or just being part of continual motion, but I feel that something larger than myself is sustaining me, that I no longer have the responsibility to divert, manage, or handle the energy I am given. I am free and it doesn't matter.

This is a wonderful time—all is motion and space. It is also a terrible time. I feel subject to forces far beyond the horizons of my control. But the wonder and terror are simply counterparts, flip sides of the same coin, one not more welcome or onerous than the other. I feel each day to be a string of days, and sometimes by evening I am still aflame, wondering from where the fuel comes.

23 / Clocktime

I have returned to work for the second time, this time for the duration of the term, and resumed the chores of my normal life. It is early November, nearly three months after the bite. I feel shaken and lost. The equanimity that I thought would never end has diminished, faded, and now eludes me as the atmosphere of my days again fills with a low-grade stress, leaving me gasping for peace of mind. An unnamed malaise again colors everything I touch. I have fallen apart and don't know how to reassemble the pieces. What do I do with scattered fragments that no longer seem to fit together?

Cold accompanies the shorter days as the winter storms begin. These are not the isolated monsoons of summer, but full frontal beasts that ride on the jet stream down from the Pacific Northwest. I find them delightful, and I want to stop the clock, stop everything, and hang out in the dark time. The prospect of shorter days as the earth pivots farther and farther away from the light comforts me. Thoreau once said he wanted to burrow his head into a hillside. I don't quite feel like burrowing, but do crave a place to hibernate, rest, heal. But the bustle of work has enlisted me a bit before I feel ready, and I reluctantly surrender, having no choice it seems but to go along for the ride.

The days begin to blend into one another as winter begins in earnest. Between the stress of approaching finals, finishing teaching for the semester, and completing my advising responsibilities, I feel tinny, thin, weak. I tell myself to hang on, that the holiday break will soon be here, that I will be able to brood and think, but not yet.

One Thursday, I cannot park on campus and look for my usual off-campus spot. I have not been here for three and a half months. It looks like some of the tenants in the area have moved, given the different cars parked in front of the houses.

I let the Jeep idle as I lock it up and get ready to swing my newly minted, bendable, fully integrated, functional leg off the seat and out over the road. Before I can reach back in for my book bag, he is there—the Dim Dog—and he looks fatter than before, stupider too.

But something is different. Yes, the barking is the same, but he doesn't bother me as much. My neck only tightens slightly, and I feel no need to taunt him or to remind him of my assessment of his mental capacity. I simply unhook the bike and make a friendly comment, to which he only snarls with increased ferocity.

I am amused, but know that the change in my response is small. Old habits die hard, and I feel the wake cut by the snaketime closing in, filling me again with the dread and grinding anxiety of work.

The lock responds to the key, withdrawing the deadbolt from the jamb. I shift the shoulder bag, stoop to pick up the laptop, and then precariously balance my coffee as I open the office door.

Good, no one is here, I say to myself as I set the laptop on a desk and slide the book bag heavy with the batch of ungraded papers off my shoulder and onto the floor.

It is the best time of day. Sounds of a campus coming to life mingle with the morning air and waft into the office. A fluorescent light blinks above me, threatening to expire before I turn it off and open the shades.

It is also the hard time, the transition time from dark to light, from calm to anxiety, from quiet to noise. The luxurious extravagance of unstructured time slips away as I look over the piles of student papers, manuscripts, and textbooks in need of editing. I cannot bring myself to engage them yet.

I boot up the laptop instead. I need to say something here, to pay homage to something, to touch something, to record something, or else the day would start off wrong footed. This is part of it, this recording, this paying and giving attention to the quiet. It is helping me ally myself with this new narrative, this new lens, this other way. It needs words. The words only come when it is quiet, at least for now.

When I can do this, I set the stage for the day; afterward, I'm only mildly irritated when I have to turn my attention to the beck and call of teaching. I rise and begin the task of pulling words out of others, into a life performing a dance that elicits, teases, and extracts what students have not yet been able to express. I know but cannot say how clearly I see the irony of being lost myself while I lead others to find what they have to say. I can see their paths easily; it is my own I have trouble with. My story traces a path tangled by cross-purposes, confusions, dead ends, wrong turns, detours, border closures, and lost time.

It helps to know this before the day really begins.

I have taught my first class, and I'm in my fog of caffeine, the speed drug. I see now that I use it as a way of simultaneously coping with and avoiding my life. Powerful conditioning paired with chemical stimulants combine to fill the void opened by a period of quiet. I am also astonished at how quickly my complicity to live the sped-up life returns. I sit in front of my computer at work and just stare, sometimes, between e-mails and teaching, mind spinning circles on itself, content and familiar in my modern misery.

My body, too, throughout, hurts, and all I want to do is sleep—a strange counterpart to the compulsive speed. There are times when my foot throbs inside the shoe that feels too tight. It is still angry and red at night when I remove the shoe and the sock. The pain does not bother me. To the contrary. I like that it is there reminding me that there are other ways to live, that I don't have to stay stuck in my angry discontent at the world not being what I want.

There are times when others carry us through adversity. Lovely Penny, the office manager of the writing program, gave me a cane she painted herself. The bright patterns and colors shine onto my dullard stress, not cracking the shell that has re-formed between me and the raw nerves of life. I feel I am dragging a cinderblock behind me on my walks to class, my forays around the house, or on errands.

David Yetman, herpetologist and host of a local television show, *The Desert Speaks*, thinks I was bitten by a "scoot," or a *crotalus scutulatus*, a mojave rattler. The neuro-effects point toward that type of snake. The chronic fatigue symptoms would be more along the lines of that kind of venom, which is a little different from the venom of a diamondback. I am inclined to agree.

My body aches, as if the nerves had been short-circuited, leaving me feeling fried. The more I try to manage and juggle the tasks of teaching, of advising graduate students, of changing gears during the workday, the more I slip into an aching exhaustion.

Inside, I've slipped back into dividing the world between good and bad.

The good I hold close with the grip of death; the bad I push away with as much strength as I grasp the good. As long as I can relax and devote my energy to healing, as I was doing before going back to work, I feel good. When I need to respond to the demands of work, return to the beck and call of the university, the more I slip into a funk of resistance, complaint, and frustration. It draws me away from something, some work that presses on me. My job, it seems, it not my work right now.

I crawl through the workday with survival as my only goal, my highest ideal. My foot hurts. The pain is in front of me, and I cannot get around it so that I can get some of these papers graded. I try taking off the shoes, but my foot still aches, still feels like it is sprained or crushed, like it has been injured by too-tight shoes.

Not only does my foot hurt, but so does the avalanche of words that pours out of meetings, seminars, conferences, colloquia, and panels—a terrible *abstraction* assaults my need for quiet. I feel outside the academic club, punished by a you-don't-get-the-joke loneliness that leaves me feeling bruised and inadequate. Teaching, grading, planning, reading, learning, reconciling old ways of thinking with the new codes and rules of engagement: these needs pull at my time, my days.

The pile of papers in front of me has grown to epic dimensions, and students are asking when they will be returned. I have to grade them. But my foot keeps my mind veering back to the ache between the bones.

Yes, there is the promise of finding better words, the right ones, that has pulled me back to the campus. Why should I go to the words? What lies there that might serve as some piece of flotsam to cling to? Is there some way to use words to get here, to get closer to the live wire of sensate and sentient moments?

Those papers, though, some of them so tortured that they assault my sensibilities of written language. So many words, so few meaningful stories. Are we writing the wrong things? I love my students, but their writing bothers me and my low-grade stress becomes the stress of low grades. It is not their fault. Is it mine? Have I connected my own story with my teaching? Have I found a way to blend patience and care—coming from the patient who has been cared for—with the needs of a large university? Again, I don't know but keep asking.

Still the papers weigh on me. I carry them everywhere and everywhere avoid them. They hunker down in my book bag, weighty and resentful at being so obtuse, heavy-handed, and vulgar. They speak in beefy, self-inflated importance on subjects they know only through distant dreams. They parrot the voices of their parents, blindly, deliberately undoing themselves in the repetition. Yet despite the odds, a voice occasionally emerges, and it shocks me with its simple honesty.

In the continual contact I begin again to see the architecture of language. In the same way that I used to read the pitch of roof, the drainage patterns, the cracks in the tar, the age and quality of the materials, I now read papers for leaks, do triage, provide estimates for repair, recommendations for replacement of conceptual structures. I read the grids and trusses of text. But there is more, something ineffable, something intangible in the potential for expression: the choosing. The choosing and honing and music making of language. With a moment of deliberation before speaking or writing, I am discovering, anyone can alter his or her perception, creating harmony rather than dissonance, art rather than cliché, wonder rather than ennui. This heady wine of potential possesses and consumes me.

I know now how to go underground, into silence. Trying on different ways of seeing things, of new words, is new and uncomfortable. The change turns me inside out. What was it James Baldwin had written? "We look forward to change about as much we look forward to being born." He was right.

I look outside in time to see that the skies have darkened and that the mountains are now hidden behind a dense gray curtain of rain. I sit and stare at the papers, raise the foot onto the desk, and wonder what I can find in that ache. It rains and I feel the now familiar rush of grief.

How long I sit I don't remember, but the storm flings hard rain at the windows, soaks the streets, and cleanses the air. The streets shine with the low sun of late afternoon. Vapor rises from the heated asphalt. I know the underlying grids and substructures beneath the road. I know why the road drained or didn't drain the way it did. The smallest minutiae of the shining pavement speak to me, and I feel the vapor, the magic of water turning to gas and rising. But more, I see the way it catches the light and dances during its short-lived visit. Such a small thing, but it fills me, gives me something to chew on, to sit with and mull over, like the cud of the ruminating cows in the pastures along the roads in Wisconsin.

I feel my heart beating; listen to the breath going in and out of my nose;

feel the surging ebbs and flows of ache in my foot, and I know how fragile this life is, know that I will not be here for long, know that my only chance is now.

The storm recedes toward the southern mountains. Cars slurp up the drying rain on their way to something lucrative. What seems the right thing to do has faded. The campus lies quiet and smells clean after the storm. The few walkers step around the puddles or jump over them if they are young and in a hurry. I look closely at the ways I might describe this aching foot and slumped shoulder, bent from the weight of ungraded papers. Another day behind me, I hope for rest.

Rainy night last night. I listened to the drops land in the bowls and buckets as the water ran through the roof. The water ran down the wall, saturated parts of the ceiling and discolored plaster and paint. It puddled in the body contours carved out of chairs around the dining room table; it pounded on the tile mosaic in front of the back door. In my mind it ran in rivulets over the gutters, through the backyard, under the chicken coop, and down to the wash, where it joined its kin, laughing in reunion, forming a stream, a rolling creek, and then a river. Sand waves carried refrigerators, oil drums, fence posts, cow legs, old tires, plastic buckets, Big Gulp cups down the big gulping wash, churning waves into chocolate foam that rolled and tossed and spit out the trash of the past year before doing it all over again. It ran out of control. I was helpless to stop it. Part of me hated it. Part of me found it charming.

The roof reminds me of all that I have not done and have not succeeded at in this life. The drops say "failure, failure, failure." I am no match for the march of entropy, and the roof won't let me forget it. I patch one crack and three more appear. It is a lost cause, but so what? It gets under my skin, making it more of a problem with me than the roof. Once one chorus gets started, more join in.

They add to the voices saying, "You have not figured out to keep water from running down the cracks in the roof, through the tar paper, past the wood that rots when it gets wet." They trigger the stinging, acid bath of finger wagging that somehow has become a habit. I listen to it and notice that I begin to believe it, to feel terrible. Why I can't just say, "Fair enough" or "I'll grant you that," I don't know. It's cowardice I guess. I don't want to look at it, engage it, or own it. I want to turn it off, but feel helpless. I am addicted to it. I am addicted to the sting.

Yes, there is that sting. But I hear something else, something quiet, behind the whining harpies. There is also appreciation for the rain, the cold storms of winter. That appreciation is bigger than me and my little house with my pans and buckets filling with rain that has traveled here all the way from Alaska.

Besides being cold and soothing and triggering my chatter, the rain brings out some unlikely critters. I am reluctant to say so, but I think they are here to remind me, to help tip the balance away from the old and toward the new. All of them are poison. All of them convene at once.

A brown recluse spider ran, and I mean *ran*, across the rug in front of me last night. It came from beneath the chair I was sitting in and scooted, rather conspicuously, across the living room tile and on to the rug. Now, brown recluses do not come out into view very often, and here was one drawing unwanted attention with its unusual haste, sprinting, as much as a spider can sprint, away from me. I lifted a paper, quickly folded it, chased him down, raised my weapon like a club, and killed the poor spider before it could escape to the safety of the couch.

This is more surprising because the night before a scorpion had done the same thing. And then there was the kissing bug in the tub, swimming away from me.

Seeing one of these creatures is rare. To see three, and in the winter, runs against enormous odds. Venomous creatures, running, afraid. I don't know what to make of this. Do I exude poisons? What is up with these infestations, these poisons that come from within and without? Why would venomous creatures flee in fear? What is going on? They are afraid. Afraid of what? Poisons and fear? Why together?

Things are moving pretty fast right now, and I don't know how much of my chosen poison I'm willing to surrender. I'm not yet ready to be unbound by habits anymore than I want to undergo another medical emergency. I am not yet ready to give up anything to meet the medicine at work in the shadows.

24 / Spiral Travel

I wake again in darkness. It follows me to the chair where I sit, one leg propped up, the other bent and unable to cross by itself. It is quiet. This moment, a minute fiber in a thin silken thread, binds me to all that is. Stars shine behind closed lids. I am part of them, they me. All is calm knowing. By the time I open my eyes, the predawn sky lightens the floor and the sleeping dog stretches. She wants to go out. I straighten my good leg. Both dog and leg are sore, getting old and stiff. It is time to care for family and make a living. It is easy to forget the shimmering darkness in the glare of morning light, but I rise and try to be kind as the world begins to buffet and knock against my vessel of calm. I may forget and get angry when things don't go my way. My ship may break apart in the storms and the rocks that wait for me. Tonight I will pick up the fragments and slowly piece them back together so that I may again travel to the stars within, without, and all around me. And so it goes. The thread that runs through my days is the thread that knits and braids me to an ocean of being that has no end.

It is Saturday, and I would like to think I have made it, that I can take a break, not just from work, but from a growing tide of old habits, poison chatter. But the grumbling is persistent; it does not take breaks for the weekend. I have healed enough to get around, to climb on ladders, do housework, to again serve as the accomplice to a culture gone mad with distraction. It is what we do, after all. My boys want a DSL line so that they can play interactive video games. I have my doubts about the need for the line, but it will help me to work from home and will make research easier and faster for all of us.

Still, I carry my doubts about the undertaking with me as I climb onto the roof that knows no seal, the same roof that reminds me there will be no victory over the running waters that travel through the cracks despite my best efforts to keep them away. I look at the job ahead of me. I will have to thread the cable down through a vent into the furnace room. Then I'll have to figure out how to get it through the wall and into the living room before running it to the computers. Not so bad. I hold the spool of line and estimate how much I will need.

The cable is light, but my thoughts are like lead ingots, dragging down both my body and my enthusiasm for the project. I drag my feet and grumble even as I persevere. There is much that I feel is wrongheaded about running a pipeline of noise into my small oasis of quiet. And then there is the actual undertaking of running the cable.

I don't know exactly how to do this, I think more than believe, and not knowing how to do something resurrects old, nasty ghosts. These twin burdens of low commitment to the cause and shame at my incompetence make for a foul and toxic mood. The mood infects those around me and is quite familiar to all of us. It is like an unwelcome guest that returns after an all too brief vacation. I am both helpless and dismayed and struggle to regain some purchase in my step as the soil loosens around me, leaving me sliding down a spillway of familiar laments.

I stop. Just stop and look at the situation, my options. I can just say no to the whole thing. Or I can keep doing what I am doing, making myself and those around me miserable in the process. I can drop my crap about it and run the cable without the onerous yammering. I could administer some antivenin right here, right now, and neutralize some of the poison running through my head.

I could just look at the task and enjoy playing around with the cable, the wires, the tool that crimps the jack into place. It might become interesting, enjoyable, and (gasp!) fun. I would be, after all, learning new skills—how to crimp and connect jacks, run cable, reformat the computer to speak to the DSL line. If I worked slowly enough, I could appreciate the craft needed to do the job well, the meditative attention necessary to the task at hand. If I did this, I might find a lightness in my attitude, a curiosity about the materials and the task.

"It *is* just a simple task," I hear a better part of myself admit. But I watch how it triggers a churning in my gut, a stream of talk in my head. Thoughts and emotions combine to fuel an inner tempest, a dance with all the demons that have lived far below this simple task. They took root long before the present moment. I am not alone on that roof. My father, mother, and brother are all standing there, whispering in my ear, sure of my loyalties to the family code: we are pissed off all the time and don't you forget it. They egg me on. I can hear the questions: Are you man enough to be miserable? Are you with us or against us? They are legion. I am a wimp.

And then there is the fact of the cable. Only I could make the thing a moral quandary. My company on the roof loved it, but dissented on the overall value of the project. It was, after all, not so much what I was doing as how I was doing it. The cable would bring entertainment, football, car commercials, sitcoms, online shopping. KC would call that one of Maslow's primary needs. Bear couldn't care less. The online universe is one he has yet to enter or even acknowledge. My mother would say "Go read a book." The code we all shared demanded that the task be a burden, that's all. The talk was just a means of making it so. Right or wrong mattered less than being burdened.

I list my objections. Here is the feed, the conduit, for more noise. Lightning will trace a path along the cable like it did a couple of years ago and will fry the computers; the kids will become addicted to interactive video; the cable will clash with my color scheme in the living room. "Here Here," "All valid," "Quite right," I hear them encourage. "Now keep working."

To simply decide whether to do so or not would make sense, would be sane, but I am not given much to sanity. I cannot help but sit on the fence of observation and watch the battle that plays out in my aching mind and body.

The operation does not go well, but I resign myself to funneling data through a cable to our virtual piped-in realities that play to the screens of our minds. I cannot quit and rest, nor can I do the task with any detachment, enjoyment, or mindfulness. I just want to let the ache drain from my joints, out of my bones.

I thread the cable down through the vent on the roof before descending the ladder, going into the house, and feeding the line through the furnace room. Here I drill a hole in the wall leading to the living room. I go into the living room to examine the wall for electrical outlets or other obstacles. It is a mess. The boys have left plates on the table, clothes on the floor, and are being hypnotized by television cartoons.

"What are you doing?" I ask, with some serious attitude.

They ignore me.

"No TV until you clean up your mess," I say, switching off the box. "You haven't earned any TV time yet. Look at the table and these clothes." I punctuate my remark by kicking a shoe across the floor. My actions told them that they were greedy, lazy, spoiled, as well as general pains in the ass.

Bottom line, my inner turmoil boiled over into behaviors that did not seem my own, that were deeply embarrassing. All this not just because they weren't doing what I wanted them to do, but because I was making myself sick. Sick feeling became sick action. I called them sloppy, got after them for not helping enough with installing the computer cable that THEY wanted. Yes, the world was doing it to me again. I could hear applause from the roof.

Kyle and Sean get upset. I can see that and apologize. I keep going and desperately try to slow down, to regain some composure, some mindfulness, to find some quiet between the compulsive stories running roughshod over my mood.

Then something shifts, something so subtle I barely notice it. My foot begins pulsing, sending some kind of blood message to my raging storm of attitude. I listen and loosen my grip on hating the task. I persevere with the installation, still grumpy but not quite so committed to advertising the fact. I do have concern about how to live with this sense of feeling overwhelmed, but that is another issue that I will deal with when my calm has returned. Even being right about keeping the cable and all it delivers out of our lives is no excuse for poisoning the day. I turn a high-intensity light on this way of talking to myself, this systematic disruption of balance, and examine all of it, study it, watch it wriggle and squirm beneath my gaze, and notice how little I am enjoying my life right now.

No, I do not say the miracle "yes" and surrender to the project. But I do go ahead, aware that I am carrying the misery of my mother and the family code of discontent on my shoulders, ever the dutiful son, the disciple of suffering, maybe keeping her close by being miserable. I am just watching the show now, not completely believing. Something shifts again. The lead weight of misery lifts, and my body, though still aching, hurts less, feels lighter, moves more freely. Those voices want to be heard, not necessarily followed but heard, let out of the bag and into the light of awareness. They have their moment, say their piece until nobody is listening. Blood carries away the waste, the unusable toxins.

The change in the air then is palpable. A quality or energy wavelength or color of experience affects all of us. I watch my sons relax now that I am working with them rather than holding them hostage. The old stories continue to make their case, that this whole operation sucks, that life sucks, that I am a pawn, a weakling, a loser, and on and on. But the frantic attorney for the prosecution of the moment fails to carry the day, and his agenda of making myself and everyone else miserable is tabled, to be taken up as soon as the light is again switched off.

The rising old tides are tenacious, habitual, inexorable, and come flowing back in, under the doors, through the windows, over and over. The old way reenters and drowns everyone present. Everybody down, we're taking hostages. No one is going to get out of here with their peace of mind intact.

When this happens, of course, I watch it, but at this point feel helpless to stop it. It seems to go with the territory of living in this mess of stories I call my personality.

I couldn't completely appreciate the lighter, "horizon-expanding" (or as L. S., onetime director of the Poetry Center used to say, the "AFGO"—another-fucking-growth-opportunity) aspects of my undertaking. I do see that the streams of noise, both the one in my head and the one coming through the cable, are not going to go away. I can fight against them, or I can cave in to them. Or I can take a third option. Rather than being gored by one horn or the other of my dilemma, I can throw sand in the eyes of the bull—neither argue against the talk, nor just knuckle under to it, but something else.

I cannot win against the force of history, against a flow of noise that is choking me. Nor can I join the parade singing the praises of distraction. I have to step back from the either/or fallacy of my response to the situation.

Either way, crusading against or being swept along only makes me miserable. The way of talk that leads always to winners or losers or right or wrong usually doesn't change anything if that's as far as it goes. The only way out is in and through. The only way to remake the stories is to look at how they were put together, to be, as I tell my students, critically aware of how we shape and are shaped by the stories we hear and believe and weave into what we call a truth. My truths, formed in the smithy of habit, pattern, and conditioning, poison just about any undertaking as long I see them as "me."

OK, I've gotten hold of a thread and will follow it as deep as it goes. Forgive me, Ed, but this path does not lead into a virgin canyon where we can light a fire, howl at the stars, share a bottle of tequila, and rail against the man. It goes where you and many others have disdained to go: the dripping miasma inside us malcontents.

Evidence of any phenomenon begs a theory, and all theories are doomed to disproof or revision sooner or later. That is the role of the upstart philosopher: knock down something and then make up something new out of the parts. Matter is neither created nor destroyed, not that it matters. So pardon please the introspective and retrospective foray. I want to hack away at the jungle of why things go bad and, since I can only affect one person, look at my part in helping them along. While your stories are distinctly yours, I hope that by way of example some of the method and concepts might be helpful.

I'll posit that my feeble mind had succumbed to repeating familiar stories—of not being up to the job (any job), of wanting to be out in the hills rather than up on the roof, of wanting to be there while I was here, of vigorously resenting new tasks and information, of feeling that my mind and the minds of my boys were being irrevocably polluted by advertisers and action movies. Many of these stories run deep into ancient history, going all the way back to childhood, the days of the dinosaurs as the boys remind me. Some are newer. The results are the same. Situations like installing the DSL cable rekindle the bad old days when I would be asked to do things I could not do. While the Bear was fighting in Vietnam, my mother would ask me, the oldest boy, to do maintenance on the house, simple things to anyone with plumbing or carpentry experience, but things that left me helpless and puzzled.

Of course, I could not do them at that time, did not know where to start. They then became paired with a shame born of incompetence that paralyzed simply learning how to do them. Emotional pain clouded and sabotaged the doing of simple tasks, sending me, at times, into a rage of self-immolation even when I was only asked to help. That is an old pattern,

one that no longer fits my station in life (gray-haired teenager). It's a vestige that needs revision, some examination, a new set of rules.

Yes, situations like putting in the Internet cable flick the switch, set in
motion familiar dynamics that grow out of old family wounds, deep emotional pain. I don't do a good job of accepting a challenging task in front of
me, and get my shorts all in a bunch when I have to do simple chores. Computers, tile work, home improvement of any kind, car repair, copper pipes,
collecting chicken eggs, dishwashing—pretty much all of it reminds me
that I would rather be somewhere else, maybe be someone else. And that is
the real problem, attending to the story rather than the task at hand. Too
bad these nasty and unavoidable little mundanities are necessary to sustain life on this planet. Or maybe a good thing. Charged situations show me
where the stories I live by get in the way. Without the breakdown, I would
not know where to begin, so I say thank you (!@#%) for the breakdown.

Once things begin to look dicey, it's time to take stock of what is really
going on. A reaction to a task becomes some physical tightness, which then
leads to an emotion, which then becomes a thought, before growing into
a full-blown story that justifies all hell breaking loose. By then it's all over.
If the upset seems unjustified given the problem, then stories are at work.
Self-talk is the real problem, not the task. I can, for example, handle putting in the cable.

The trick is to catch the rising waters at the start. Listen for the rumble of the flash flood of emotion coming down the canyon, gather up your
cookware, get to higher ground on the bank, and let it flow by. Watch the
small stuff.

It is here in the small and ordinary upsets of living that reframing the
story can first be considered. Microscopic stimuli, still at the level of nano
self-composing, form the site of possible revision. Here, where the emotions and the stories are still embryonic, is where I think we can have an
effect on how we react to those stories as they gain a full head of steam,
before they go from simple thought to a blinding, if constructed, reality.

To watch this requires an effort not unlike that of a runner pushing
to the very edges of ability. Only it is attention, along with the white-hot
desire to focus, that burns like lungs and legs that scream to be released
from all-out effort.

While watching the changes, I have to not buy into, identify, or believe
them, but instead let them run their course, which they do. Things don't

escalate. How can this be, you ask? I don't quite know. But I do know that during the snakebite healing I somehow severed the power stories have over me, somehow better accepted "problems" as just things to deal with, things not worth making up a big story about or complaining about. And frankly, liked that better than being pissed off all the time.

I have the pain in my foot to remind me that the current of noise is just noise, from which I can stand back or not. I can shake my head at the foolishness I believe to be real. It takes some work and some effort after getting the general idea and finding some reminder. It looks like I will have to work for what I want, and what I want is to wake up.

Buddhists talk about two levels of mind. One of them is the one we use all the time to get through the day, to solve earthly problems. Often this mind identifies with lack, incompleteness, and unfulfilled desires as it creates a kind of delusion that results in suffering. This is the mind that operates in the ways of the world. It is this level of mind that says "this is good" and then hangs onto it while rejecting "that which is bad," pushing the bad thing away—attachment and aversion, as the Buddhists like to say. This mind confuses happiness with classifying and controlling outer, material reality, to shaping it to fit with desires.

The second level of mind is the "true mind." This mind watches the stories created by the lower mind and does not respond to them, but appreciates the present moment as just what it is, a kind of imperfect perfection. It sees that problems arise from our reactions to circumstances over which we have no control. The third noble truth of Buddhism claims that we can be happy only when we move beyond the lower mind, beyond believing its stories, beyond identifying with the noise and illusions of craving. If we can shake off "attachments" that color and distort all we see in front of us, we simply see things as they are, without a need for them to be different. When we see what is simply and really in front of us, the thinking goes, we end suffering. The old bliss of the here and now. That simple but not that easy.

"Right mindfulness" requires attention to the body, the emotions, the lower mind, and continual vigilance of the stories that spin out of simple stimuli. The stories activate old pain and create a need to have things be a certain way by force of personal will.

Of course, the world does not comply much with personal will.

I think I confuse the two levels of mind. I think I "am" my first level, that I "am" the anxieties, fears, and compromises that go along with working in a large organization. I need that mind to make it through the day, but I haven't yet learned how to stay detached enough not to believe every crisis and drama it sends down the pipe. I haven't yet learned how to inhabit one while using the other, or to switch, to become more "ambicerebrous."

When people ask me how I am now that I am back at work, I notice how I return to the old stories of being overworked and underappreciated. That is a story I tell to keep my place and my stance familiar and constant. I can hear my mother behind that lament. I suspect I have not forgiven her for being so unhappy with her life, but the talk does more than that. It *serves* me somehow, or else I would not have refined it so. I hear how committed I have been to playing the loyal son, following her desires with no hope of fulfilling them. She loved books and art. I have made letters my life and struggle valiantly to create beauty. She wanted to live in the desert. Somehow I have ended up only a few miles from what might have been her chosen place.

But most of all, I hear her saying that her life was not good enough, and that it would never be good enough, that it is a son's duty to rail against that unfairness.

I have so much to tell her, but now she can't hear what I have to say. I can't forgive her yet. Back and forth, back and forth, from one mind to the other. Yet a third part of me knows it doesn't matter, that this is the life I have and that it is a contradictory, rambling, wonderful mess. When I hold my mother in my thoughts, I am still close to her, still connected.

My complaint serves to keep me unhappy, and unhappiness becomes an end in itself. An acquired taste, it still becomes addicting. In a way, it keeps me from the real joy and real sadness of my life, not unlike many more accepted poisons. I see it happening, watch the chain of talk, hitch a ride on them, even though I no longer believe in them. If I am unhappy at work and that consumes my awareness, then I don't have to look at the fact that my mother is dying of Alzheimer's. I don't have to see the desert disappearing beneath a sea of tiled roofs. I don't have to acknowledge that my aging face tells me that my time is shorter than I want to believe. Real grief, not neurotic suffering, feels like it will kill me.

It may be hard to hear, but sleep and distractions are no longer the only options. It's time to wake up, because the old talk just doesn't cut it anymore. It's time. You know. The days of running away have ended. When you stop believing those old tales, you'll begin to see what I mean. It's like watching a film being made. When you see how it's put together, it loses some of its power; it's never again quite so real.

OK, and so what? Do I really need to hear this? It is funny to me that as I feel better, I feel worse. As I physically heal I want to return to the old way; the "egoic mind," as my Buddhist friends say, gains strength from a body that can temporarily support the illusion that it will not die. That mind still lays claim to dictating how I should live.

Why can't I simply look at things the way they are and be content with that? I am pretty unremarkable, enjoy only moments of brilliant clarity, make little use of limited talent, am quite ordinary, but this is the only life I've got.

My unremarkable life is pretty remarkable in that it is a life, "one that we peel, crying," as a lugubrious French saying has it. What the heck? I may as well drop into this black pit here, having no idea if I'll get out in one piece. Down here, I can hear the spelunker saying as in a nature docutour, is where we find the elusive raw nerve, the unpleasant fact that life is tenuous, passing, that all of us are slowly dying, no matter what we say.

It's time to face the serpent that really scares me, to put the theories to the test. Onward, out of the heart of the desert and into the lair of the beast. I am going home.

25 / Holding Breath

The Bear has elected to have two knees replaced a week before Thanksgiving. We children have organized around going back up to Wisconsin to serve as his nurses. Maggie, one of my older sisters, is trained as a nurse and will coordinate the care and shifts. She'll come up from Florida, Lisa from Texas, Sarah from New Mexico, and I from Arizona.

I simultaneously dread and look forward to the prospect of going back home; it reminds me of my failures to meet the expectations of my family while kindling hopes that this time we might meet on fields full of light and play. I have run back to them, but perennially fail to reach them, to make contact, whatever that means. I broke out of the orbit of the family right after graduating from high school and ran as far as I could, toward something in the West, something in the mountains, something promising and liberating. I needed to be away from them, all the while looking for something to take back. I have been the dutiful son, looking for what was missing, looking for something that I hungered for, that I was sure the family hungered for, that we had somehow lost. I have found what I thought was some meaning, some happiness, but they have declined to accept what I offer them.

The last time I went back I began to give up on them ever being different, but I still hung on to hope.

Rewind to six years ago and the front seat of another of my father's new cars. He has picked up me and my sons from the airport and we are going home, to his house.

He drives off the end of his driveway, over the grassy berm in his neatly trimmed front lawn, beneath the silver maple, around the crab apple tree, and along the lilac hedge up to the back of his patio. "One of the benefits of owning your own property," he says. He lives according to a nobody-can-tell-me-what-the-hell-to-do attitude that I grew up arguing with. I don't own much of anything myself and live on cooperatively held land, do group decision making, eat a diet of something other than beer, cheese, and brats, and like long lonely runs in the open desert, land nobody owns, or more accurately that we all own.

My way is no better. It is just a way, and I wait for someone in my family to see it, not necessarily agree with it, but just see it.

I am home to give my father more time with his grandsons and to give my sons a taste of Midwest celebrating of Norwegian culture, Syttende Mai, Norwegian independence day. The grandpa time is a tradition. The festival is an extra. There will be dancing, food, a parade, lots of ethnic hoopla. That our visit coincides with a Norwegian festival in this small town is subordinate to my other motive, an ulterior one. Part of the festival includes a twenty-mile run from the square in Madison, Wisconsin, to the small town where my family moved when I was in high school. I never rooted there. They did. I still try hopelessly to reach across a gap between me and my brothers, me and the town, me and a life I respected but could not live.

The Syttende Mai Run was something I didn't dare try until I was long gone from high school and the stigma that came with just running, not running for football or wrestling, but just running. Not many locals did the run, and I had to move away before I could appreciate it enough to try it, at first to establish my difference and later to try to get back to my family in ways I couldn't before. When I was a student at the University of Wisconsin, I decided to do it as a kind of "look ma, at what I'm doing" trick that I hoped would make me more visible to my family.

And I still want to please them, be acknowledged by them, and I continue to bring hope-filled expectations back home like a bad habit or a drunk's hope that by continuing to drink he will somehow solve his problems. I come alive on epic runs in the mountains. I and my aging cronies go for hours and emerge sweaty, sometimes bloody, and depleted. We are happy then, and not just for the "high" but for the contact with a wild place, for an immersion in something grander than our day-to-day lives. We used to be adrenaline freaks who spent more on outdoor gear than on our cars, but have gotten serious, married, and responsible, sort of. These guys are my tribe, a bunch of weirdos who find God between the saguaros on a trail run or in the plunge pool of a box canyon. They are the timeless moments, where I am "at one" as Zen friends say of meditative clarity. I feel we see each other in ways I want my family to see me. Out there, where I'm tired, grimy, exhausted, but glowing with peace and contentment, has become my church, and I want to bring the gospel or part of it home.

I am not a fast, race-winning runner, but I hope my running twenty miles will convey some of the magic I have found living away from this town, these people I call family. It is the only gold I can bring them. The wealth of my experience is not something material, but is as real to me as a truck axle.

I am happy in the mountains and offer that to my blood tribe. "We'll have none of that," they cluck. Not surprisingly, my visits are perennially disappointing. I hope this one will be different, that I can stand with my sons in my weirdness and not cave in to trying to meet and beat my family at games I don't otherwise play. I can't keep up with them in the cars they drive—showroom shiny four-wheel-drive pickup trucks—or in the discourse—the inside jokes and stories of people I have never met, the impenetrable histories of years of living together in a small town.

My hopes are intact as we unload the car. We pick up our bags and move in to a small room we will share. I spread two sleeping bags that date back to my own childhood. They are covered with scenes of mountains and bears and the lining shows through at the edges. I remember being eight years old and using these sleeping bags camping with my dad and brothers when we lived in Alaska, mythological times of running rivers, deep woods, giant red salmon. The reverie begins to fade when the Bear knocks on the door telling us to get ready; it's time to go to eat.

We head to a café downtown that has spaghetti, a place where I can "carbo load" for the run. Talk over pizza turns to friends and acquaintances with whom I graduated. One is an investment banker who lives in California in a home overlooking Manhattan Beach, 6,500 square feet with an ocean view and rare art furnishings. "He got his MBA," my dad reminds me. I got a degree in English.

The talk moves around to current events, and the Bear reminds me that he will be speaking at the Memorial Day parade and that my nephew recently finished boot camp in the marines. The family seems to agree that military service is a good thing. I had crusaded against it, preferring independent critical thinking to taking orders. Times have changed, and to my family I seem as wrong about the military as I was about impending peace in the Middle East.

I then hear about the neighbor who bought stock in a company that gave a big raise to the executives while putting many in the community out of work. But the stock went through the roof, making the neighbor, who is retired and set for the rest of his life, richer, a multimillionaire. "That was all while you were in South America working for peanuts, teaching and climbing mountains," he reminds me.

"Yeah, but that was what I wanted to do," I say almost apologetically. What I meant to say was that I had no choice. I had to go. It was like some kind of bug inside me would have eaten me alive if I did not surrender to it.

The values of life-long learning, traveling as a quest, and living simply all seem to have hit the rocks and broken apart in the storm that is twenty-first-century culture. The celebrity worship and fascination with wealth have pushed gaining life experience to the margins. My father and brothers, who laugh at my choices and wave off any travel stories as pure folly, have done well, but are afraid that their prosperity will disappear. They don't want me, don't need my ideas or suggestions, and would be worse off if they had followed them.

The spaghetti comes and my two sons eat fast. They are hungry from traveling all the way from Tucson. Kyle chews his pizza with the sides of his teeth because where the front teeth should be he has the eight-year-old gaps and gums. He looks like an old man with none of the shame of a toothless grin.

The Bear tries to show enthusiasm for the run, but this kind of endurance sport is something whose appeal escapes him; it doesn't have the speed, excitement, or sexiness of skiing or motor sports. "That one time you did the run, you lost four toenails, didn't you? You looked like a tortured Christ when you finished." He lets out a little laugh and shakes his head. It was a bit ridiculous.

"Yeah, I ran that without training, something of an impulse with shoes I had found at Goodwill. Ninety-nine-cent running shoes. I guess I got my money's worth."

That time had been grueling. I remember cramping, having to walk, finishing in just over three hours. I hadn't trained. It had been an embarrassment. Another time though, one he forgets, I had finished well, crossed the line in less than two and a half hours, picked up my shirt and left. No applause. No pictures. I think I went to work that afternoon washing dishes and cooking pizzas.

That was almost twenty years ago. Here I am again, a middle-aged father running the same course, hoping to get it right this time.

Kyle eats so fast he gets a stomachache. "I feel sick," he whispers to me, leaning over, a bit sheepish. The Bear is impatient. I mother Kyle in ways that make my dad fidget. It will be a disappointment if I end up watching him tomorrow instead of running. The thought leaves me feeling irritated at my son. I notice my irritation and guess that I have more at stake in this "lark" of a run than I tend to admit. I take him to the bathroom past the video games and the candy machines and stand guard over the door so he can have privacy. While I wait, I wonder why being here, in this place of memory, of unresolved unproven test so long ago, is so important, so bothersome, so persistent. Why I keep hoping to either get my family to see things my way or at least stay unhooked from their needing to see things their way.

When Kyle emerges, he is pale but seems to feel better. The Bear is up paying the bill, a sign that he is ready to leave. I notice a man wearing an old T-shirt from a year long ago, one of the years I ran before. I no longer have the T-shirt I earned for running so many years ago. I gave it away or threw it out after using it for a rag to clean the Jeep. I wish I had that shirt now. It might give me some identity, some credibility now when my own seems so fragile.

As we walk back to the car, a storm threatens, then arrives in great sheets of rain and lightning and thunder. We drive back to my dad's place peering through the windshield between the high-speed swipes of the wipers. The Bear takes a turn fast. My boys notice and tell him that he took the turn really fast. "Grandpa likes to take corners fast, to cuss, and to drive on his yard," he tells them.

"But only when it's safe," Sean, the younger son responds. He is his father's voice.

"Right, only when it's safe," the Bear concedes.

None of us sleeps well, and the boys join me in bed. They are afraid and sandwich me on either side as the storm lights both the walls of the room and memories I thought I had lost. It lasts only part of the night, and the day dawns clear, windy, and cool.

My brother comes over to take me up to the start of the run. At first my boys don't want to go, but I tell them about the start, about the Capitol building, the farmers market, and the possibility of getting a treat afterward, and they consent. On the way, we stop to get a Gatorade. My brother, KC, buys Sean an entire box of white powdered donuts. I hate these things but relent since we are on vacation.

The race start is a dream. My father is there. My brother is there with Sean on his shoulders. Kyle stands on the side, and when I hand him my hat says, "But papa, you haven't run twenty miles in practice, how can you do it here?"

"I'll do it," I say to him.

"Just in case you don't make it, do you want us to meet you somewhere? Have a backup plan?" asks my brother. His doubt in me stings and burns.

"I think I'll do it."

I join the crowd of runners and wait for the gun. When it goes off I feel like sprinting to the head of the group, but know better and hang back. At one mile I feel heavy and want to quit, but keep going. We run into the wind, a little under seven minutes per mile for four miles before runners begin to spread out. It's time to run my own race, and I settle in to the rhythms of breathing and heart rate I know I can sustain. The second-to-second breathing turns to minutes, which stretch to an hour. I run steadily along country roads, up and down rolling hills, trying to keep my neck and shoulders relaxed. I try to fix on goals along the route, but come back again and again to right here, right now, this breath, this moment, this calming of the urge to tighten up, to freeze, to stop, to walk or sit or lie down along the road and quit.

I wonder where this running comes from and remember a time my father and I did a canoe race. My first stroke snapped my paddle in half. I was crushed. We didn't have a spare. I wondered aloud whether we should quit. The Bear just muttered "Never say die" and fished a decrepit, waterlogged, moss-covered, misbegotten root out of the current and said he could use it to steer if I would paddle like hell.

We finished, even passed a few stragglers.

So I keep going. Stopping is not an option. At eight miles, I see them seated in their car off the side of the country road. My boys get out as I approach and give me a big hug. KC gives me the Gatorade. They ask how I am doing. The Bear, in a reversal of the usual bear/man photo op, takes a picture of me from inside the car.

"Do you want us to meet you farther up or are you OK if we see you in town?"

"Town's OK," I say, noting lack of enthusiasm to cheer along the route. But they meet me up ahead anyway. "Come on, Toso, suck it up! Let's see some speed." The encouragement, though a bit facetious, helps me along. Any recognition, even crumbs, is nourishing.

The run courses along rolling hills lined with oaks, maples, elderberry, all in new leaf. Spring is in full bloom. I head down a long grade, letting the legs fly despite the pounding, and another hill takes the place of this one, and on and on.

I remember a time when I rode with my brother who worked driving a semi one winter. One bitterly cold night found us struggling with gelled diesel fuel, which meant the big rig lost power on climbs in the Poconos on the way from the Midwest to New York City. On the shoulder of the highway we raised the cowl covering the engine and fiddled with the fuel line. My brother had his hands in the shadows of the engine compartment. Only a week before, in an identical situation, my brother's gloved hand passed between the pulley and belt of the idling semi; I can almost imagine the crunching ca-thunk before he winced, hard. Now he had to deal with the same problem, his hand a thick wad of gauze. It had been bad and no one had been there. Now I was there to help, but was not a diesel mechanic and could do nothing beyond watching him fuss with hoses before getting the truck to run right. Guilt punched me hard in the gut.

What if I had been there when he had lost his finger? I could have done something, made something up to him. I was the big brother who abandoned him, and that had created a void that might never be gapped.

"I'll get help," I might have said after getting him back in the heated cab and wrapping his hand.

I could have run up the slope toward La Crosse, hailing passing cars, running for miles until someone pulled over.

KC might not have lost his finger. If I had run, gotten there in time, it might have gone better.

The image lingers. Others take its place. I can't help but love these people, even if I don't register on their radar. I want to tell them how much I want to reach them, how far I will go, how much pain I will endure. But it all falls short somehow. I need a minimum of recognition to give them what I have to offer.

At two hours, I'm at fifteen miles. I lock in on the finish and begin counting breaths to offset the traces of cramping. I unroll a Tums and chew it, hoping the calcium will counteract the cramp. My heart rate stays high even though my pace is slowing. I am pushing past the envelope of my endurance. "Come on body . . . no cramping . . . no bonking . . . please." I'm running the possibility of failing through my mind's eye. It doesn't look good. To stall in front of everybody lining the route would be too much. If all I have to show for a different way of living is to quit, I tell myself, I'll lose all credibility.

I slow my pace to over eight minutes a mile. Not the speed I want, but better to finish slow than not at all. Runners pass me. I pass some that are walking or who sit on the shoulder of the road, DNFs, Done Fors. No. No. This is the only way I know. They are a reminder to take it easy, to run my own race. The course joins a highway. Now away from shade, in the late morning, I can feel the heat. I have three miles to go. I try to smooth my stride, to keep my chest an even line, to glide through the growing urge to pull up and off along the road into the ditch. Cars speed by not far off my elbow. I can see the town, the center of which contains the finish. Church spires, a Wal-Mart sign. Of course, Wal-Mart has found the place that is lost to me. We leave the highway and pass through a sprinkler some generous soul has set in the street. The chill is one I can't distinguish, between one induced by evaporation and one by heat. Right after mile eighteen I see the family. Brothers, sister-in-law, niece, nephew, father, and sons are lined up on lawn chairs along the road. I pull out of the line to join them. I give the niece a hug, the brothers a high five, and sons a kiss before continuing. They call after me, saying they will see me at the finish. Even if just for a moment, the barriers relax; it's the crumb I have come for.

The last two miles drag by. Cramps hover just around the edge of my resistance to them. I run into the downtown past banks, hardware stores, body-piercing parlors, across the river and up the last hill. I ignore finishers who sprint the last hundreds of yards to gain a few places and shave a few seconds from their final times. I work at hanging on to the elation, the lightness, the desire to weep, the floating dreaminess of the finish.

Whether they see it or not, I want this to be my metaphorical coming home. The sum of efforts to reach my family has to exhaust me fully, completely, past all barriers to feel real, satisfactory. I am putting everything I have into reaching them, hoping to build a bridge from my world to theirs. I had hoped this could constitute a common ground, an effort we could mutually understand.

Here is the scene I hoped for: the announcer says over the PA: "Here's one of the Toso boys, from Tucson, Arizona," and I hold up my arms as he adds, "but we think he's really still a hometown son." I continue to run as I nod theatrically. I am home. I am seen. The crowd erupts in cheering and the scene turns hazy with joy.

My family is there, waiting. They crowd around me and want to know more about who I am, how I live, where I have been all these years.

The actual finish line has one brother there, waiting impatiently. He lets me know that the first runners beat me by almost forty-five minutes, looks at his watch and says, "Let's go get some breakfast."

He seems relieved that it is over. The Bear is pleased, but he too is distracted and pushes the boys toward me in a gesture of turning their care back over to me.

We all ride silently back to the house, where talk again turns to the Packers, hunting, weaponry, and motors. I listen distantly and offer some unqualified comments, but clearly see them drifting away, uninterested, back to the familiar, well-worn tracks of topics and conversations. My hopes of a bridge forming between their world and mine evaporate as the car winds up the hill, away from the river, past the cemetery.

I miss my world and want to get back to it, away from this longing, this hunger that knows no end.

26 / While I Was Gone

How will I go back to Wisconsin this time? What will I do with a heart that feels stripped, exposed, flayed—open to the wind, diesel fumes, and video mayhem of star-spangled America? What will they say when I show up as innocent as a sun-baked gecko, crippled as a three-legged kit fox? Who will I see? How will I define myself? Running, the best I had to offer, did not work last time, did not work for a family that idolizes play, dual incomes, action, physical appearance. What can I offer this time, now as a neophyte mystic bearing tales from the underbelly of free time? What will I hold up as likable, attractive, desirable? All of these questions form a soundtrack playing behind my search for tickets, my finding a substitute for class, my packing and finally departing for the sweet dairy air of Madison.

I can travel fairly easily now that the wound has shrunken to a weep hole that needs only a small bandage. Swollen and red, it speaks to me, reminds me, pulls attention back to here and now. It and I are at home with each other. It serves as talisman speaking to something beneath the need to be liked or to win approval.

I dreamed last night that I was in the water, in a swamp of some kind, when an alligator began to pursue me. It was clear to me that I was about to be eaten, to be torn to shreds. Yet behind the alligator, a large snake, a cottonmouth or something like that, slithered into the water off a floating mat of debris, an island of roots and tangled fiber, not unlike the decaying prickly pear pads in the desert. That snake, cousin to the rattlesnake, a kind of viper, drove away the alligator.

I take it as a good sign.

There are not many rattlesnakes left in Wisconsin. When I was in high school, some buddies used to kill them for a five-dollar-a-tail bounty. Their numbers declined so precipitously that the state rescinded offering the bounty in 1975, but stories of snakes overrunning the place continue. A farmer once told me he found a den of snakes that numbered in the thousands and that he had to dynamite the side of a bluff to get rid of them all.

The rattlers in Wisconsin are more timid than those of Arizona and tend to stay in rocky areas along the Mississippi and other steep, difficult terrain. The timber rattlers, especially, stay away from people and tend to be secretive rather than aggressive. Their camouflage makes it very difficult to spot one, and they seldom move even when hunting. There are others too, very rare, but equally retiring. The massagua, or swamp rattler, lives in the marshy areas around the big rivers. Between the two types, only about one bite every four years or so occurs in the entire state, if you don't count those occurring after drunk rednecks decide to play with snakes.

No, the rattlers of Wisconsin are not exactly power players. I doubt I can hope for much help from them or from human sympathy toward them.

The day I leave Arizona, a rare rain falls in thick, flapping, unruly curtains that blow in gusts across the streets. Snails have taken over the front porch. Rain like this leads a cold front; a big storm is coming in. I park the Jeep at the airport as the wind begins to blow in earnest. Low, thick, dark clouds move in from the west and turn the roads to rivers. Tucson has terrible drainage, and when any amount of rain falls, water runs muddy and fast down the most benign of parkways, turning them into churning arroyos that sometimes carry away small cars and unlucky children.

The plane is delayed on the tarmac by wind, which is blowing at over fifty miles an hour. I sit in my seat and calm myself, get mentally ready to return to see my family. I will have to enter the insular world of my brothers, resume the put-downs and pecking order that we learned in junior high but have yet to outgrow. We play out male affection clumsily in tight, closed circles.

The plane is almost empty after a layover in Minneapolis, so I put my foot up on the seat. It is throbbing and bulging from so much sitting. I look down through the cold darkness as we fly over Wisconsin, imagining the lives down there beneath the single mercury lamps lighting the pump houses and barns of the farms below. It is not hard to hear the dinner talk or to imagine the smells of manure, of iodine for cleaning the teats of milk cows, or to hear the pump moving fresh milk, thick with butterfat, to the stainless steel rake that will stir and cool the immaculate liquid, the tinny clank of buckets.

I can hear the stories between fathers and sons, between brothers, and know what binds the thinking and what closes the doors. I can hear it like I am sitting at the table, but still I feel the stranger in a familiar land, perhaps seen by some as disloyal for bowing to other stories, embracing other ways. I don't blame them. There is other glue that binds us.

Yes, it's true. I don't bleed the green and yellow of the Green Bay Packers and I did not join the army and I don't buy a new truck every other year. Those are not the only ways to assign value to a life well-lived. That they are necessary is a line that has gotten a bit long in the tooth and loose under the chin.

I can hear the false bravado behind my words. The gut tells it differently and does not betray the family truth so lightly.

We are at the Bear's house the next morning for breakfast. My body has gone heavy, opaque, mute—enigmatic as a sphinx. Whatever was there before that allowed me to step back from the grip of family stories has been taken back behind locked doors, encrypted again, beyond my easy reach. I bang on the door with my fist, but get no response.

It has returned to secrecy of darkness, where it was before the bite. It is out of reach. It has been kidnapped by loyalty to family ways.

Friends say it gets worse before it gets better when they talk about breaking out of old ways of thinking. It is bad. The old anxiety, the taut cords of my neck, the pissy complaint—I must be getting close.

Why is it that in these moments I ask for the help of a god? I think it is because I again fear death. When I fear death, I throw up my hands in helplessness and go running to the arms of a protective deity. Yet when death is near, I cherish precious life, breathe the air of immediacy, contact, mystery, and calm.

If we could feel death close, we might begin to see each other and Earth differently. The miracle of them would be more immediate, the need to care for each other more urgent. It is this complacency of security, this attendant running from the pulse of mortality, that deadens my touch and closes the doors to presence in flesh, care for myself and the Other.

I learn from the Bear that Johnnie is home from the marines. The day after he got in, my brothers took him to a football game—the Packers and the Broncos—a record-setting game for attendance at a Packers game played in-state. Today they will have breakfast and will go up to the land, where Johnnie will pick out his deer stand. They will give him the best one because he will hunt for only a day before he must return to base.

Of course, KC and the boys were late for breakfast at the Bear's. KC needed more time to get ready—take his eight o'clock shit, shower, and powder pat. He's a big man and has to listen to at least a full CD of Garth Brooks as he moves between the tub and the commode and the closet and the kitchen in order to go out into the world without stinking or itching or feeling irregular.

Bear had breakfast ready at eight, just as he said he would. He sits for an hour next to the wilting, cooling food, piled high on plates in the middle of the table next to the window overlooking the cornfield and highway before anyone shows up. KC makes it a point to show up late and has ever since Linda began staying overnight with the Bear. The Bear prefers now to sit out on his porch in the mornings with Linda while she smokes and has her cup of strong coffee. The Bear, retired soldier, never used to sit with anyone, including our mom. But since my mother went to the nursing home with advanced Alzheimer's, he pretty much feels he deserves to do whatever the hell he feels like doing.

It's been this way between them for quite some time. The Bear and KC are like two old grouches who can't stand each other but who can't quit each other either. Gus, my other brother, stays clear of the mud they throw around and has begun to extricate himself from the whole family drama. He has three baby girls. I wonder how they will grow up in this family of boys.

Gus, the youngest of the three, is also late for breakfast, but I get to talk to him after talking to the Bear. He's glad to be taking a day off work to go with the boys up to the land to fish and scope out the hunting that is only a month away. Johnnie arrives as I'm talking to Gus. Johnnie looks every bit the same young kid I knew before.

We start out talking about the snakebite and how horrible it must have been, how malicious, slimy, cold blooded and on and on that rattlesnakes are. I try to explain that it was an ordeal, but that not every aspect of it has been bad; in fact, some of it has been good, helping me to appreciate my life.

Johnnie looks at me cross-eyed, as if he can't focus on me, and then recounts an encounter he had with a snake on maneuvers in southern California. He vividly recounts how his skin got all tingly and creepy before he and his buddies decided to kill it, contemplating even eating it. From there, every sighting of a rattlesnake and every fear of seeing one ends up with the predictable conclusion of an ugly head reared, victims saved by a gallant spray of machine-gun bullets. All join in the chorus of "if I had been there, I would have killed the snake."

We exorcise the demons and I show them the foot. It is suitably off-putting and only confirms Gus and Johnnie in their fear and loathing of anything mysterious and reptilian. Johnnie finally says he hopes they are hibernating today because he'll have his deer rifle.

They see only the wound. It touches a reflex humans seem to have in the wiring of the psyche. Their response is one we have learned, but only one of several possible. They don't see another side, the awe that is the counterpart of fear, that comes from a creature with such power, such mystery. They don't see that by killing the literal snake, they destroy the mythological gifts the snake can bestow. All are cheated and lowered. Awe exits stage left. And we get another beer.

I see in the talk that I can no longer sit by and just let the conversation slide. It is an affront to me, and to them, though they do not see it. It is a slap in the face of coexisting with other creatures, of waking up to a kind of sacred pact that we broke long ago and of which we need reminding. It's part of a dangerous narrative stating that we, humans, are separate from, and somehow above, the natural world.

"Yeah," I begin, "and it hurt like hell . . . but I have to wonder what the world would be like without snakes, especially rattlers. They keep rats down, but it's also exciting just knowing they are out there."

They look at me the same way the Rural Metro EMT looked at me when I said I didn't hate them. Only this time, I keep talking about it.

"I think, sometimes, dangerous things are good things. Like, you guys like motorcycles. They're dangerous, but they make you feel more alive, make you wake up, pay more attention. Snakes are the same way."

Gus absently looks over me toward the TV, looking for answers elsewhere. Johnnie begins working the pop-top on his morning Mountain Dew. He looks into the darkness of the can for something hiding down there. I know that look, those searches. They have drawn me in the same way to nowhere, always nowhere. I am waiting for an answer that would never come because I have to go find it myself. I know I have to get away from the droning televisions, the endless cans of pop in the morning, beer after noon.

I am losing them. How can I explain something I do not know well enough myself? I am still looking in different places, tracking down something in the same way that they will soon be tracking down the deer on opening day. Am I vain to think I can find it myself when so many easily adopted substitutes lie ready and waiting for any who ask? What is the story about snakes anyway? Don't snakes add something as subtle as it is valuable to the experience of hiking in the woods or on the desert? Can't they see that? If we lose the literal snake, don't we also lose the mythological snake, the redeemer, the awakener, the other, wildness, mystery, and mystique? The answer I'm sure would be, Hell no, with a tone of bullshit, blasphemy, and paganism.

Normally at this point, I would start to argue, to confront and refute. That has never worked in the past. But I cannot just sit there either. I realize I have to find a new way, some approach that will not threaten but engage. I have learned a lot about snakes, but not yet enough about people.

I lose my train of thought for a second and KC fills in the void.

"OK, so there's this guy, right?" KC begins, apropos of nothing, "in Prairie du Chien, you know that place down by the Mississippi, that place that almost got taken over by rattlesnakes a while back . . . well, this guy gets a new pair of boots, see, and he goes for a hike. He gets bitten by a rattlesnake and dies before the sun sets."

We all look at him with some incredulity, but willing to play along.

"Anyways, his wife was just waiting for this all along and has her lover move in the next day. Of course she kept the dead husband's boots to give to the lover. Well, the lover tries them on, gets sick, and dies before the sun sets the second day."

There we are, hanging, wondering where this thing is going, when he finishes. "Turns out the snake fangs were still in the boot and poisoned the second guy."

We all stare at him for a moment, in silence, as it dawns on us.

"Serves him right," Johnnie and Gus both agree.

"Be careful next time you put on your boots—those things'll kill you even when they are dead," KC says to the whole group. We laugh, and it feels good to laugh. It is a step and is as far as we are going to go.

The conversation winds circuitously to other necessary subjects. Yes, Johnnie still has the same girlfriend. Yes, he plans to see her and to go golfing with her parents. I quiz him a bit on his life. Oh, he's been running and lifting weights. He can do a five-and-a-half-minute mile. Have I done any 5Ks lately? Yes, but I won't be able to for a long time, if ever. My ankle and knee are too weak. Pause. I hope you and Gus can run sometime, I say, referring to my other brother, who was also quite a runner in his day. Yeah, Johnnie muses, I'll have to take it easy on him. Since he had the girls he's slowed down quite a bit. A head start's a good idea. Oh, and you're going to recruit? I ask. You get to spend an extra month at home if you get more of the town kids to sign up?

Here I feel them again sliding away. I had hoped that Johnnie would go to college rather than join up, like Bear had, and Gus, and how KC had wanted to.

I wanted him to join me on a walkabout, a trip to the mountains, in the woods, or in my dreams, to wander, or quest, or whatever it was that called me away so long ago. Some story found me and possessed me at his age, and I had to follow it. Its siren song was the mountains of the West, the desert, outgrowing something, becoming something else. I still carry that odd need to wonder about strange places; it is as useless as a third leg in this group. Johnnie was always gentle as a boy, and had a way of seeing and understanding people and animals. I see him now through the aging uncle's eye, as fit, handsome, young, bright, appealing, doing his best to lure kids into the marines.

I can remember the persuasive pull of recruiters myself and how I barely escaped joining and submitting to the orders that might ask me to kill, taking directions that would determine the trajectory of my life. I remember that night in my parents' dark living room: the recruiter, a shadow in front of a window as I was looking out onto the last light of the day. "We can do this. We can go right now—to sign up. You can get what you want." His words hung on the thick summer air. All I could mouth was "I don't want to kill anybody." Silently, exasperated, he stood up and left. I don't know where those words came from, but they served to tear some of the fabric that wove me into the family code. The belief that fight was right was never spoken out loud, but was inscribed on my brothers like a tattoo. Somehow that imprint did not take on me, and I don't know why. All I knew was that I had to follow another path, a path below me somewhere, over which I would stumble for years because it lay in darkness. I followed it, heart hard with betrayal, guilt, and loneliness, breath as shallow as that of the dead.

Military hierarchy defined my father's world and, for reasons better left for another discussion, I swore I would never be part of it, that I would find something better. I ran to the university. I see now that going 180 degrees from something only to create and identify with its mirror image is not an escape. Instead of generals, my world has regents' professors; instead of colonels, full professors; instead of captains, assistant professors. I have identified with a parallel hierarchy, ending up no happier, maybe even less so, than my father. I see that I need to do more than simply run away or define myself in opposition. I have to look at the defining stories, even if I feel they are "right," and see how they keep me away from living, from forgiving, from being present with my nephews, father, and brothers.

Here I am still, the pacifist cactus hugger, in the company of my gun-toting brothers, sticking to my guns as staunchly as they are theirs, rigid as rebar and getting nowhere. The past still stands between us, in spite of my having pushed it deep into the recesses of my mind. I haven't given up hoping to change them. Maybe it is time to rebuild some bridges, to make some peace with them.

When they take off for the land I again realize how I have left, or maybe abandoned, the men in my family. I try to make my way back to them, to present my case for doing things differently, but they recede faster than I can approach.

I make my way through the rest of the day without them. I'll take the Bear in for his pre-op appointment, then what? My steps from here are tenuous. I feel that from here I swing my feet past the edge of solid ground and onto air. I don't know if faith will support me or if I will fall the fool's plummet. When I look at my own boys, I wonder what I will teach them, what I have to offer them. And I am clear that I can't do this alone. I need to get right with myself, to look for my tribe, a culture deep and vital enough to sustain them on their way into a world larger than I and the men in my family have imagined.

27 / Learning to Breathe

The Bear's surgery went well, but he is in more pain than he wanted to be. He cussed out the nurses when they told him he had to stand on his new knees. They will keep him for another couple of days.

I am free to wander around Wisconsin and go up to Portage to visit my brother KC. When I pull into the driveway and see his pickup truck, I know he is home. I called ahead but got no answer. I left a message letting him know I was coming.

Deb, his wife, is home. She tells me KC is out deer hunting and does not want to be disturbed. Rain is falling. She tells me that he will be disappointed. At first I think she is referring to me, that KC missed seeing me, but then realize that she means that the hunting will not be as good.

She shows me the "cabin" where the hunters stay during the hunt. It is really a shed in the backyard. Inside the large heated shed, they have erected a tent, have full coolers of beer, bags of snacks, a stove, and a display of "racks," or antlers, from the last hunt. Of course, one of the racks is small and belongs to my youngest brother. His is in the spot reserved for the "wall of shame."

She lights up for a second, remembering something. "Oh, KC wanted me to tell you that we've got snakes on the property. He saw one last summer. He thinks he knows where they might be sleeping for the winter. He's probably going to have to kill them. We don't want what happened to you to happen to Reggie." Reggie is the dog.

Deb returns to the display and makes some comment about the youngest brother, Gus, never getting a big deer, and then chuckles to herself.

Ah yes, the pecking order remains. There are hats, with KC getting the one embroidered "Camp Boss," with the silver leaves of rank spread across the visor. The men have gathered to smoke cigars, drink whiskey, tell bad jokes, and carry on the rituals of boys bonding.

I flirted with the life of a Midwest redneck for a while, but the call of State Street in Madison and the life at the university and then the myth of western mountains proved to be more than I could resist. That one step, that change of course, shifted everything. A gate closed behind me and I know I could never return, that they would never forgive me if I did return. I betrayed a family code by entertaining other codes. That was the real sin, and there has been a price to pay. I still envy what I see to be their ease, their comfort. I remember the simplicity of the tavern life, the low lights of TVs playing the latest game, the shared world of trucks and football. I don't blame my brothers for staying but know I could not do so. Too infected with visions of the mountains and wanderlust, my redneck impulses fell to the crashing waves of hippie intellectual. I will never be forgiven for leaving.

Perhaps forgiving is ultimately up to me.

I leave without seeing KC and make the hour drive back to Madison with rain streaking the windows. Maggie, one of my older sisters, will arrive soon, but I'll have the Bear's place to myself until she does. I drive in quiet and make my way almost automatically back to Dad's mobile home park. I know I am close when I smell the water treatment plant across the street. The smell of shit seems oddly appropriate. I lock up the car and enter the dark double-wide.

I'm staying in his study. This is his place. On the wall hangs an oil portrait a friend of his painted of him forty years ago. I admire both the work and the subject. I had forgotten that he had an oil painting; its hanging here demonstrates the value it has for him. In it he is still young, excited, and idealistic. That was before Vietnam, before his daughters' divorces, and before his wife's Alzheimer's. The past rises like a tide and I gasp for breath in the flood of it. I need to learn to swim in it.

There are also photos of him flying his beloved Mohawks and Hueys, his dream come true. He wanted out of his family too, or at least out of the confined horizons of a small town in northern Minnesota. Flying took him away, but extracted a price. When I asked him one time to teach me to fly, he declined, saying something about not wanting to remember his days in the cockpit. In these old photos, though, he smiles, strong hands at the controls, calm, confident.

There is also the large TV and various remotes controlling the images that bombard him and the rest of us who are here to help. It is the constant.

Wherever one travels, there is the same fare being ladled out from the tube, a hugely standardized model and frame of how to live, of what to do, of what not to do, of what to fear.

Outside, it has gotten cold, below freezing. I'm a little worried about ice on the sidewalk when Bear will have to navigate on crutches. The quiet of the place soothes, and for the first time since I arrived I have a chance to sit. The turbulence in my head, the noise about being back in my father's house, the cultural confines of the Midwest that I have worked hard to escape, all come roaring at me. I want to weep in self-pity, but don't. Instead I fight. I fight against them until I can get quiet enough to hear a weak voice coming from outside the periphery of my mind.

It reminds me that I have not been given a dividend of days so that I can sit in judgment of anyone, least of all my brothers. I know that even days like these carry gifts within them, no matter how they fail to live up to some kind of imaginary standard. Yes, an older form of me found these things to be an intense dislike. It is not my place to question the forms of days that come to me. It is my place to savor, to revere, to embrace, over and over, this grief, this hopelessness, as if this moment and all others were the last of my life or the ideals of my choosing.

Maggie and her lover, Earl, arrive late. We cook salmon and have a ceremonial reunion dinner. I have not seen Maggie for many years, and she looks younger than I remember her. She is trim and tan from days of yoga and sailing and an easy life in Florida. She listens to my laments and commiserates.

The next morning we check on the Bear before going to a Bikram Yoga session, the strand of yoga Maggie has studied and in which she instructs others.

I am about as tight as a person can be, and my foot makes it hard for me to stand or balance on one foot, so I suffered through the poses. I could not cross or braid my forearms, point my toes, sit on bent legs with tops of feet flat on the floor under my butt, or arch my back. Through the fogged-in windows of the heated studio, I could make out the traffic of a city I knew too well. I felt I was pushing against old stories as much as a resistant, bound-up body. My injuries and mental noise notwithstanding, the session worked my heart and body in ways that I needed, and I felt very good afterward.

In one of the poses, blood rushed into my foot, and it turned bright red and hot to the touch. Immediately following the session, the swelling went down, and for the first time in three months my foot was not red at the end of the day.

Of course, vain child that I am, I felt like a fool in the session. I could barely approximate the poses and could not escape the fact, as there were mirrors on all walls. The tight outfits of yogis emphasize the forms of the body. My body, embarrassingly, looked old and overweight. It was not the body I remembered having in college, in another life in Wisconsin, yet another reminder that those days are gone.

An aspect of the scene appeals to the narcissist in all of us. Body, mirrors, form, heat, glowing chambers of sweat and sexual tension, pull me ahead and into a world alien to those I know. The heat of attraction, sometimes, is enough to draw us into areas we would not otherwise explore. It is to spiritual practice what romance is to marriage. No one would get married knowing the depth of the ordeal were it not for the siren songs of lust and the promise of bliss.

And so I open the door to this new heat, this loosening that may help to dissolve old ways of moving, ways that have resulted in stiff and calcified joints and postures.

I try to quiet the beating heart that wants to flee the strange smells and light of the yoga chamber. My heart feels tiny and weak, and I don't know if it can stand what I have to do.

We picked up the Bear from the hospital and took him to a nursing home that he would have no part of. He sat on the bed for all of a minute before cussing and grabbing crutches and declaring. "I've had enough of this shit. I'm going home." We did get a free lunch out of it though.

He wants to be at home and is grumpy enough to break the policies of recuperation to do so. He is astonishingly spry, given that he just had two brand-new titanium knee joints pounded into his femur. He is able to stand, even take awkward, tentative steps, in spite of tremendous pain.

It's a risk, but we agree to let him go home and drive him there. He's still in his postsurgery antiembolism stockings, and his gown is sprawled over the backseat like some enormous cabbage leaf that he wears out of modesty as we maneuver through traffic. I look up and see geese flying overhead in a perfect wedge. I think of the wedges that divide us: the deer hunter and the wildlife lover, the townie and the university dude, the soldier and the sensitive, literary wife, now far away in her dementia. It's a weak but poetic thought, a bit laden with bathos, but it stings nonetheless.

My overly active mind keeps nattering on about the cold wind and the melancholy clouds as we pull into the parking lot and unload the Bear. He is now on the ferocious road to healing, and it is my turn to change bandages. We do so as we watch the smoke rise from the mobile homes, their Packer flags waving in the breeze.

Coming home to help the Bear heal new wounds has uncovered old wounds of mine. It has unearthed relics from another life, fueled reminiscence. This place is rich in memories I have not entertained for thirty years or more. I ran away. It's that simple. Now I am back and have to make some kind of amends, ask for forgiveness where I know there will be none. I am not so afraid of it as I once was. All of my transgressions gather around me and want to be wooed back, to come to rest.

After changing Dad's dressings and putting on clean hose so that he doesn't clot, I leave him with my nurse sister and drive into town to visit my mother. She has advanced Alzheimer's and is bound to a wheelchair. She is in the cafeteria when I get there and looks about as bad as I imagined. But I am not so repulsed that I turn away or withdraw into numbness until the visit is over, as I have done in the past.

I approach her and take her emaciated hand. She looks up at me for a second, then, as if trying to remember something, looks away until she can gather her thoughts.

I know questions are pointless, so I do the talking.

"Hi Mom. It's me, Erec. I like your outfit."

I do. She is nicely dressed and her hair has been combed back. I am again the son, looking for some shared piece of memory, some floating flotsam in the murky doldrums of dementia.

Then we just sit there for a bit before the nurse takes her tray and lets me push her back to her room. Here, it's more private and I want to make the most of the time. I doubt I will see her again. I know I have things to say but can come up with only, "The boys are growing like weeds. You should see them. I think Sean is even lankier than I was." I pause. These are not the words I need to say. I gather myself and step through some self-made barrier.

"You were a good mom," I blurt out, surprising myself. "Thanks for what you have done for me, giving me Dostoyevsky, Tolstoy, and Turgenev, and Whitman, Frost, and Eliot. I remember you shoving the Time-Life art books across the coffee table and saying, 'Take a look at this. What do you think of that Da Vinci? Isn't he something?' modeling what it means to love beauty." I sound hokey as hell, but irony doesn't seem the right tack to take here. There is no need to couch a message, only a need to take hold of the mane that is this running horse of emotion. Then I go silent, aware that I have not really learned what she tried to teach, that I have missed something, some piece. She had found peace between the lines in Russian literature and tried to pass that along to me. I was still looking. She looks at me again, then away. I am tempted to run my hand over her stringy hair, or to set my palm on her tight, shining fist. She seems to be waiting.

Next to her I see a wooden bowl filled with carved fruit. I made her that bowl, a long time ago. I fall back into a memory over which I have no defense.

When Mr. Cummings unlocked the door to the bulk wood storeroom, the smell of the exotic lumber filled the shop. He went ahead of me into the dark, locating by habit a string that switched on the overhead bulb. He stood there in the center of the room, a giant in the cramped space. I could see the rough-sawn oak racks that held the boards we could use for our projects.

"You want mahogany?" he asked. "It's over there." He pointed to some one-by-ten boards stacked on the scaffolding in the corner. "You'll only need one, max two," he said. Mahogany. I liked the sound of the word, and it was the same wood my father sent back from Vietnam. He sent mahogany carvings of fruit: grapes—held together with primitive leather laces that served as stems—pears, heart-shaped fruit that I could not name. The mahogany carvings arrived accompanied by ornate, porcelain elephants, brass scales, and cutlery. When mom went to visit during his R and R, she brought back more brass, porcelain, and silk purses for the girls. She populated our living room with the Southeast Asian exotic. Maybe if I made something of mahogany it would please her.

Ever since Dad left for his "tour" as they called it, I had felt like some-one shaved off the protective fur between me and the world. Everything felt raw and too close. I was supposed to be grown up now and help out, be the man around the house, but I didn't quite know how. Mom was beside herself sometimes, screaming at us kids about how she just couldn't do it all anymore. One time, when she was cutting my hair, she slipped and cut a big bald spot on the side of my head. She tried for a while to comb over it, but the hair that was left just couldn't cover it. I could tell she didn't know what to do either, so she just left it. When the kids laughed at my haircut, I just walked away until I could no longer hear them and went to that place inside where I felt safe and quiet.

Normally, I breezed through schoolwork, but for some reason that year I fell behind. Algebra kept us guessing about quadratic equations, and the books in social studies didn't make sense. Mr. Cummings, however, ran his class differently. After two weeks of showing us how to use the different power tools in the shop, he turned us loose to design our own projects. We drew up designs, made a list of the materials, and proposed a time line. He reviewed the project, made revisions if necessary, then released us to do our own work. At first I thought this would result in chaos, but it didn't. Even the tough kids seemed to take an interest in making things. They could tell that Mr. Cummings tolerated no goofing, and I never saw anyone test him.

I slid one board off the pile, held it against my side like some long book, and headed back to the door just before he switched off the light and left himself.

"We'll need to cut it into squares, glue it, and get it as round as we can before you put it on the lathe," he said, a bit absentmindedly. He then pointed to the table saw and told me to come and get him when I was done cutting.

I took the board to the table saw and cut it into squares. I was careful to use the push stick, like Mr. Cummings had taught us the week before. This was my first job without direct supervision, and I didn't want to lose any privileges. The sawdust from the board was dark and mixed with the lighter pine dust from earlier jobs. The wood smelled dusky. When I had the pieces I would use for my project, I carried them to the glue and paint shop.

There we smeared the boards with white glue and clamped them together with vises made of wood. Mr. Cummings spun the threaded shafts of the clamps with his thick hands. The reddish hair of his forearms curled over the rippling sinew as he cinched the clamps down. Glue squeezed out the side like frosting out the side of a cake and streamed down the boards, leaving a white trail behind each drop.

"You better put some paper underneath that so it doesn't drip on the table. Then come out and help clean up. Bell's about to ring."

I looked at the square dripping mess of edges and wondered what I was thinking when I decided to craft a wooden bowl.

When I told Mom about the bowl, she seemed pleased, but didn't make a fuss over it as she cleared the table. She had a lot on her mind and told us all to go watch TV. I always liked watching the news, hoping that they would mention the place where Dad was living, the place I couldn't pronounce. It was on some big bay with an airstrip with giant C-130s parked all over the place. He told us about the tennis courts and how he was getting good. In letters to mom he also said the place was hotter than the tines on the gates of Hell and full of mosquitoes. I told him in one letter that I was learning to whistle but did not know what tines were. He wrote back that he liked Muskie better than anybody else who was running for president.

The news never did show that place where he lived, but they did show lots of bodies being carried out in bags and told us how many Americans had been killed compared to the VC (Vietcong), or "gooks" as my mom called them. It was a massacre. We lost about twenty-five sometimes; and they lost thousands. I figured it couldn't last much longer at that rate.

I wore goggles while the band saw sliced through my bundle of glued boards. It was hard to follow the circle I had drawn on the top. The wood seemed to resist the bite of the saw. The wood inside was lighter than that outside, and the seam between the boards all but disappeared when the edges were flush.

I trimmed the edges as well as I could, using the blade of the saw as a file to smooth the edges. When it was almost round, I switched off the machine.

"Looks pretty good, but those edges will still catch on the chisels when you start spinning on the lathe," Mr. Cummings said when I showed him my work. "You'll have to center the mount on the base before we can get it completely round," he said as he directed me to a series of round metal plates.

I placed one of the plates over an X I had scribed into the base of the wood. I then screwed the plate into place with short heavy-gauge countersunk screws. With the mount secured, I could thread the bowl onto the lathe.

The lathe was a lean, powerful-looking machine. Belts ran from an electric motor up into the housing. To change speeds, I had to switch the belt from one pulley to another. We set the machine at the slowest speed in order to do the rough cut. It reminded me of my grandfather's garage. My dad had never liked to go in there much; he was too busy with his brothers drinking beer and Everclear to work in wood. My grandfather was missing a couple of fingers, but he didn't complain. "Price you pay for having such big hands," he told me once. And his hands were big, as big as Mr. Cummings's. My uncles and father seemed to tolerate the old man more than admire him, but I thought he was royalty. He seemed to know how to do whatever they wanted to do.

One time they decided to make a pickup truck out of an old Ford sedan. My grandfather gave them the idea of turning the blade of a circular saw around so that it would cut metal, and they tore into that old car with the creative gusto of mechanical Van Goghs. Within a day, they had shaped the car into a rough facsimile of a pickup. With the old man's help, they made a bed out of wood and put in a rear-facing window. After that they took off driving around town, drinking beer and puffing on cigarettes like Hollywood studs.

If it weren't for my grandfather, I doubt I would have found out much about tools, not that I knew all that much before the shop class. The lathe was new territory.

Mr. Cummings rested a cutting chisel, a gouge, on a guide that he situated next to the spinning mass of wood. He eased the chisel forward. "You don't want to move in too fast or else the chisel might catch and go flying. It's sharp, and I don't have to tell you what might happen if a chisel went flying through the shop."

The chisel caught the edge of the wood and his body shook with the force. Chips of mahogany flew from the spinning mass in sporadic flurries. He worked the height of the cylinder methodically, painstakingly, back and forth, back and forth. Each pass cut more smoothly, and the sound of the cutting became finer, more even.

"Now you try it," he said, handing me the chisel, handle facing me.

I moved the chisel toward the spinning cylinder, slowly, slowly. Then contact. The chisel came alive as a fine dust spun away from the wood toward my hand. I watched as the piece gave way to the pressure I put on it. The wood seemed more like clay than a rigid material and submitted to the shaping power of electricity and steel.

For weeks I shaped the outside until it took on a graceful arc from the base to an apogee before curving back slightly to the top. I moved from the gouge to finer chisels with sharper cutting edges, narrower blades for finer work. I then cut out the inside, being careful not to leave the walls too thick or too thin. I cut the base of the bowl so fine that the screws holding the mount began to show through.

I moved back and forth between the worlds of the shop and of home, the two linked by feelings of dread. I knew Mom needed help, I just didn't know what to do. I tried doing the clothes, moving the bundle from the base of the chute to the washer where I dumped it all in with the detergent, but she said the clothes came out as dirty as they went in. I didn't know how to cook anything but a hot dog in a frying pan or the doughy frozen pizza that tasted like mold; so that didn't help much either. I did what I could. I mowed the lawn, raked up leaves, cleaned out the rain gutters, kept the tires of our bikes pumped up, but there was a nagging voice that whispered "It's not enough. You're not doing enough." The voice took root in the back of my neck where the cords there became so tense I could barely turn my head. I gnawed on the question of what I should do in my sleep, carried it with me in the joints of my body, the small of my back. Things moved so fast that they froze. I felt I could barely move.

She told me that I could help her most by just staying out of her way. "Just go watch TV or something."

Watching TV didn't help much with schoolwork, and I continued to fall behind. The equations in math and the experiments in chemistry left me baffled. I struggled to catch up, very aware of how little the man of the house I was becoming. Only shop class seemed to match my rhythms.

With the shape of the bowl set, I worked at the finish. I used wood filler to level out the pores of the wood before moving into an interminable series of sandpapers. I worked the wood down with the finest sandpapers available in the shop and then began to steel wool the sides. By now the wood developed a luster of its own, and other boys in the shop came by to admire my work. I looked forward to getting into the shop and polishing the bowl. I was in a hurry.

One day, instead of tightening the bowl onto the lathe by hand, I set the mount on the thread, turned on the motor, and let the lathe do the tightening. The mount snapped into place in a split second. I spent the hour polishing the bowl, thinking about which finish—walnut or oak—I should rub into it. When it was time to clean up, I couldn't get the bowl off of the lathe. The mount seemed married to the machine.

I got a friend, but the two of us couldn't get it off. Mr. Cummings saw our problem, came over, and looked at the lathe. "I'll try to get it off, but it might wreck your bowl," he said calmly, matter-of-factly. He took hold of the top of the bowl with both hands and set himself against the lathe for leverage. We all stood back, sensing we were about to witness some great effort. He heaved. Nothing. Again. Nothing. He heaved, turned red, strained, seemed about to explode when the bowl came loose, intact.

"Next time, thread it on by hand," he said, handing me the bowl to lock up until the next class.

I went with the walnut stain. That color would contrast, I thought, with the lighter-colored mahogany we had decorating the tables and book-shelves around the house. The stain was a deep brown by itself, but the wood made it look red. To my delight and surprise, the grain in the wood shone through the pigment, and the contrast between the dark end grain and light cross grain gave the wood a jewel-like brightness. I used a satin finish to seal the bowl and put it onto the lathe one last time to polish it. I threaded it on slowly, enjoying the routine, savoring the spinning, the final step before calling the bowl done.

About that time Dad came home for a visit. He was tan, "permanently," he said, and fit. But there was something distant about him too. I told him about the bowl I was making and he nodded, but his eyes didn't really look at me and wandered off. He seemed happy only when he sat in his chair with a beer and watched the vacant TV. Still, his eyes failed to focus on the program, looking instead through, or past, the screen to something on the other side of the wall we couldn't see. They seemed incongruous with the rest of his face—sunken, old.

The trip to the airport was red meat raw. I was sure that everybody in that car could feel the acid air burning our skin. We were not up to the task of saying goodbye. There was and never would be enough time for the burn to go away, time for things to return to some balance, ease, comfort, innocence.

"You're the man of the house," he said with his predictable aplomb. "Now take care of your mom and the rest of the family."

"Yes sir," I answered obediently, absently, full of shame knowing I could not do what he asked, that I didn't have the tools or the skill to even begin.

He turned away, looking cut, smart, sharp as pressed khaki, and walked toward the plane. He did not want us to see the tears welling in his eyes. How long the rest of us stood there, I don't remember, but it was a while before Mom could get up out of the hard plastic seat. We kids stood around her, our hands on her arm, hoping that she would be strong enough. "So much to do. So much to do," she kept saying.

With a thick cotton rag I made sure no part of the bowl didn't shine back when I looked into my reflection. When the finish shone as much as I could get it to shine, I took the bowl off the lathe, removed the mount, and carried it over to Mr. Cummings for a grade.

He sat at his drafting table—a working-class prince—all muscle and grace. He turned the bowl over between his strong hands, looking at it from the top, side, and bottom. "You did a good job," he said. "And this bowl took you eight weeks. After gluing it, I could have done the cutting in twenty minutes, the finish in a day." He looked at me. I knew that I had taken too long but felt that the bowl somehow wanted my time so that it could become beautiful. "But it needed the time," I wanted to tell him. "I needed the time."

I can hear the echo of that voice. It resonates within the piles of papers on my desk and the scribbled errands in my Day-Timer. Between the lines it whispers about the perils of efficiency with no regard for priority, appointments with no sense of importance. How many things have remained unbegun because I didn't have the time?

Now I can see that I had been working on the mahogany bowl in another understanding of time, a time things take to become fully crafted, a time I crave but have forgotten. I live in a time that has no room for what needs to happen. Speed has superceded the journey and the destination. Expedience is valued over beauty. I live in a time where production is a tyrant and results are god.

I gave that bowl to my mother, and I see it here. It has traveled across the years to this nursing home room table, some thirty-odd years after I made it. It still shines and has lost none of its deep red beauty. It is one of the few things, if not the only thing, I have made that has not been colored by the visceral need to hurry. I want to go back to that lathe and work. I want to work on something, heal something, something that will become beautiful; I want to work and abide without the need to finish anything before its time.

I have lost that ability, but want it back. We all have lost it. And we're conspiring to keep it lost.

I look at my mother, realizing that she did not intend to teach me to speed up, but that she had to in order to survive those times, those fierce years. She passed it on to me.

It's time to let that go, to let her go, to give up trying to prove her right.

Now I look at her, look her in the eyes, and say what I have to say before it is too late.

"Mom, it's OK if you want to go home. We're OK. My boys are strong and happy. My marriage is a good one. We'll get along fine with what you have left us." She smiled a bit, I think.

Then, all of a sudden, she laughed a light, delicate laugh. It seemed like she relaxed. One of the nurses was surprised by the laugh and wanted to know what I said. I did not want to tell her that I had just told my mother that it was OK for her to die.

It was not our way, the family way, to laugh. We were always the serious type, the Norwegian bearers of the flag of melancholy burden. We showed emotion best when things did not go our way. Then we cursed at them, literally and figuratively. We learned to swear up and down if a toilet so much as plugged. Doing so did not get the toilet to flush any sooner, but we believed that if we got nasty enough, that things would shift, go more the way we wanted.

No, we did not laugh much. Things had to be really good to get a laugh.

Mostly things were bad, just bad. Life, we all chimed in together, was not something that one enjoyed but something one endured.

It seemed to me that Mom didn't really buy that line anymore either, and that she did not seem afraid of anything.

I let Mom's hand go and just sat until the nurse said it was time for me to leave. Head back, Mom slid into her cloudy stare, seeing not much, in this world anyway.

Death was there too, but this time not for me. I did not mind that, but still bristled at the incessant fact of it. I could see the first traces of death in my mother's eyes, but saw something else. I saw that she was ready to go, that whatever she had been hanging onto was now gone or finished. I have to confess that I got the sense that she was content, ready to go home. I told Mom one last time that I loved her, and then stood, turned, and left the confined air of the nursing home. I wanted out, fast. I pushed through the swinging doors into the latest round of mist, darkness, and freezing rain.

The tears hit me hard when I leaned into the wind and pulled up my hood. I wept and walked, then ran. I ran. I could feel the strain on my foot, the rush of blood to muscles that had not moved in over three months, but I ran. I could feel ligaments straining, threatening to tear, but it did not matter. My feet moved by themselves, as if it was the last thing they would do in this world. I ran choking, almost convulsing, to the car. After unlocking the door and climbing in, I let the hard breathing help chip away at years of frozen emotion.

I have to let her go, give her back the gifts she gave me. To survive, I learned to medicate pain with television, streaming music, alcohol, and later drugs. I chose distraction over the here and now of my life, and protected that distraction with a wall of woe, a cloud of complaint. The facts of the moment were too much to bear at one time, but now they are what gives me life. My mother is dying. My step has lost its spring and I am becoming an old man. The desert is turning into a sanitized playground for golf carts. Just facts. A direct experience of them feeds me, plugs me in to the live wire of living. Running away from the monsters of death and loss has been my way, the family way.

I see it now. The golden fleece is right there, and it is guarded by two ferocious dogs: the dog of loyalty to the family way and the dog of fear at having to live by another story. I have to choose between comfort and chaos, between the perennial chore of keeping reality at bay and surrendering to my humble role in living close to what is. Either of them will eat me alive, but only one will awaken me to that fact.

I had been given a taste of presence when death sat next to me. I was not going to give up a chance to find it again, no matter what the cost, whether it be time, money, or the comfort of habit. A brilliant wash of lightness and relief pulsed through me. There was no more need to pretend or to force things to be any way other than what they were.

I dreamed that night that I was running, in the desert, at noon.

In the dream, I focus on the horizon beyond the far mountains and pick up my pace. I attend to my breathing, feeling it rushing in and out, belly expanding and contracting, nose burning with the heat of summer air. The cords in the back of my neck grow tense as steel cables, then loosen a little. The ache of strain comes and goes in the thigh, then the calf. An old muscle tear remembers its insult and sends a dull reminder that it could tear again if I push too hard.

I am going to make it, whatever that means. I am going to cross some line, some goal, something that is all I really want. I see friends, and I watch the streaming collage of random memories, plans, urgencies, fantasies, and stories that play on the screen of my mind and try to stay out of their grasp, their demanding dramas. It is on the stage of running where I meet them, where we converse and negotiate all that has been unsaid, unsettled, despite time being up, game being over. Yet the drama is played in the wings.

All I am doing is running, and the joy of focusing on one thing pulses with energy and concentration. One thing, one place, one moment is enough, will always be enough, if seen through eyes clear enough to perceive the mystery. I keep my attention on the footfalls, the shock on joints, and the slight sway of muscle and loose flesh. The ground moves steadily by beneath my stride. And then I realize that I will never arrive, and that this moment is the goal, the whole point, that the horizon beyond the far mountains is here, where my foot falls each time it strikes.

The heat sinks deep enough to trigger chills, a strange paradoxical sensation felt somewhere before, as if in another life, and I marvel as goose flesh and shivers run in waves down my arms. The periphery of sight dims and blurs, but the center stays bright and sharp and I continue to look through it. I speed up. As I accelerate, my hands begin to tingle, and the tingling spreads up my arms and then legs toward my trunk, slowly, steadily. I push harder, approaching a sprint. Just as I can take no more and approach the brink of collapse, I reach the end of the run, tap the bar, stop the clock, bend over and breathe. The desert and I absorb each other's heat.

And then I know that everything beyond this moment, this breath, this sensation, is a fiction.

My mother, who I doubt ever ran more than a few steps in her adult life, is standing there. She seems to know that I know. Her expression says "Lighten up." And then she is gone.

The image snaps me out of sleep.

Today is Thanksgiving.

His body speaks armor. Shoulders, neck, arms, stance are all those of a man in full battle gear. But his armor is flesh, bulk, tension, a kind of emotional scar tissue that has built up over years of toughness. He is man in dominion over the beast, a creature apart, a hunter. And what he does not like, he does not do. Our mother ceases to exist for him. No visits. No talk. He and I are cut from the same cloth. He is my brother. I begin to understand why this is so hard, why I don't want to look at him, reach out to him. Thomas Merton says that the only way to make people worthy of love is by loving them. Easy to say.

His life has not been an easy one. As the second son, he had to survive me and my treatment of him, then my father, then early marriage and fatherhood—lean years of odd jobs and unemployment until the air traffic controllers strike of the early eighties opened up possibilities. Without a high school diploma, or the advantage of military service, he made it through the training and went to work as a controller, replacing those President Reagan had fired for organizing and going on strike. It was the Reagan way to cross picket lines, to take care of oneself no matter what the cost to others. That way has gained momentum over the years, and KC has ridden the wave with sass, skill, and impressive opulence.

The affluence, power, and comfort that came with that job proved to him that anyone can make it and that making it is all there is, a story he clings to like he clings to life. He has woven his life out of a story I know well. I remember it from the days in the factory before I went to college. The old men looked past the confines of the assembly lines, through the haze of welding smoke, beyond the prison of days between them and retirement, to an ideal: the mythological ideal of a cabin, cold beer, a new truck, Packers on the big screen, a Harley in the garage. It did not matter that these things were an escape, an illusion, a salve for the pain of drudgery here and now, nor did it figure into the conversation that these things were all but unattainable. They were the shared story, the illusion that made life on the assembly line bearable. KC has fought his way through to the ideal, and he holds it up like a trophy. All else is pushed into shadow. All doubts. All questions.

I have my illusions as well: those long miles in the mountains, a life of letters. Our antagonism is one of stories competing, colliding. And so it will be until one of us drops it, gets off evangelizing his beliefs.

I see KC, maybe for the first time. He is dressed in his stories. He needs them. They have sustained him, given him meaning. He carries a shield and sword to defend them and welcomes those who share them. He knows too well I do not.

I stop fighting and let him have his stories. I release the possibility he will ever see mine, much less understand or share them.

Yes, he is the camp boss, the alpha dog, the big fish in the woods, with a hand-hewn cabin and a new Harley to prove it. Yes, when he doesn't like something, he lets you know it. And he is afraid, just as I am afraid, that my stories will not keep death from coming for me.

He is a man of few words. In being brothers for forty-four years, he has written me one letter, letting me know our dog had died while I was away at college. It took death to get him to reach out. And death has only been close to him once, so far.

For now, he is master and hunter and lord of his hilltop.

To his eyes, I have neglected the manly arts of dressing deer (though I first introduced him to hunting) and football. I no longer care about the Packers. I don't need a new truck or rifle every other year. I never lived up to his standards, as I'm sure he felt he never lived up to mine. We did not want the same things, still don't. On top of it all, I left, committing the ultimate sin in his eyes, cowardice and abandonment.

Yes, there is distance between us.

I call ahead and ask Deb if she minds if I do the prayer for the Thanksgiving gathering, an old twelve-step prayer about humility, about gratitude. The prayer addresses what I want versus what I have, about asking God for things but being "given life that I might enjoy all things." I want KC to know that I am glad to have been given more life. I want to tell KC that I am learning to be happy with what I have rather than yearning for something more. It is my way of saying we are brothers here; let's not need it to be other than what it is.

The cabin shines in the honey light of a sentimental painting of family holiday ideal. More than we could possibly eat set in greater comfort than we could ever digest, the grilled turkey, roasted turkey, fried turkey, two kinds of cranberry sauce, scalloped potatoes, mashed potatoes, sweet potatoes, steamed carrots, sourdough bread, wheat bread, white bread, and more are spread over the tables. My people are dressed in new sweaters in fall colors and look scrubbed clean. The television is tuned to a country music station, and speakers quietly play plaintive crooning while the television tells you who is singing, the name of the song, and brief videos of the artist. KC and some others are drinking beer and watching.

It is a beautiful and smug setting. I have to watch my reactions and stay distinct from them. Others greet me and are friendly, but KC manages to ignore me, even when I ask to see his new Harley. I almost crack and take the whole thing personally. But I stay the course. I don't give in to the temptation to argue or to snipe. I try to see these people, my blood, just for what they are. To forgive them for that, to forgive myself.

We socialize and marvel at the decorating, the quality of the cabin's construction, the beauty of the woods. Reggie, the giant chocolate lab, weaves his way through the party looking for table scraps. Refrigerator doors open to reveal stocks of canned pop and beer and packaged food. This is abundance, an American cornucopia.

Then it is time to eat. I recite my prayer. It hits home. People are quiet. Midway through the prayer, probably to defuse some tension or atmosphere he finds uncomfortable, KC reacts by cracking a joke. No one laughs, and I keep going. They are good words, bigger than I am, bigger than KC, but part of both of us, part of all of us. I talk about asking for power, but being given weakness that I might learn humility, about asking for wealth and being given poverty that I might learn gratitude, and being given all things that I might enjoy life but being given life that I might enjoy all things. The prayer looks past the illusions of what I want and squarely at what I have been given.

When I finish, Andy, KC's favorite son, the large and gifted athlete, applauds, then others join him and we relax and break for food.

I don't much remember the rest of the night other than working hard to listen, to let KC be who he is without punishing him for that. I also remember feeling like the bottom had fallen out of my emotional container and that I had to give up the hope that things would ever be different. I felt like I was bleeding inside, and I just let the blood drain out, kept the wound open, like the hole on the side of my foot, so that it might heal from the bottom up, from the inside out.

Through the windows I could see that rain had slicked the roads, that the light from the sodium lamp was caught and reflected by the blacktop drive. The night would be cold, and that sheen would soon freeze. I remember Jack Kornfield saying something like, "My family hates me when I am a Buddhist, but loves me when I am a Buddha." I wish I could play a part in this story that was easier—Buddha or cheesehead or whatever. This curriculum felt too much too soon, but I knew the only thing standing between me and being happy to be there was me, me and my pouting arrogance that this moment was not something else that I happened to like better.

It hurt to be there, and we stayed late.

I slept on the floor back at the Park House, the Bear's trailer home, and then got up before dawn to drive to the airport. Beneath the light of the half-moon, we left the house, feet crunching on the frozen crust of new snow. I followed my shadow across the open yard and walked with the Bear to the waiting car. We unlocked the doors, threw in my bag, and silently drove to the airport.

As we drove across town, I realized that compared with Tucson, Madison is a small town. It used to seem so big.

It took us twenty minutes to cut through the heart of the city. As we drove the windows fogged up, then cleared. I watched the streets, each loaded with memories of a different time, pass by the misty screen in the window.

So many stories here, so many beginnings and bad outcomes, each of which triggers memory trace, a pit in the gut, or a fantasy of what might have been. I study my father's hands on the wheel. They are still large and strong and they are bare. My hands are gloved. I see he is sad, but he says nothing.

When he drops me at the airport, he thanks me for coming, thanks me for what I bring back to the family. More he cannot say, but I see him stifle a welling up, a sob? I take off my gloves, and he gives me another hard pat on the back before telling me to call when I get home.

I left after the Bear was able to stand on his own, glad I had taken the time, but with a storm breaking in my heart.

29 / Sunrise

The sun rose while I waited for the plane. The east-facing windows framed its glory, and the light of it pinned me to my seat. I was going home. Life pulsed through me, free from the clogged patterns of habit. I saw a deer down by the marsh.

To anyone who passed me, I was just another traveler on the weekend, heading home after Thanksgiving. Yet something was happening. Old ice floes were breaking and moving. I was in the grip of an ongoing healing and warmed my hands at the changes of season.

When we see snakes braided around the caduceus, the symbol of professional medicine, we associate them with healing. Culture has given snakes this symbolic power, even in our technological, science-driven mindset. Ironically, we fear snakes, in spite of the healing energy with which we endow them. Healing unites fear and hope, surrender and courage. The serpent, or the symbolic vestige of literal fear of snakes and reverence for their mystery, persists.

I think we forget the healing power snakes represent. In much of Christianity the snake has been vilified. The story has it that because of the snake we tasted knowledge and were evicted from paradise. But other strands of the Christian tradition, such as gnosticism, see the snake as the beginning of knowledge, of awareness, and of consciousness. Without the snake there can be no conscious appreciation of paradise, of knowing that there is something else.

The snake, then, can represent both healing and awareness, energy and wisdom. The snake around the caduceus is braided to the vertical axis of the cross and intersects with the horizontal day-to-day awareness to pull us out of unconscious horizontal material reality. It snaps the rigid, lockstep patterns of conditioned talk and holds us spellbound and suspended above the sleeping lifewalk. In the presence of the serpent we behold the mystery of life and death. The vertical axis, connecting heaven and the underworld, gives depth and spiritual context to the seemingly endless life miles we travel.

My snake hit me in the middle of life, the middle of my journey along the horizontal bar. I was between childhood and old age, between conception and dissolution. The strike came at the heart of my life-road, locked me into the interstice between past and future, between, as Thoreau puts it, the two great eternities, past and present, between youth and age, and pinned me between terror at dying and ecstasy at still being alive. The two great eternities, however, are nothing compared to what binds them, what creates them: the present. Those eternities are like the bark and the heart-wood of a tree, both dead, held together by the thin layer of living cells, the cambium, xylem, and phloem, the only place where life really happens in the most enormous of trees.

To live at the intersection of the vertical and the horizontal is to be suffused with awe and gratitude at the gift that life is. But that is what habit fears most. It calls it crucifixion.

If crucifixion is the charged moment when daily life becomes infused with a spiritual depth, then my cross is one spiraled by a winding serpent. At the intersection lies a spiritual fire that burns all that is transient, a momentary awakening to the ephemeral embers glowing within.

In the same way that the vertical is anathema to the day to day, the snake is other to human life. It is the "otherness" of the snake that speaks to the mystery of death, of the unknown lying outside the boundaries of living. Our knowing the domain of the snake is as likely as our knowing that of death. The snake reminds us, scares us, fascinates us, unites us with those things that cannot be known or even imagined.

I will never be free from stories. I need them like I need air and water. Stories tell me who I am, make sense out of a senseless world, give me meaning. They come with the territory of being human. If I do not write my story, it will be inscribed upon me by someone else. Stories hate a vacuum.

I will never be free from them. But when I choke on them and begin to drown in a sea of received stories—whether from the powers that be or the irrepressible craving of distraction—when I substitute my preformed versions of how the world works, who is bad, good, or expendable, for a direct taste of earthly contact, they function to keep me from the here and now, the present, ripe with flowing aches and delights.

Stories can blind, poison, and imprison me as much as they can sustain me. They can be toxic and they can be life affirming. They give form to mysteries, shine light on the incomprehensible, on coming to terms with the unrelenting "Other" of a turbulent world, both inside and out. Stories, at best, can help me embrace or coexist with the Other, or they can convince me to reject the Other's right to exist. The Other *is*, and I can live by stories that acknowledge that or not. If not, the Other may come around to bite me, so to speak. The Other can be constructed of disowned and exiled parts of myself, or it can be characteristics of others that I do not want to see. I will never fully understand the Other, but I expand when I bring it into the light of my awareness.

Rattlesnakes, in particular, jump-start the engines of storytelling. Human reflexes form the raw material, create the need, form a crisis of necessary response. Snakes create an opportunity to respond to the mystery of the Other. The involuntary, hardwired reaction opens the door. What we do with that reaction is optional. Whatever assumptions we carry about snakes will steer the resulting story. If we open the gap between stimulus and response, just slow down the reaction and make it more conscious, the story we tell can better fit and serve the questions we have, the needs of the moment.

The rattlesnake opened that gap for me. It interrupted my stream of stories, allowing me to stand apart from them enough to see how they kept me from seeing what lay in front of me. The confinement following my injury freed me from the opiate of motion and distraction. Together they took away my "fix" of running, my identity as a man in motion, a man disconnected. Harsh facts, from which I ran, could then enter the space created. I could not and cannot change those facts, but I can see them and grieve and accept my place here and now.

I doubt I will ever be free, but I can become conscious of the ways those stories organize, make sense of, and then govern my actions and emotions. I can live in stories even as I change them, compose them so that they push open the doors, peer into the bag, lighten the loads created by fear and grasping.

The stories I tell guide my steps. They can be framed to accept the invitation contained within all experience. My actions can be knee-jerk, one-size-fits-all reflexes, outdated but cherished myths, or they can be answers to a world in crisis, a world calling out to me to respond. The desert is calling. I need new stories, new myths about how to live with the desert, how to coexist with rattlesnakes, mountain lions, and pup fish.

Stories that organize our place in the world need to be revised in times of crisis. Now is just such a time. We need to get out, to wake up, to unplug, to slow down, to stop long enough to realize that the old stories of snakes as slimy, evil messengers from Satan no longer work. The stories of a desert that will support massive, water-hungry cities no longer work. The story that life is a burden to be endured no longer works. The stories that we don't need a wild nature to define us as civilized no longer work. It is time to re-write, re-think, re-see our stories. It is in that rewriting that the experience of being alive can shift from fear to awe, from subjugation to coexistence, from poison to medicine.

It is this world, radiant with meaning, in which I sat that morning: radiant in the sense that it hummed and confirmed the vitality of a life in contact, aware of the braided threads that defined its passing. It was not my usual passive inertia of disconnect. In some ways I sat with those things I fear most: a desert under the blade, my mother's illness, my brother's guarded distance, my place as the black sheep in the family. They shimmered as part of this day, shimmered because I did not run but called them home.

While I held them close, I was awake, and this I believe is what we fear most about the serpent, the cultural, iconic power of the snake. It is not the poison or the difference so much as it is the need for vigilance, for mindfulness, for presence in the domain of the serpent. All things are as they are if we merely witness them without the distance, without the spin we weave with our streams of habit and fear.

The sun and the serpent, the winged Quetzalcoatl of the Aztecs rising before me, left me quite simply conscious of the life running through me. The Serpent is a river. Words are a river. We are part of a sacred and flowing mystery. A story born of blood pulsed in me.

Even death moved down a few seats.

30 / Cultivating Balance

The path disappears below and in front of me as I roll toward the lip of a jagged outcrop of granite. Too late to bail I say to myself, stretching my arms to full length and dropping my butt off the back end of the saddle.

I pick a line no less steep than the others, but smoother, and let the bike drop into a descent along the primitive, harshly sharp granite wall. From this point of entry there can be no retreat. As the front wheel falls away, I feel the rear unweight and threaten to rise forward, potentially throwing myself and the bike into a cartwheel down a bone-breaking slope of naked rock. I feather the brakes so the front will not lock up and pitch me forward onto the unforgiving stone. I sit farther back and drop my rear lower still, almost scraping on the rear tire as my abdomen rests on the seat. Trust is Allah, but move your butt. This is it, the balance point, beyond which any steeper angle of descent will toss me into space.

The bike rolls forward, the front fork absorbing the punishing terrain, keeping bike and rider from stalling.

Now I can see the line around the steepest section and take it, this time nailing the curve perfectly as the rock outcrop ends and the trail levels out onto packed dirt.

I catch my breath and settle into a rhythm, cutting through the tight curves of the fast, rolling, hard-packed trail. I cut the corners close, just missing the overhanging cholla burrs that, if touched, can attach themselves to a shoulder or knee and burn there because the spines pull the skin in too many directions to easily dislodge.

Now it is just the serpentine line of the trail and my breathing as I hunt for the zone, the zone that heightens attention and reflexes, lets me breathe through the pain rising and falling in neck, triceps, the burning legs. I move fast, but find some inner calm; I move as fluidly and gracefully as water running through a gauntlet of boulders.

Yes, it is here that I am at home, oddly and paradoxically—still in mind while physically flying—at speed, dizzy with exhaustion and endorphins. It is the only other place I feel the peace like that after the bite or after long runs. Finding that peace now is work; I have to make time and let the murky waters of my mind settle so that the silt sinks to the bottom, leaving clear water, serenity, acceptance. I take it wherever I can get it. Gradually, I get longer and longer stretches of calm, greater and greater quantities of energy, of heartache. I long to make them last.

I can see nothing but the trail in front of me, hear nothing but my breath and the pounding of blood in my ears, feel nothing but the desert terrain traveling through the aluminum of the bike frame in the form of shocks to hands, wrists, feet, and butt. My body shakes as it absorbs the vibrations, muscle flapping slightly in spite of being tensed to control the trajectory of ground flight along the desert crust.

Stories come and go. Scraps of love, longing, and loss drifting in and out of my awareness. KC, my mother, Megan, my sons—all are here with me, pumping through me. I know of no door that is locked, and all the stories are free to come and go, to have their moment, to play across the screen of awareness, but only so much. They do not pull my attention from the trail, the need to attend and respond.

My foot throbs but gamely plays along, doing its job. This is my new running, my communion with this threatened but still open desert; these wheels, this incessantly chattering mind, this quiet, popcorn-eating witness—all intensify this moment. I wish I could approach everything with the enthusiasm I bring to moving freely over the winding trails of the high Sonoran Desert, but I don't yet. I won't say can't. Someday I will be balancing my checkbook and grading papers with the same joy of quiet deliberation that I bring to these forays into the cactus forests. If I spend enough time out here, anything is possible.

Right on cue, I roll past a coiled rattlesnake in one of the sandy sections of a wash. We eye each other as my foot passes within a foot of its head, easy striking range. Nothing happens.

Within two years, this desert will be bladed to make room for six thousand homes. There will be no trail, no rock to ride down, no snake to roll past, only a water-hungry sea of tiled roofs.

I nod and keep rolling, more awake for the encounter, reminded of the work that still needs to happen. It is a long haul, a journey taken breath by breath. I am delighted to be alive and to answer the call.

I chew away at the miles and lose track of time. Angry gnawing in my belly tells me I have been out for a while. An hour? Two? It doesn't matter. I see the Jeep in the distance, close the gap, and then it is done.

I flip open the skewer holding the front wheel, pop it off, and lift the frame onto the bike mount on the roof. I like the mechanical efficiency of the task. The front wheel joins the helmet in the cockpit of the Jeep before I open the side door to extract some clean clothes for the trip home. I sponge off with some camp soap and rinse with cold water. The cotton shirt and cargo shorts feel good as I reenter the anonymity of everyday costume: I am now just another guy on the road, heading home, back to life, back to the stories that still need to be told. The words are writing themselves, taking this life and wringing out of it what they can. They come slowly, carefully, and I listen, learning to be still and patient. I feel a vague tingling sensation in my arms, a light in the back of my head, and an urgency to get to the typewriter.

I harvest the words I need to write my life, to try them on for truth, and then to put them to work. This singular, precious, weightless gift of spinning words out of heartache has been something I was running from. I embrace it now, dream it into being, enjoying the fit of it, the comfort of the weave.

Epilogue

I have dropped the boys at school. We will run together this weekend, I slowly limping, humbly accepting that my twelve-year-old will beat me in the Race for the Cure. It is a first, but not to be a last. They are overtaking me in their speed and their algebra. It is their world now. It is my place to move over and make space for them, to care for them, to give what I can to them.

I will take them to a canyon later in this month, a protected place, a sacred place. We'll backpack in and maybe will see some bighorn sheep, or coati, rattlesnake, or maybe a mountain lion. They would prefer to stay home and sit with the computer or watch TV, but I ask them to come with me. Once they are out, they begin to see, begin to pay attention. They do a better job than I at watching the turns in the stream, at spotting the silver flash of the spikedace, suckers, and loach minnows as they swim ahead of us, in tight packs, shoulder to shoulder, taking cover beneath boulders or in caverns carved and scoured by the running waters.

This stream is one of the few that remain. Others, like the San Pedro, are having the lifeblood pumped out of them by thirsty golf courses, unconscious money-hungry developers.

The water still runs. The story can change.

The evidence of flood in our canyon rests high on ledges above us, driftwood lifted twenty feet by flash floods, and all around us, in branches wrapped around tree trunks.

I will find the "zone" walking over uneven jumbles of river stones, of moss-covered roots in the trail. Even the chaotic choke points, the massive products of avalanche and erosion with conglomerate blocks the size of delivery vans, will allow a kind of rhythm that beats to the swing of my hiking stick. I will stroll into the current up the mouth of the stream as we push deeper and deeper into the canyon. The emerald water will cool our exertion in a narrow band of desert jungle. Dense stands of alder, cotton-wood, sycamore, oak, ash, walnut, hackberry, willow, and other deciduous giants will all vie for space on the floor of the canyon meander, darkening the floor with their shade. We will trace a serpentine trail of green beneath the desert scrub surrounding the canyon. We will find the mysteries and secrets of the side canyons—Hell's Half Acre, Painted Cave, Horse Camp, Paisano, Parson's, Booger, and Hell Hole; all waters drain from the rim to join the main stream. Palisades of sandstone stacked high above the volcanic tuff, the red porphyry, the buff conglomerate will draw our gaze skyward. Boulders of serpentine, quartzite, and polished granite will line our path and tower over us.

Brilliant tanagers—both red and yellow—vermilion flycatchers, black phoebes, orioles—dashes of orange, yellow, streaking red, will flit from tree to cover, betraying their hiding places with their extravagance. High on the updrafts golden eagles will circle, meditating on the wind. We will all be "extra-vagants" in the archaic sense of wanderer, as wanderers beyond the borders of settlement, of habit. They, cloaked in color, I in wet shorts: both bird and man will be at home in the canyon. The trill of the canyon wren will cascade down the scale, the notes falling down, down. In the canyon of laughing waters, as some translate, or of many wells, as others hear it (I just say many laughing well), we will listen to the falling notes that mimic the moving stream, traveling from high to low. It is the law of the canyon: all things move down. Even the mountains above us are only a freeze-frame of collapse. We are all falling down, falling apart, laughing. True. Sad. Beautiful.

Still, we fight gravity's tug. The trail will be the stream, and we will follow it higher and higher into the canyon as it narrows and deepens. Volcanic bedrock, pitted by ancient explosions of volatile gas, will stand in front of the mouth to one of the side canyons. The ancient bubbles now lined with crystal casings the size of eggs glitter like stars in the deep gray matrix, a fearsome and lonely aspect. But we will enter. We will clamber over, around, between, and under them, like ants, before gaining access to a geologic cathedral punctuated by waterfalls and clear plunge pools.

This is the water that transforms, that sculpts, that turns a desert into a paradise. It was here before these mountains; it cut this canyon. Even as the mountains rose, it flowed steadily, patiently, from one side of the range to the other, slicing neatly through eons of volcanism and ocean sediments. We will read the story told by the rocks and marvel at the wonder of it. It will feel right to be humbled, to be small, to be present, part of the running waters. We will filter the water and drink from the flow of time. It will then be part of us. We will take the canyon with us.

For now though, I live in a world that is both natural and full of artifice. My desert is a desert of silent canyons and of deafening cities, of stillness and tail-chasing speed, of streams running dry and streams full of lost hope. To believe otherwise would rend a soul.

It is warm. Spring is coming. I park off-campus and wheel the Jeep into my open spot, free street-side parking. I'm looking forward to the bike ride from Jeep to office; it gives me time to think, to get ready for the coming pressures of the day. "Embrace each moment as if you had chosen it," says Eckhart Tolle. As if you had chosen it. What does he mean by that? Yet another enigma. He probably means that choice has little to do with the moment you get and everything to do with how it is lived, the stories told about it.

I say "Don't tempt honest people," hearing the Bear, and spin the key in the lock of the Club and extract the faceplate of the radio. Then, right on cue, as if from some other lifetime, the Dim Dog notices my lockdown procedures. The agitated bark, its shrill pitch grating the air, makes the hair rise on the back of my neck. I sense it before I hear it, feel it on my arms, react instantly.

Like a rogue wave flushing through my nervous system, it breaks, travels up the beach, and recedes. That is all. The Dim Dog goes off on his mission to protect his territory, and I try to move out of there as quickly as I can without hurrying. I simply take down the bike, throw the bag over my shoulder, and go about my business.

In some residual backwater, I can hear the usual litany, the voices shouting in my head as they circle the wagons, preparing to meet an enemy I cannot change and then launching into the attack. "Damned Dim Dog," "stupid dog," and on and on. But the voices and noise and neck-tightening reflex are farther away, one step removed, and frankly I find myself not believing them. They are more of a curiosity, more of a "now look at that, I wonder why I do that" kind of event. These reactions still have a life of their own, albeit now somewhat quieter and more distant, receding like galaxies viewed from an open-air campsite.

Within a few yards of my rolling, the Dim Dog has turned back to his yard and waits for the next chance to proclaim himself vanguard and sentry, protector of the tribe. He has a job to do. We both do.

I have to speak up for the desert, for what we are losing, even if there is no hope that anything will change, and do so with as much care as I can muster, with as much love as I can stand. I am in mourning, will always be so. And it is morning. Who knows what might happen today? Time is precious, opportunity limited; the last running waters and wild places are almost gone. This is my battle, my time, my song, the voice I have been looking for my entire life, my story unfolding. Could anyone ask for more?

I bow, ask for permission to continue, agree to the ransom of having to learn, to make it up as I go. I surrender to the work ahead of me, whatever it will look like. It may be following snakes that have radio transmitters embedded beneath their scales; it may be speaking and reading. It may be asking my students questions about how they live in a fragile desert. It may be just showing up and listening until I get my chance to plant the seed of a new story in my sons. Everyone has some role to play in this epic defense of what is wild and free.

I don't know what lies ahead, but I know that I have to take it slowly and attend to one situation, one moment, one word at a time, not asking them to be anything other than true and alive. I will embrace them as I do my dearest, closest, chosen friends.

The first warm wafts of afternoon mingle with the cool morning air moving past my arms and face as I roll my way into the possibilities that await me. I glide over a pavement of chance and privilege. Like tiles set on the slant, taking on the shape of diamonds, my life has a pattern, and I see myself in it. I am surging, pulled forward by a winding mystery, a shimmering, ringing heartbeat.

Acknowledgments

This book would not have been possible without the help and support of friends, family, editors, and publishers. I stand on their capable shoulders. My desert trail buddies Chris, Bill, Dave, and the Danimal provided moral support and brotherly encouragement when I wanted to drop the whole thing and sit on a saguaro stump. Michael Robinson, Rebecca Salome, Sydelle Kramer, Ken Bacher, Tom and Ginny Beal, Dee Wildermuth, and Marianna Cacciatore all read versions, offering thoughtful and constructive guidance for revision. The California Writers Club and the *Briar Cliff Review* both buoyed me when I needed it most by publishing excerpts. David and Joyce Rychener of Aravaipa Canyon Ranch shared the healing waters of the canyon, demonstrating by example that dreams can come true if one is willing to do the work. To my family, my brothers by blood, I love you more than I can say.

About the Author

Erec Toso lives in a crumbling adobe house just outside the city limits of Tucson with his wife Megan and their two sons. He has written essays for *The Sun*, the *Briar Cliff Review*, *Northern Lights*, and other literary journals. His nonfiction and poetry have won awards from the California Writers Club, *Writer's Digest*, the Academy of American Poets, and others. He teaches writing at the University of Arizona.